BEIJING
TAI TAI

Life, laughter and motherhood in China's capital

TANIA McCARTNEY

EXISLE
PUBLISHING

First published 2012

Exisle Publishing Pty Ltd
'Moonrising', Narone Creek Road, Wollombi, NSW 2325, Australia
P.O. Box 60–490, Titirangi, Auckland 0642, New Zealand
www.exislepublishing.com

National Library of Australia Cataloguing-in-Publication Data:

McCartney, Tania, 1968–.

Beijing tai tai : life, laughter and motherhood in China's capital / Tania McCartney.

ISBN 9781921966156 (pbk.)

McCartney, Tania, 1968—Family.
McCartney, Tania, 1968—Travel.
Expatriate authors—China—Beijing.
Authors, Australian—China—Beijing.
City and town life—China—Beijing.
Beijing (China)—Social life and customs.

305.824051156

Designed by Christabella Designs
Typeset in Sabon 11/15
Printed in Singapore by KHL Printing Co Pte Ltd

This book uses paper sourced under ISO 14001 guidelines from well-managed forests and other controlled sources.

10 9 8 7 6 5 4 3 2 1

For Ian,
without whom this tale would never have occurred,
and our lives would never have been so enriched.

tai tai (noun. f.) wife (the word is also used by expats as a tongue-in-cheek description for a woman who lunches, shops, has her nails done and probably fills her house with orchids)

The Announcement

How the news was broken, like a china teacup

When my husband first announced we'd be moving to China from one of the quietest, most charmingly provincial state capitals in Australia, I was 95 per cent horrified.

From a Californian bungalow with glossy floorboards and Tudor glass windows to a precariously constructed cement block in the sky? From streets with manicured lawns and the echoing pop of tennis balls to spit-laden, noise-polluted racetracks? From sunny strolls with the pram to harried, seatbelt-free taxi rides that strangulate the function of your heart?

How to forgo the comfortable Known in favour of the scratchy Unknown? How to release breakfasts of pouncy bread, gourmet muesli and silky yoghurt with essence of dried fig, in favour of — er … what *do* Chinese people eat for breakfast? And do they even *have* bread in China?

I was a well-travelled, thirty-something woman when we received this 95 per cent horrifying news. I was well-educated, well-read and well-versed on the world, having already schlepped my working life around Europe and nearly every Australian state. I was liberal, open-minded, travel-hungry, ready for change, ever-primed for adventure, not a scaredy-cat, never shy of a challenge — all that.

So it surprised no one more than me to learn that the prospect of living in China for four years made me 95 per cent horrified.

Maybe my initial terror was due to the cushy life we'd been languishing in for so long. Maybe it was due to the rush of human rights

propaganda that invaded my post-birth brain after a fifteen-year sabbatical. It may also have been the fact that China has remained towards the end of my lengthy travel list. I've never felt that 'pull' for China like I have for so many other countries around the globe. The Great Wall? Sure, I'd love to see it. The 1703 summer retreat of Empress Dowager Cixi, surrounded by the world's largest classical imperial gardens and eight minority temples?

Huh?

Simply put: *I just didn't know anything about China.*

There. I said it.

My fears were probably also compounded by the fact that the world was no longer about me and my husband any more. It was purely and simply about two other people. Our daughter Ella was three and our son Riley was just one year old when we received The News, and so our family was still heavily invested in a nappy-padded world — a world where everything is pastel and whimsically aesthetic and smells like lollies and cloisters snugly inside mother's groups.

I've never been part of a mother's group. Having wanted and struggled to have kids for longer than expected, however, I had *so* bought into this artificially 'perfect' world of babies and toddlers. A world of sweet, harmonious perfection, tucked inside a pretty house with echoing floorboards, white rugs, hand-knitted toys and un-mineralised baby oil. Oh, and popping tennis balls.

There were carefully structured days of best-for-baby routine coupled with pedantic meals served in expensive ceramic dishes with silver baby cutlery. There were daily *Baby Einstein* DVDs, mini-maestros music education and Gymboree, all bundled up in flashcards, fluffy toys and fun. Essentially, I was up to my eyeballs in the whole coo and caboodle.

Having this idyllic routine unplugged was a precarious position to be in. With babies, life isn't about challenges; it's about *eliminating* the challenges for the sole purpose of clinging onto any semblance of sanity. And the ideal way to do this is in making life routine. Making it easy. Focusing, honing and committing — not diversifying, risking and free-wheeling.

Going to China with two small kids and leaving our nappy-padded comfort zone was going to need more diversifying, risking and free-wheeling than I'd ever called upon before.

My life called. It was time to tuck a baby under each arm and plummet into the abysmal Unknown. No wonder I was 95 per cent horrified.

The Adelaideans

Be careful what you say out loud ...

I've revealed many things to my Xiansheng (pronounced 'see-an-shung', aka my husband) over the years — from my fear of untucked sheets to the fact that I would follow him to the ends of the earth and live in a tin shed if I had to. I specifically told him this: 'I will follow you to the ends of the earth and live in a tin shed if I have to. In fact, I will move anywhere in the world with you except Adelaide and China.'

Be careful what you say out loud. Six months later, we were posted from our home town of Melbourne to Adelaide, and now eighteen months later, we are on our way to Beijing.

Not a word of a lie.

Moral of this statement? Just be really careful what you say out loud, because the all-permeating, all-knowing caretakers of Karma will hear it and will *stick it* to you. Not such a bad thing given that whatever we avoid in life probably needs to be *part* of our lives, as was the way with my facetious comments and subsequent uprooting from our beloved Melbourne.

Adelaide, the capital of South Australia, is in many ways a world-class city, but in many ways it's also a large country town. The capital

is known for its clique of long-term Adelaideans — the offspring of a long line of South Australian residents so thick, even their accent differs from the rest of the country. Many Adelaideans will probably agree: unless you're born inside it, you're always a bit of an outsider. As a result, Adelaide pulls the reputation with other state-dwellers for being a little, well … let's just say it's hard to get into the well-established 'clique'.

I was nervous about this reputation, and having already lived in most Australian states by the time we left for Adelaide, it was with some authority that I abided by this somewhat tongue-in-cheek character assassination of our South Australian capital city; an assassination similar to the rivalry between Sydney and Melbourne as the cultural capital of Australia, and the affectionate stab at Queenslanders for being a little — er … slower than the rest of the country. It's wonderful that Australians have such a great sense of humour and hefty aptitude for self-mockery.

So, typically, because of this somewhat ridiculous paranoia, Karma swooped down and gave us a posting straight to the inner 'burbs of Adelaide.

We stayed eighteen months, and — surprise, surprise — we loved it. It was a wonderful experience. And I was let into many a 'clique'. In fact, I easily slipped into some of the loveliest cliques I've ever had the fortune to be cliqued in. Some fascinating women welcomed me (and the kids) with open arms, and our time in this town holds some of the fondest memories of my life. So much for clichés, let alone cliques.

It was when we left Adelaide, however, that I realised a clique is only a clique if you're standing on the outside of one. When we left, the bubble enclosing my clique healed over almost instantly, shutting me outside. I was given a send-off fit for a queen, yet once the Adelaide hills disappeared from view, it was as though I no longer existed. The gates to this town closed, the vortex sucked back in on itself and everything within it was swallowed up in that lovely little world, with the door firmly shut. Telephone calls and emails may enter that place but it seems they rarely leave. So I guess, after all, Adelaide did live up to her reputation — out of sight, out of clique.

No matter. My memories are still fond. And anyway, we had larger seas to navigate; the China Sea, in fact — and it would take all our focus to deal with the potential cliques ahead. In Beijing.

Like I said, be careful what you say out loud. Or better yet, go ahead and make your grandiose statements and ponder hard on your rut-like beliefs, and then wait for the biggest dose of reality since crow's feet.

Reality, here we come.

Beijing Bound

Can long-held preconceptions really shift?

If there is anything (beyond apathy and the violation of human rights) that gets my guns blazing, its parochialism. Living in a one-horse town doesn't make one parochial; it's purely a mindset. It's the ludicrous (and dangerous) idea that nothing actually exists (or matters) outside one's own immediate area — or worse — outside the confines of one's own skull.

I like to think that my aversion to living in China has naught to do with parochialism, but rather a distinct Lack of Knowledge or a decided desire Not To Know. It may also have something to do with my self-righteous opinion that because of a), b) and c) from the annals of world history, China would not be a good place to live. If you asked me what a), b) and c) were, I probably wouldn't even be able to tell you any more — the opinion is just that fiercely and innately ingrained.

But I do have other reasons, beyond human rights and history, to be sceptical about life in China. Trips to the Chinatowns nestled deep in Australia's capital cities had often been a sticky experience in my younger days. Noisy, cramped and perennially grubby, the food was always too saucy, too salty and too pineappley for me, and the service officious and oftentimes cold.

I've often wondered if our petite but ballsy Asian neighbours simply dislike tall blonde Western women, particularly after a visit to Hong Kong in 1987 with a friend. I'm not sure if we were tailed by the curse of the Blonde Demon Dragon or whether we just looked suspiciously whorish, but both of us were consistently treated like crack hookers in Hong Kong way back then.

Hindsight being a wonderful thing, we were pretty young, pretty wild and pretty much drank our way through every bar in town before raping the shops of every high-heel shoe known to mankind (to be worn with black leather miniskirts) and smoking our way around the night streets. So, admittedly, there was a distinct possibility we fitted the 'Oh look! Two Western sluts — let's snarl at them, shove them off the escalators and spit in their general direction!' (yes, this actually happened) picture.

I also remember a Chinese woman I used to work with in Sydney. I was eighteen, she was a 36-year-old life insurance underwriter, yet her only means of verbal communication was to giggle. And yes, she could speak fluent English. It drove me bananas.

So, yes yes, because of the Ignorance and Fear behind my lifelong reasoning on China, Karma swooped in and posted us to Beijing. It said: 'Cast aside thy disposable nappies and thy expectations for low-fat vanilla soy decaf lattes and get thee to a flat, grey Communist city where you may just be subjected to dislike. Get thee there and findeth out.'

And so I'm having one last low-fat vanilla soy decaf latte. And like all good followers of Karma, we are going. Tomorrow.

The Wild Ride

It's only just begun ...

I won't go into the shenanigans surrounding our journey to Beijing. After the intense stress of dividing and packing every earthly belonging, the heavy immunisation schedule (we are still pincushion sore) and my attempt to coordinate the upheaval of an entire family with only a small part of my brain functioning at full capacity, I was hit suddenly by the crashing reality that we had missed our flight.

I was standing in the middle of the busy check-in counters at the airport, clutching the handle of our overloaded luggage trolley when the realisation hit. I just sort of slid to the floor in a silent cry that gave way to a series of horrendous, very public sobs (I'm *still* embarrassed). The kids instantly took pity, and stood over me with their hands on my head like mini popes blessing a heathen. Poor Xiansheng ran around like a chook with its head cut off, trying to pinpoint the reason we got our flight time wrong and who was to blame. It didn't matter — the sobbing was out of my control now.

After a stiff gin and tonic and a bracing swim in the airport Hyatt, we settled in for the night before leaving for Beijing early the next morning.

Would this mix up and delay be a harbinger of doom for our new adventure? We were now arriving on the fourth of the month and the number four is a seriously ill-fated number, according to the Chinese. The Mandarin word for four — *si* — is very similar in pronunciation to the word for death. What would this terrible omen mean for us?

Now, on this Mach-II day of departure, Riley, only just past the age of two, slept in for the first time in his life. He was also grumpy, noncompliant and incoherent to any instruction, especially when it came to customs or immigration officials. But it was okay — I was armed with Vallergan, a behaviour-numbing, sleep-inducing drug for

tots. I packed that bottle in my hand luggage, fully cohesive of the warning that in a small percentage of children, the drug has the opposite effect and instead turns sleepy children into banana-wielding, lemonade-spurting maniacs.

No problem — it wouldn't happen to me.

Halfway into our nine-hour flight to Hong Kong, I was ready to pop the aircraft's rear door and parachute to freedom. Riley went bananas all right. He reacted so adversely to the Vallergan that 'running amok' took on a whole new meaning. He actually acquired the ability to ingest only and exclusively lollies, chocolate, apple juice and plastic texta lids. I remember at one stage taking him into the toilet to give the other passengers five minutes' peace, but our darling little boy screamed like a banshee and unravelled every toilet roll in fury. He refused to go to the toilet at all costs and subsequently wet through every nappy onboard. He then, out of sheer exhaustion, fell asleep for a grand total of twenty, twitching, heart-stopping minutes (I don't think I breathed the whole time and God forbid if anyone pressed a call button). Of course, because Riley had already used up all his nappies by this time, he whizzed in his sleep — right through his clothes, my clothes and the fabric seat, and we all three stank to high heaven for the rest of the trip.

Now, before you think Xiansheng and I have raised a harem of monkeys, I have to mention that our daughter Ella, three months shy of five, sat in her seat and read a book, played a game, ate her dinner/lunch/snacks, watched TV, chatted charmingly with the hosties, played more games and read some more. She did not pee *once* during that entire nine-hour flight, and did not utter a single word of contention.

Point made.

Meanwhile, back at the Riley camp, when we finally got off the plane and into a nice, clean mini van, our son brought his eighteen-hour travelling circus show to a grand finale by vomiting all over the van's seats and onto my shoes.

The Chinese have a saying: the more 'challenging' the child, the greater the man. Truthfully, I am living in hope and will listen to anything they tell me.

For now, though, I have China to contend with.

We are here.

The Fourth of May

Welcome to Beijing

When our aircraft landed in Beijing, I was nervous. Would a series of strategically placed cameras *really* follow us from the aerobridge to our bedroom door, with nary a moment of blank space betwixt? Oh, the propaganda in this propaganda-paranoid place!

Disembarkation, immigration, luggage, customs — all uneventful. Easy, even. Then it was through the sea of Chinese faces waiting at the international gate, then out into the balmy Beijing night — so fuss-free, I kept looking behind me, waiting for a hand to descend upon my shoulder. Instead, it was the Beijing air that grabbed me by *both* shoulders and quite literally took my breath away.

A yellowish cast was veiling the starless night sky — a sort of choking haze that grabs the inside of your throat as it goes down — and there was a distinct smell that I will never forget. It was sort of a smoky aroma, draped fragrantly between egg noodles and dust, blended with a very ancient low note, sort of what I imagine frankincense would smell like.

Starry-eyed and too exhausted to cough, we clambered into the mini van and travelled along the airport expressway, all of us sitting quietly and staring at the rows of poplar trees lining the roadway. Through the tollway with the gaudy Chinese gate, then more road and more trees, until eventually the city of Beijing unfolded like a pop-up map, and we were swirling in on the new freeway extension to the Third Ring Road, and there we were, cruising the late-night streets of Dongzhimen, to our apartment (whereupon Riley promptly vomited).

The Chinese reception staff in our building were really interesting to

me. There wasn't a hint of surly Chinatown waitress in sight. These people were *lovely*. They laughed off the vomit. They darted around to fetch our bags. They smiled. They grinned. They spoke English. They welcomed. They — they — seemed to *like* us.

Despite the vomit, it was a nice introduction, our first night, and as we scaled the heights to our apartment, the view clean knocked our socks off. The night sky may have been hazy from filth but the coloured lights of the city's buildings, surrounding us on all sides … it was just breathtaking. As we twirled around the floor of our massive, open-plan living area, we marvelled and grinned. We were right in the middle of it all, like a pin in the middle of a pincushion of pins.

With the kids bathed (in an effort to rid Riley of Eau de Wee-Wee and Spew) and straight to bed, Xiansheng and I settled down with a glass of wine, while resting our feet on ten unpacked suitcases. We had eyes only for the view.

Three hours in and China was going okay. So far so good.

First Full Day Overload

It's the little things ...

Things smell funny. Not in an unpleasant way, just a different way. And the strawberries taste like candy. The apples look different. The milk pongs. The bread crumbles upon contact after toasting (yes, they have 'bread'!), and the yoghurt tastes like it did back home in 1982.

It appears the Chinese actually enjoy sleeping on hardwood planks; our aching hips are screaming out for inner coils. There are no ceiling lights and not enough lamps in the apartment — we fumble around in a state of dim. Things break with frightening regularity. A parade of strangers turns up at the door and waltzes through our apartment almost hourly, fixing things, helping themselves to an unabashed eyeful

of our private life. I mean, they *stare*. Things seem to take forever to get done and explanations are rarely forthcoming.

Welcome to our first, scratchy day in the capital. Our comfort zone is being pressed and prodded already too soon.

For all this, though, there are white slippers for our feet. And the teabags have that 1950s retro charm, and the loose tea — saints be praised — it overwhelms me. The green tea, the *pu-erh*, the barley tea, the jasmine, the rose, the chrysanthemum flowers that open like magical anemones in your teacup.

Today we wandered Xin Yuan Li wet market, awash with more green leaves than the Amazon jungle. The tofu section had me stunned with the seemingly endless ways the humble soybean can be stretched, soaked, shredded and moulded. For less than a dollar, I took home an entire shopping bag of cherry tomatoes, bursting with red. For not much more, I secured my weight in cucumbers. And the lychees and cherries and guavas and mangoes … too fragrant and pennywise to mention. The variety of mushrooms had me skipping for joy through the imaginary fields in my mind. It is a chef's haven here — a foodie's paradise, a pomelo-addict's nirvana. It's a fruit salad of scrumptiousness.

We've only been here a day but have already learned that *pu-erh* tea makes you lose weight and bamboo extract soothes a lost voice. We have learned that drinking cold water is an assault on the body and warm water cleanses you through. We're learning quickly that the Chinese live according to the seasons and that this seasonal living has its charm — it allows us to live within the rhythms of mother nature, to sample her finest at its best, straight from her earth rather than a simulated greenhouse with a chemical addiction. It also allows our bodies to become analogous with the air — the temperature, the time of year, and so with it, enjoy warm foods when we should, cooling foods when we must.

Coming to live in China is a little bit like stepping back in time. Could it be possible that this step backwards will create a better future for our family?

It's an intriguing thought. We shall see.

The Square

It's the big things ...

It only took two days to follow in the footsteps of scores of provincial Chinese tourists and haul ourselves around Tian'anmen — the world's largest city-central square. This small action sent us hurtling towards a glimpse of stratospheric super-stardom. We now know, all four of us, what dodging the paparazzi in La La Land might be like.

We were famous. We were trailed, pawed, revered, snapped and begged to be part of family photo shoots. Being wide-eyed and bushy-tailed, and typically friendly Australian *laowai* (foreigners), we said, 'Of course!' Big mistake. Photographic Group Number One paved the way for Group Number Two and Three. By Group Eight, we had to say, 'No more photos, please!' as a queue started forming around the Square.

We should have charged money. The locals would have.

Apparently, provincial people use photos with foreigners to wangle tourist visas for travel around or out of China. Urban myth or not, the aggression with which these people sought our photographic autograph was a little unnerving, as was the way dark-skinned, country bumpkin parents shoved their achingly shy toddlers forward for a photo op. Little darlings.

Our very white-skinned, blonde-haired Ella was so freaked out by all this attention, she jumped into Riley's stroller and pulled the hood down over her face. This did nothing to stop the Chinese from shoving their phones under her protective awning and snapping a point-blank photo of her face, or reaching in and wiping their grubby hands all over her cheeks. I was swatting them away like flies. Riley rode up high on Daddy's shoulders to escape the pawing but they still grabbed at his legs like pagans revering the Madonna. A wailing Madonna in the form of a terrified little boy.

Yes, Tian'anmen was a pretty full-on introduction to China for us. Not only were we foreign but it seems we were also the only people in Beijing to have a blonde girl in a hot pink dress jammed into a baby stroller, and a green-eyed two-year-old riding 7 feet high in the air with dangling legs so adorable that no one could resist a tug.

The Chinese, God love 'em, couldn't help themselves. And the more the kids cried, the more adorable the locals found it, and the more snap-happy and pawing they became.

It's amazing how fast a crappy old stroller can go when you push it hard enough, because we pushed that thing across Tian'anmen like a Formula One race car. Scary that our admirers happily hotfooted after us, their little red flags flapping madly. It wasn't until we were in the safety of a cab, with ruddy faces jamming smiles through the windows, that we finally escaped our provincial friends, waving and calling out to us long after we evaporated up Chang'an Jie.

Mark my words, this experience will benchmark a whole new reality for our family.

Food Glorious Food

Beijingfan? We're already hooked!

Our very first Beijing restaurant experience was a culinary wonder. It was typical local fare in a large, very busy restaurant — always an indicator of good *Beijingfan* (local food). Four adults and two kids ate and ate and ate with much gusto. We supped like gluttons and we even drank beer (well, except the kids). So you can imagine the look on our faces when the bill was delivered, announcing the whopping total of 97 yuan. That's about sixteen Australian dollars.

We carried on like ecstatic maniacs for 25 minutes about this (much to our expat hosts' eye-rolling), then we went home and slept and came

back the next night. And the night after that. We love, love, love it. We love the oil, the salt, the dumpling wrappers, the plump minced pork, the herbs, the egg pancakes, the mushy rice porridge with shreds of savoury chicken — the whole shebang.

This is not Chinese food! Not the Chinese food we once knew — the shiny, sticky, sesame-seeded stuff from the suburban Cantonese restaurants back home. Mandarin food is *different*. It's like a whole new cuisine has slipped over on our tongues, and we've fallen ravenously in love.

The *al dente* bounce of *jiaozi* (dumpling) dough on the teeth. The satisfying lump of hot fried bread studded with green onions and zinging with salt, passing into the gullet. The crunch of silky, wilted greens bathed in fresh garlic and a slip of oil. The chunky shards of cucumber with a sesame tang, tingling the centre of the tongue. The fizz of local Tsingtao beer on the lips. The curl of cigarette smoke in the nostrils and busy chatter of voices and natter of chopsticks in bowls (no forks here).

I love it all. Yes, even the smoke, in a Parisian-café sort of way.

And what I probably love more than anything is the kid thing. Our kids can do no wrong. Our kids are still settling in; they're disoriented and ratty. They whine, they bang their chopsticks on the bowls and stick them upright in their rice (both a terrible no-no — the former imitates beggars banging their bowl for money, the latter imitates incense offerings stuck into sand for the dead).

Our kids won't sit still like the perfect Chinese tots around us. They squiggle and squirm and hop on and off their seats before chasing each other around the tables, bumping into scurrying staff carrying hotpots of scalding stock.

This kind of kiddie behaviour is grounds for restaurant-divorce in Australia. Here, it's all … it's all … should I say it? It's all *okay*. The staff *love* the kids. The fellow patrons *love* the kids. Instead of stares and glares and rolling eyes, there is naught but compassion, grins and encouragement. I am stunned. What the …?

The staff actually scuffle to entertain the kids, to pick them up, to trail them, to cuddle them, to pinch their faces, to whisper sweet Mandarin nothings in their ears. They quite simply adore them. And let's not even mention the security guards in our building whose faces light up and knees bend to the floor the moment our kids appear as silhouettes in the distance.

And of course, like a puppy, the more over-attention you give it, the more it wants to squirm away. Our kids are like, 'I know how much you wanna squeeze my pink cheeks. I know you want it bad. You gotta work for it, baby.' They torture these poor, sweet, young *laowai*-obsessed wait staff. One minute the kids are using them as swings, fire engines, even horsies; the next, they're running away on their sneakered feet, teasing with pale-iris eyes and scampering away like evil snow pixies.

And the staff just love it all the more. It's a bizarre dance.

Apparently, pixie-like behaviour is condoned in China, and if it means Xiansheng and I don't have to step in and/or gush apologies to crabby fellow patrons — hey! We're happy! We can actually spend time chatting to each other as husband and wife, or — God forbid — actually even swallow some *food*.

It also doesn't seem to matter when the kids gnaw the back of their chairs, shred their paper napkins or spread their rice from here to kingdom come. Even the bad-luck act of dropping chopsticks on the floor can't besmirch the attractiveness of our kids. The staff just rush forth to pick them up and replace them with a freshly sheathed pair (though not before Riley shoves the filthy ones in his mouth).

No wonder we are regulars.

Baby School

Today my baby started little school in big China

I'm fine. No, really.

Today Ella left for full-time Reception at the British School of Beijing, and I was actually ecstatic. Sure, she was a little nervy but she jumped right on that bus (well, she was nudged) and when she got home this afternoon, she was buzzing and smiley and chatting non-stop about all the exciting things she did, just as I knew she would.

She needs little pushes, our Ella. Riley might be different, but Ella needs a gentle nudge. Not a brain-washing, thought-controlling shove. Just a little prod towards the fear — and then she can walk right through it, of her own volition.

We've often done this with her. I remember the first time she sat in the bouncy toddler seat anchored to the front of Riley's pram. She had refused to get in. Categorically refused. She carried on like a maniac for twenty minutes before I simply lifted her up and plonked her straight in. Sure, she screamed. For about three seconds. Then she promptly stopped and started bouncing up and down in the seat with glee (and then refused to get out, but that's a whole other story).

Yes, a little nudge can be a good thing.

So, after less than a year of part-time kindergarten in Australia, my little tot, who had not even begun learning phonics, has been 'nudged' into full-time, big-girl school, entering a curriculum around eighteen months ahead of her Aussie peers. How will she cope? I'm not too worried. We'll take things a day at a time. She only has six weeks of school before the summer holidays, so things are in wind-down mode anyway. I'm actually more worried about how we're going to cope with the long summer than I am about her grades.

But back to why I was ecstatic. This ecstasy is not for me — it's for Ella. What an opportunity. Firstly, to have the chance to go to an

international school (a reality I honestly never configured into my lifetime as a parent), and secondly because she is *so* ready for this. So so ready.

I have a deep belief in allowing kids to be kids (read: have unstructured fun), but I also believe education doesn't have to be 'work'. And to enjoy the myriad educational wonders at the British School — I'm just so, so excited for her. Excited she is starting so early on this journey to independence and adventure, something I voraciously encourage in my children, even at this tender age.

Meanwhile, little Riley and I are left at home, wandering the empty halls. But we aren't crying and lamenting. We are kicking soccer balls! And ruining pots with homemade playdough! And talking about the day that Riley will join his big sister. And when will that be? Straight after summer when he is two-and-a-half years old. Straight in the deep end for my kids, thankyouverymuch.

That'll make 'em good swimmers.

On a Plate

But sometimes not easy to swallow

It's an understatement to say that moving to Beijing has been a breeze for us. We really are being well looked after and I'm kind of reeling at how easy this settling-in period has become. From the helpful reps waiting at the airport arrival gate to the cushy apartment, everything seems easy and pretty much served to us on a plate.

It's day six. Xiansheng started work today and our *ayi* (housekeeper/cook — the word *ayi* means 'auntie') started work on the same day. An ectomorphic, fuzzy-haired sixty-something-year-old woman, things seem to have started out well. She is enthusiastic, excitable, accommodating, polite. She uses the polite form of 'you' *(nin)*

rather than the less formal *ni*, and calls me *furen*. This will probably be the first and last time anyone ever calls me Madam, so I'm relishing it.

Having an *ayi* is beyond my wildest dreams. Most *tai tai* in Beijing have one and they perform many tasks from cooking, shopping and cleaning to washing, ironing and child-minding. For me, having an *ayi* means I can have a few moments a day (for the first time in a very long time) to rediscover my writing, and perhaps even rediscover who I am. It's going to be an interesting process of rediscovery on many levels, and, of course, giving up the scrubbing of toilets for a while is a delightful little bonus.

I must admit, though, having an *ayi* unnerves me. Having someone work for me, in my house, in my space. Dealing with my *underwear*. It's creepy creepy creepy, for so many reasons. I'm so damned self-sufficient and have never leaned on so much as a benchtop my whole life long … so to have this woman cleaning our toilets, scrubbing our floors, making our meals, ironing Xiansheng's shirts and folding my smalls … it's just weird, and yes, it's difficult.

Ha! you may well laugh or even roll your eyes in 'yeah right' sarcasm. But it's true — I've been feeling lazy, awkward and intensely uncomfortable since Ayi started. Especially as our paraphernalia from Australia hasn't yet arrived and all I have is the television and a handful of books and toys for the kids. The days seem long, drawn out, with not much to do except … nothing much, while Ayi cooks, cleans, dusts, polishes, scrubs and mops. And I can't even help because apparently, if you do that, *ayis* feel they're not doing their job properly and this leads to *ayi*-paranoia and that's a whole other kettle of *jiaozi*.

So I don't help. I hang around and do unspeakable things like write in journals and send emails, play games with the kids and watch cartoons.

Yes, living with house-help should make me ecstatically happy, but for now, whenever Ayi's key turns in the lock, I break into a cold sweat. She lopes in with her bags of shopping and a big '*Ni hao, Furen!*' and proceeds to chat with me as though I'm completely fluent and she's known me for years. I just smile a lot and try to avoid her and smatter

the air with lots of '*ting bu dong*' (I hear you but don't understand what you're saying). It's awkward. It's weird. Having her here is really the equivalent of someone standing and staring at you for eight hours straight.

I. Don't. Like. It. There, I said it.

I mean, you can fart but it has to be silent, and you can pick your nose but you have to flick it somewhere strategic, and you can't gorge yourself on chocolate all day or get stuck into the sherry at 10 a.m.

Yesterday, while Ella was at school and while Riley napped, I sat at the dining room table, wasting decadent hours journalling on the laptop. Ayi stood 3 metres behind me, ironing a mountain of clothes like a pack horse. The house was silent, my back was vulnerable to her gaze and I just wanted to fold myself up and slip under the door like a telegram. My swallowing hurt, my skin prickled and tears wallowed in my eyes. This woman is old enough to be my mother and she toiled silently through a creased bundle of cotton the size of a small car.

I imagine she resents me. I'm sure she takes exception to these wasteful hours of gluttonous memory-cataloguing — so self-indulgent. The silence hurts. Listening to that iron glide and hiss over cotton actually *hurts*. I can't bear being the princess in the ivory tower, doodling in the middle of the day like a debauched wench, while this frail, borderline poverty-stricken woman tapdances for pennies.

It got too much to bear. I closed my laptop, checked on my sleeping son, phoned a neighbour and slipped out under the door like a telegram.

Princess in the Ivory Tower

It's not all it's cracked up to be

Well, I'm slipping a little deeper into a new comfort zone.

As previously lamented, you'd think I would be skipping for joy over home-help. Not so. I *want* to skip for joy. I'm *trying* to skip for joy, but all I can manage right now is a lopsided lope.

I met my neighbour at a local coffee shop today and when I told her about my *ayi* 'issue', she laughed so hard, cafe latte nearly squirted out of her nose. A veteran of nearly three years in Beijing, she thought my story was typically ridiculous. She reminded me that I've just spent six months reconfiguring our Aussie life to fit awkwardly into the template of a life in China, husband and two kids included. No wonder I'm emotional.

Then she said something that has changed everything for me. She said I'm forgetting Ayi is actually — here's a thought — *being paid* for ironing our small mountain of clothes and folding our smalls. *Paid*. It's her *job*.

To hammer the message home, my coffee-spurting friend kindly pointed out that my *ayi* has a Good Job. I mean, a really good job. In a country where much of the population work too many hours for too little yuan, Ayi has a good job. In a lovely, temperature-controlled apartment, with light duties and using quality equipment (she's using a very good German iron designed to be easy on bird-like, sixty-odd-year-old wrists, after all).

My face lightened when my neighbour pulled these facts out of the Beijing smog. I smiled. I'm not imprisoning or debasing this woman after all. I'm sort of *looking after her*.

Good, saintly me.

So, this afternoon, after my totally private conversation at the café, the oddest thing happened. Ayi moved her ironing board from our living

room (where her presence so tortured me) to the small storage room located at the very back of our apartment, with the board games and the cleaning equipment and the change of clothes she keeps there. Feeling bad about it (and admittedly, quite suspicious), I told her she could iron in the living room but she told me the light is better in that tiny room (it isn't) and that she likes ironing in there (how could she?).

Hmm.

I'm off to frisk the jacket I wore to the coffee shop.

Ashes to Ashes, Dust to Dust

The never-ending attempt to shine surfaces

When you come to Beijing, it's not only the flavour of the air you have to get used to. It's what's *in* the air. And what's in the air (among other lung-paralysing things) is dust. Fine, powdery, silt-like, greyish white, pervasive, insistent Beijing dust. This stuff is so insidious, you could find it on the inside of a can of tuna. Indeed, it has been found on the inside of many a perfectly sealed package in our house, so you can imagine its presence on the inside of our lungs, eye sockets, arteries and perhaps even filling our hair follicles.

Right now, my house is Bizzaro Dust World. Any self-respecting housewife would run in terror at such a pervading presence in her home, particularly since this substance requires a bare minimum of four hours to resettle on every shiny surface (and most particularly the television screen). *Four hours.* Yes, you read it right — a dust-settling timeframe that takes four *weeks* in Australia.

Where this dust comes from is questionable. The shockingly rapid rate of development in Beijing at this very minute, as I type, is barely

short of implausible. As the *hutong* courtyard houses crumble into piles of brick and high-tech Taiwanese shopping centres pop up as though pulled by strings, the building sites alone cause enough dust to cement the bowels of hell. Then there's the outer reaches of the Gobi Desert, inching closer and closer as the planet is twisted and skewed and pulled from pole to pole as we heartlessly screw with its ecosystems.

The northern belt of China was recently touted by a British newspaper as the most consistently polluted stretch of land on earth. Beijing factories (which have all been evicted to the surrounding countryside) are churning out more produce than ever before — quite a feat considering China is already the world's leading manufacturer of anything and everything. Local production of cars is growing exponentially and vehicles are entering the streets of Greater Beijing at an astounding 1000 units per day. Coupled with the fact that the steering, accelerating and halting of vehicles is not a mastered art here, and gridlock, here we come.

The origin of this all-pervasive white soot, then, is probably insignificant when compared to the prevailing questions: how to deal with it, and how to keep as much of it out of our lungs as possible.

So what to do? You wipe. You have to. And closing windows and cupboards won't protect you, my friend. If you use a feather duster, the silt will fly into the air and resettle on the walls of your bronchi within the half-minute. So you have to wet wipe (or have Ayi do it for you). Then you have to do the same thing again the next day and the day after that. If you leave a photo frame one week, your beloved family member will go into soft focus. If you leave it a month, it will look like it's been sitting in a be-sheeted mansion for 25 years.

Air filters, cleaners and humidifiers are supposed to 'help' with the dust. Whether they actually do anything is negligible, but it can't hurt to try. Humidifiers wet the air and weigh the dust down onto furniture more quickly; not so good for the furniture, but helpful for keeping lungs pink.

This morning I leaned against the window of our high-level apartment and feasted my eyes on the swirling white muck, grey-scaling

down through the atmosphere and onto the streets below. It creeps down to the pavement. It lingers with the people. It turns your hair dull in hours. It dries out your skin and cements the walls of your gut.

My God. What are we doing to our kids?

Christmas in June

Our stuff has finally arrived!

I'm loving our apartment. We were allowed to choose our paint colours — the living room has a chocolate wall and a mint wall and a cake-coloured wall. I could make dessert with our walls, they're so yummy. There's loads of space and we can now fill up that space because … drum roll, please — our stuff has arrived from Australia!

It's been like Christmas unpacking it all. Ayi has a permanent, gawping look on her face and ceaselessly tells me we brought far too much with us. If you call eight million books too much, then it's too much, I suppose. There were several uncertainties about coming to China and one of them was the English-language book selection, so we are well prepared, that's all. Our family reads voraciously, and frankly, books cost a lot to ship, so we stocked up. And up and up.

We also brought every toy we owned so the kids could grow into and through them, as well as four massive cartons of food: breakfast cereals, Milo, Aussie chocolate and other snacky things we weren't certain could be found here. We brought a few sentimental items, too; things I couldn't bear living four years without. Like the kids' baby books. Our scrapbooks and journals. Framed photographs of family and friends. That kind of thing.

So, it was like Christmas opening all the boxes. Suddenly our life feels more real. We've got more of an anchor to help us connect with our new life here because everything still feels surreal. I'll be walking

past the window and I'll look outside at the massive cityscape below and I'll just sort of gasp quietly as though it's only just materialised there. It's so easy to become cocooned inside the shell of expat living and forget where you are.

Oh my. We're living in China.

Cycling Beijing

The bold and the brave

We may be nuts, but we've purchased new bicycles with kiddie seats attached to the back … and we live smack-bang in the middle of a ravenous city, right between two major, knock-'em-down-like-skittles roads. Of course, we have bike helmets for the kids and we use the bicycle lanes (also frequently frequented by motorcycles and cars) so I'm sure we'll be fine. *Eeep*!

I have a very loud bell, which I use constantly, and the kids — who seem to have an inbuilt desire for thrills — *love* it. They love it when Dad and Mum race to be the fastest (it's always Dad). They love watching Beijing whiz past without having to walk in the heat. They love the bumpity bumps in the road. I'm sure they love the physical agony Mum endures after a particularly long bike ride in this stinking heat, too.

Oh, it's luxury being a kid!

But, of course, parents are fools for love and we wouldn't have it any other way. We've been out and about on these bikes every weekend and even nipping out in the evenings to our local haunts for dinner.

We were, of course, stupid enough to buy good bikes — top-of-the-range. This means we need to buy a bicycle lock that costs the equivalent of a security guard's monthly wage. Just our luck that one of the few petty crimes that occurs in Beijing is bicycle theft. As a result, we park our bikes (with Fort Knox locks) in full sight of wherever we dine.

The *one time* we left the bikes out of eye-shot for about ten minutes, we returned to see someone had attempted to free them from their Fort Knox locks. Clearly frustrated with their failed attempt, the wannabe thieves decided if they couldn't have the bikes, they'd make off with my removable basket. Not the sharpest knives on the block, they failed to notice the easy-release mechanism and instead, probably in a flying panic, forced the basket right off the frame. This did naught but break the mechanism and leave the basket hanging loosely from the bicycle like a broken bottom lip.

Very annoying.

So we're nervous about the bikes now. I've not once taken mine shopping for fear I'll come back to a vacant space and a gently dangling lock.

Nonetheless, we're totally enjoying riding the bikes for fun rather than transport *per se*, and we're getting to know The Jing's warren of streets even better as a result. There's nothing more luscious than scooting through the soon-to-be-razed *hutongs* near Sanlitun Lu, kicking up a breeze, darting through the dappled sunshine. Just lovely.

And having wheels is also lovely because it makes us feel that little bit closer to feeling welcome — to feeling we're not just tourists on a quick jaunt; that we are *living* here now. And even though we know we could never assimilate into a country like China, it will be great to feel even a teensy bit local.

A Mother's Day

The Taipan experience

Without wanting to come across as pitiful, we left behind a challenging part of our lives in Australia. You probably know all about it: huge mortgage, two small kids, a mother who chooses to stay home rather

than work, a life far away from family and hands-on support, the mind-bending price of disposable nappies, among other consumables. There was many a night when Xiansheng and I wrung out the last drops from the foil bladder of a cask of wine (then inflated it and used it as a football; cheap wine does that to you).

Like many expats, coming to China has provided a wonderful opportunity for our family to have, well, a little more. The cost of living is low, the cash flow is good and the lifestyle easy. Let's just say that we are kind of like sugar-deprived kids in a well-stocked candy store.

On top of this, my role as a mother back home was pretty much all-encompassing. Although it wasn't always easy, I wouldn't trade a minute of it because I was blessed to stay home with the kids in their formative years. Like most mothers, however, I lost a large part of myself when I became a mum. That part is still there, it's just deeply stashed behind the needs of Everyone Else, and although we've only been in Beijing a short time, it's been rather exciting to see that young woman, with a fresh face, bright eyes and bouncy hair, peeking out from behind the ratty, exhausted carcass I dragged over from Australia.

So, when Mother's Day came around, it was with dedicated excitement that I slipped out of the house, at Xiansheng's insistence, for a pampering session at Taipan.

Taipan is quite simply a place you need to frequent if you want a too-good-to-be-true treat. From the orchid-studded wooden walkways to the dimly lit, be-curtained rooms, scented candles and smiling provincial girls with a knack for kneading, this is just heaven for the harried mother.

After I had changed into my little cotton shorts set and ordered my freshly pressed pear juice, I succumbed to the incredulous goose-tingling stress-release that is a Chinese massage.

There *really* is nothing quite like it. The pressure points, the kneading, the rolling, twisting, pushing ... grinding elbows and forearms and fists into constricted muscles. The cupping, flicking, striking that sucks the blood up to the skin's surface like a rouge-daubed sponge. It is one of the most wonderful things you can put a

human body through, and the experience was very overwhelming for me, especially after many, many months of pent-up stress and angst.

When my too-short hour was over, I lay delirious on the massage table in my crumpled shorts set like a rag doll after one too many mocktails at the Toy Inn. I waited until the masseuse left, then I lay in that beautiful, darkened room for a few precious minutes, and wept my heart out.

It really is the simple things that count, and mothers are so good at appreciating them. A massage, a cup of tea, a hug, a card with buttons stuck to it, a butchered breakfast served up sloppy by the kids. Sure, it's tempting to flaunt diamond-bare earlobes in the weeks before the event, but it really is the little things that make the heart toasty.

My most treasured Mother's Day gift is the small dry-mount photo album Xiansheng gave me on my very first M-Day, with black pages and slippery rice paper between each sheet.

Each year, I carefully paste a photo of myself with the kids inside this book, and it's such a precious memento of my motherhood. It's also mildly confronting. I'm not sure I want to watch myself shrink, grey and crinkle over the next 45 years, while my babies grow into tall, spotty, hairy, potentially smelly creatures. Indeed, my husband tortures me by suggesting the trace notes of baby smell still pooling in the crook of my two-year-old son's neck will quite soon be replaced by sweat, pimples, and God forbid, hair.

Being a mother is, of course, a process. It's a journey of the years and an entity of many incarnations. It's something that grows and shifts and moves over time, and each year brings with it a new challenge and a new beauty.

So, regardless of how old or smelly your children are, when M-Day dawns far too early for respectable eyelids to open …

• When the house-husband and scurrying-mice kids batter their way around the house in an attempt to be inconspicuous …

• When you smell the burnt toast curling in under the door crack …

• When you blindly reach for pillows to prop yourself as a child-propelled tray heads towards you, with slopped tea and dismembered fruit …

- When you sip the sloppy tea and the love infused in the brew reaches your toes …
- When you tear-up over the card made with smudged crayon and decorated with mismatched buttons …
- When you giggle and coo at the homemade presents of sagging clay pots and long-forgotten Pokemon cards wrapped in tissues and bound with sticky tape …
- When your daughter reads you a poem that wraps around your heart …

When all of these things happen, you will realise that nothing is better than this. This is as good as it gets. And you wouldn't want more.

Well, except maybe that massage at Taipan.

Acrobatic Marvels

How do they *do* that?

Every country has its thing — often several things — and for China, one of those things is acrobatics.

Having a general aversion to anything too 'touristy', we headed off to Tiandi Theatre with mixed expectations. How impressive was this really going to be? A bunch of skinny work-whipped sad-sacks dressed in yellowing leotards, leaping for pennies? It was kind of awkward going along to see this — a bit like the feeling one gets when visiting an under-funded zoo. But boy, were we in for a surprise.

The show was wonderful. Performed by the China National Acrobatic Troupe, even Riley (not yet two-and-a-half years old) was mesmerised. We sat three rows from the front, our heads resting back, our mouths hanging open with wonder. And what was our favourite? Almost impossible to choose.

Was it the gorgeous bird-like girls with a single feathery plume spouting from the tops of their heads, flinging diabolos around on strings, tossing them into the air and catching them with absolute precision and perfect timing? What about the fact that they danced and kicked their legs like burlesque flamingos at the very same time?

Was it the young boys in gold leotards who projected themselves dart-like through flimsy, bespangled hoops and scaled 30-foot poles like monkeys, only to fling themselves down the poles again, coming to a halt with their chins poised just millimetres from the ground?

Was it the woman who juggled a young boy with her feet? Was it the eight-year-old who rode a unicycle on a high wire? Was it the fifteen or sixteen (I lost count) women who piled onto a single bicycle and rode around and around the stage, stacked and fanning outwards like a peacock tail? Was it the two teens who juggled and bounced twenty balls in a hailstorm, their hands ablur as they walked up and down a staircase? Was it the archetypal girls tossing noodle bowls onto a lofty stack with their feet, or balancing stemmed glassware on their foreheads while performing back-cracking contortions? Was it the young men flinging themselves around underneath a series of seemingly motionless straw hats like crazed, gravity-defying scarecrows?

Or was it the young woman, whippet-thin and constructed entirely of sinew, balancing atop a long pole, slowly meandering her limbs around her head in a pretzel-like fashion? The strength and flexibility had our eyes watering.

So, I'm happy to say we were more than impressed by China's acrobats. The costumes were lush and spangled. The sets and lighting were visually saturating. The music was compelling and the acts were indeed breathtaking.

Frankly, I can't wait for our first round of visitors so we can go back again. And again. And again.

Market Mecca

Where do I begin?

I feel a little embarrassed talking of my first Beijing market shopping experience. And it wasn't to the famed Hongqiao Pearl Market, Silk Market or Ya Show, no no. It was actually to the Tianyi market in the east of Beijing, with several very seasoned Beijing shoppers who knew a thing or two about … *da da de daaaa* — wholesale! (Collective gasp, please.)

Now, you have to understand that a Beijing market experience is a wonder to behold. Sure, it's migraine-inducing, even a little suicidal at times, but it's also a wondrous experience of designer joys for very little cash. It would be easy to go a little coco bananas in a Beijing market of any kind, but a *wholesale* market — where items are at *wholesale* prices? I mean, this is where the marketeers from the Silk Market go to find their wares! Imagine!

Also imagine, if you will, a Western woman (tragic first-timer) exiting Tianyi after two hours of solid acquisitioning, waddling out with five times her girth in black plastic garbage bags. A suburban pack horse (or garbage tip).

Yes, this is what happened, readers, I'm ashamed to say. I pack-horsed my way out of that market and I brought home so much junk, I thought I might faint when I unpeeled everything from the bags and spread them across the lounge room floor.

Coco bananas, all right.

Two Hermès copy bags for the price of one plastic number at Target. A stash of wrapping paper and shimmering ribbons that would take me seven years (and a month's wages) to amass in Australia. Converse shoes for the price of shoelaces. Gap hoodies cheaper than a pair of socks. Diesel t-shirts for the price of a latte.

It was like being stunned with the slap of a wet fish, only it didn't stink at all. It was a divine and surreal experience. I was hopping around

like a gluttonous flea, barely able to contain myself from tearing open my bounty. Heavenly and heavens of heavens.

So now I only have three problems. One: where on earth am I going to store all this stuff? Two: how can I justify this appalling consumption of consumables to Ayi and Xiansheng, let alone myself? And three: which market next??

Spitting and Whizzing in the Street

As opposed to the toilet bowl

You may have heard of split pants — those crotchless duds Chinese babies wear from the early months through their first year. It doesn't take these kids long to toilet train, and neither would you if you were allowed to whiz and poop on every surface, including the lounge room floor.

Initially, this toilet-training method kind of makes sense; it's quick, easy and extends well back to the familial roots of our ancient ancestors, whereby mothers instinctively knew a bowel movement was nearing the end of their child's intestinal journey, just by glancing. It's quick, no fuss, runs on instinct and teaches kids early control. But then, a really important component called Hygiene rears its sparkling head. Not much hygiene going on in a house where one can find whiz and poop on the floor. Nor in the streets, where it's pretty much everywhere. No wonder the Chinese take their shoes off upon entering their homes.

So, despite an admiration for many Chinese ways, this is not one that I (along with most Westerners) understand nor condone. Most of us take years to train our gag reflex to cope with squat toilets let alone a go-anywhere-you-like system. Many a time I've watched children as old as ten toileting themselves in the street. Whizzing in the bushes is

perhaps okay, but laying a turd in the middle of a city sidewalk … Forgive me if I poo-poo that idea.

I'll never forget watching a grandmother dack a two-year-old, who promptly squatted and emptied its bladder in the middle of a pavement of pedestrians, despite the multitude of grassy patches, trees and other options only centimetres away. Even one *side* of the path would have been more acceptable than right in the *middle* of it.

So, this is something I'm struggling with, along with the spitting. I remember my first spit experience. It was in our first week, at one of The Jing's nicest department stores, in the lamp section. I slipped on one — green and plump. I think I threw that shoe out, and my stomach still turns at the thought of it.

Since then, I've mostly just encountered them on the street, and this has led to an uncanny ability to glaze my eyes over when walking on the pavement. Now I just see a haze of pale green spots which I quick-step and trit-trot over like an Irish dancer in need of the loo. You just can't think about it too much. And God forbid if the spot is brown.

There are some things you have to accept in life. Doesn't mean you have to agree with them or even like them, but you may just have to live with them. And the faster we learn to live with these natural Chinese phenomena, the closer we'll feel to fitting in. Hygiene notwithstanding.

Scraping the Sky

Those magnificent men on their dental floss strings

Today we saw something outside our window that had us tearing around the apartment screaming. No, it wasn't Armageddon rolling over the distant northern mountains. Neither was it Santa performing practice laps in his sleigh over the Worker's Stadium.

It was window cleaners.

I mean — *how?* Twenty-six storeys high? On a single rope? Come on. That's just crazy. I would jump up and down until the centre of the earth shattered if my son told me he was going to scale buildings like King Kong and scrape squeegees over windows while dangling from a piece of string.

There's a lot of building going on around Beijing right now, and plenty of suspect safety laws in place (or indeed, no laws at all), so seeing these men dangling from that piece of string, hauling themselves from window to window with no other safety harnesses, no platform, no protective gear other than a pair of overalls and a wet rag ... it was extremely unnerving.

The kids, of course, thought it was brilliant. Those poor puppets on strings became supreme entertainment, and all credit to them for keeping totally immersed and professional while my kids clambered on the windowsills. They'd obviously been told to respect the privacy of the tenants and virtually treat our windows as mirrors — not once did those fellows show even the slightest indication they could see us. Their eyeballs instead stuck firmly to a depth no greater than the actual surface of the glass. Very impressive.

And our windows? Thanks to these daredevils, we can now see forever. Well, as far as the Beijing smog will allow, anyway.

The Great Outdoors

Beijing's death-defying playgrounds

Ah, the great outdoors — Beijing-style. An outdoors fraught with all manner of death-defying excitement. Why not go outside and try it today? Kids can watch in hilarity as parents fuss themselves into a lather over cat whiz, dog poop, human saliva and shards of metal or broken wires jutting from the grass, park bench, wall or children's play equipment. The entertainment value for kids on parental distress cannot be underestimated.

Indeed, probably the happiest outdoor place for expat kiddies in Beijing is a Chinese playground, conveniently located in a cement-padded, shadeless spot in most Beijing parks, and boasting trains, dodgem cars and oxidised merry-go-rounds from 1952. There's Ditan, Ritan, Longtan, Tiantan — park location not important. Wherever you choose, a stressful experience is guaranteed.

The good old 'pay away' system endemic to these playgrounds is a great way to lose post-baby weight. You enter the playground, select a ride, then traipse around looking for the appropriate ticket booth, which could be up to 50 metres away. Not a good thing when you've just installed toddlers, prams, feed sacks, drinks and discarded shoes next to said ride.

So, you grab protesting be-socked babies, pack everything up, traipse over to the ticket booth and attempt to explain the ride you want, complete with barking, mooing, whooshing and bouncing until your bra snaps. You'll then be given a ticket for a ride you *don't* want (who knew a helicopter charade could pass for fishing in a plastic pond?) or it won't be for the right time of day or is unable to be used during February or if your name ends in R.

I'm *not* exaggerating.

Your intense frustration will then be heightened by your wailing babies and the sudden blast of screechy pop songs and Christmas carols from the 1970s, as another rusting ride cranks into life.

Yes, these outdoor playgrounds have enough adrenaline-gushing risk to send any kid into gung-ho superhero mode, impervious to any danger. You will grit your teeth as the rides rattle and roll and careen; yet, all the while, your kids will be totally entranced, totally immersed, overcome with the cranking, joyous noise of it all — the kitschness, the subtle protruding-wire danger, the … the … Chinese-ness.

And, amidst the noise and the squeals, you'll actually feel like you're achieving something by keeping your toddler relatively safe in these crazy surroundings, where Chinese kids run amok and get good and filthy without a wet-wipe in sight, and their faces are glowing and their parents (or more likely grandparents) are gazing at them with such love and such all-encompassing adoration.

And suddenly you are filled with a renewed sense of love for your own children, and even though your eyes stay locked on their every move, the intensity of your gaze softens a little. The muck and the protruding wires and the rusty patches seem less threatening ... and you remember where you are on the planet and you just feel *good*.

Oh, hang it. Wet-wipes, please!

Taxi!

To ride or not to ride ...

Today I had to stuff our kids into a taxi with no seatbelts. It was horrifying to me. How incredibly negligent to ride the hazardous streets of Beijing completely belt-free. I mean, come on. This kind of thing attracts a whopping great fine in Australia and is absolutely unheard of; you just wouldn't get into a car without a firm, operational seatbelt for every occupant. Well, anyone with a brain wouldn't, anyway.

Beijing is a little bit different (along with most of Asia, for that matter). But then I guess if people are riding motorbikes and bicycles without helmets, and if parents are dinking kids on the back of their bikes with nary a harness nor protective head gear in sight, and if window-washers dangle from 30-storey buildings by a piece of dental floss, I suppose seatbelts in cars are also an afterthought.

So what to do? Stay out of taxis? Stay at home and never leave? We have a car but Xiansheng uses it for work and if I need to ferry the kids around during the day, what do I do?

It's a rarity, but I did need to take them out today, and a cab was the only option. Oh, the parental guilt when I stuffed my two-year-old and four-year-old into their first belt-less taxi. The shame! The negligence! Terrible mother!

I tried to justify the trip by telling myself it was only around the

corner, and that the traffic in Beijing is so bad we can only travel a few kilometres an hour. But the raging guilt continued so I grabbed both kids and locked them in a vice-like grip in the back seat, mentally prepping every swerve with preventative safety measures. The kids didn't utter a word of protest as I avidly braced for the possibility of a bingle (probably because they also couldn't breathe).

Anyway, we made it there and back easily and without a scrape, other than two very sore diaphragms and a mother who stumbled out of the taxi wild-eyed and bushy-haired.

Will I do it again? Maybe. After all, we also brought our kids to a country with the highest hepatitis rate in the world, an almost non-existent percentage of canine rabies vaccination, and pollution levels high enough to turn your lungs to pus.

Frankly, *every day* is like a taxi ride with no seatbelts.

Liangma Flower Market

The first time ever I saw your blooms ...

When we first arrived in Beijing, we were taken to the Liangma flower market near the north-east Third Ring Road. It's quite a small market, yet when we pushed through the front doors, the assault on my senses was something I'll never forget.

Visually, it was a *Wizard of Oz* movie-set of wonder: rows and rows and rows of blooms in every colour and variety imaginable — so bright, so luscious, my eyes boggled. I actually had to close them to cope with the beauty.

There were white lilies popping from dark green sticks like clusters of stars and roses in every imaginable hue, each sweet head encased in a soft netted bonnet, to keep the petals from furling outwards. Some bonnet-less roses even had their petals dipped in sparkling blue glitter. There were

orchids, too — elegant painted ladies dipping their heads into the fragrant perfume of purple hyacinth below. There were pastel lisianthus, miniature daisies and blousy collections of flouncing pink peonies.

Our eyes were awash. And that was only our eyeballs. You know that wonderful, musky smell you get when you walk past a florist? Well times it by one hundred, and that is the scent that descends upon you when you enter Liangma for the first time. It slips up your nostrils and turns on something wonderfully floral in your brain.

Needless to say, when we left the market, I was toting several forests of flowers, and Xiansheng was also lugging an Amazon jungle or two. And I mean lugging. We had three white orchid plants, a couple of small green shrubs, and probably eight or nine bunches of blooms. And the most blissful thing of all? The entire lot cost the equivalent of a single bunch of flowers in Australia.

Floral heaven.

I now visit weekly and know the vendors already. I know the ribbon lady on the first floor who lost her husband in a car accident (one of the many Chinese to suffer this fate; seatbelt, anyone?). I know the check-out chick upstairs who is pregnant. I know the lady in the plant section who gives me the best *laowai* price on orchids in Beijing. It's a community of plants and flowers, and every week, I return home with my arms piled so high, I can't see over the top.

Ayi just stares at me when I struggle in the door with my forest of flowers, horrified at such a flagrant waste of money. Indeed, it seems cut flowers last half the length of time they do in Australia — probably a combination of the questionable water and the chronically drying air. Peonies are particularly prone to this phenomenon; they seem to last just minutes, but boy do they put on a show. Blousy, pouffy, delicate, succulent — no one could stare into a peony and not want to bury their nose deep into its folds. No wonder it's China's national bloom.

I'm burying, sniffing and drowsy from the perfume … and making the most of every scented moment.

the Ayi Love Triangle

Parenting is a relative concept

The gods are smiling on you, little one. Who is she, this dark-haired angel on earth who will acquiesce to your every mortal and spiritual need before the demand has even arisen? Part psychic, part adoring fawner, this woman has been sent from above to provide all that your mum and dad will not. Yes … even in a pink fit and during a blue moon.

Of course, you are naturally oblivious to the tension and frustration this total compliance causes your mum, but what does it matter? At least *two* of you in this parental triangle are happy. You have the need for adoration and Ayi has the need to give it … a pure and harmonious union that Mum will never understand. Instead, Dragon Woman watches from the sidelines, trying not to sweat the small stuff; hoping, in her heart of hearts, this will not turn you into a discipline-deprived despot before the year is out.

No, this is not a description of my son and his *ayi*. This is a description of someone else's son/daughter/dog and *their ayi*.

My *ayi* doesn't seem to be developing this kind of relationship with my kids. She's not overly warm nor affectionate, and, frankly, she's much more interested in just getting her work done and getting out the door. This suits me okay. I don't want a mummy replacement in my house and I don't think I'd want the deep emotional attachment I'm watching develop between other *ayis* and their charges.

Each to their own, but I wouldn't want the drama. Nor do I want to be squabbling with another adult over the best way to discipline or raise my own kids. This is bad enough in the West, and Lord knows the Chinese do things very differently here — the whizzing and the pooping is only the tip of the iceberg.

Yes, I'm glad my *ayi* is just getting on with her business and skirting

around my kids. Maybe it's a good thing. Or maybe I'm just telling myself this because I see those other *ayis* smooching their charges and fawning over their every move ... and perhaps I'm jealous.

Just maybe.

Our First Tea Ceremony

Oh joy!

In a nutshell, life is made up of these things: mental, physical and emotional challenges; wondrously huge life-changing experiences; plenty of mundanity; and those little 'moments'. Those moments that make life beautiful. They can be short moments like when your child encircles their arms around your neck and lands their sweet lips on your cheek, or when you catch them chatting to imaginary friends. Or they can be longer moments like hikes between the Jinshanling and Simitai sections of the Great Wall ... or Chinese tea ceremonies.

Ah, the ceremony of tea. Such a lovely thing to do — and a bonus if you like tea, particularly green tea. I could bathe in green tea nightly, so quaffing the stuff, in an extensive range of styles, is quite all right by me.

Today we went with the kids to the network of streets just south of Qianmen Dajie, to a little teahouse with beautiful girls in green silk standing outside, lulling you in with the waft of oolong. We walked to the back of the store, past the glass containers housing grassy tea, to a nest of tables topped with beautiful serving trays and teapots in glass and clay.

The girl who took the tea ceremony spoke a little English, but even if she hadn't, the beauty and understanding that comes with this ancient ritual really defies language barriers.

This is what they do ...

First, boiling water is brought to your table and placed on the carved wooden serving tray, then the server will tip the steaming water onto dried green leaves in a glass teapot. She will swirl the leaves briefly, then tip the water out (to clean the leaves). Then she will add more water and replace the lid. Here she will pause.

After a few moments, the server will pour the tea into very small, tube-like cups and top them with little handle-less teacups, like a jiggly lid. She will then hand this capped cup to each guest who will pick it up, flip it upside town and pull the tubed cup out. The tea will *schplonk* into the lid and then everyone drinks — three sips to drain the cup is best. When the tea is drained, you smell the cup and then bring the tube-like vessel close to your open eyeball, to glaze it with hydrating steam.

You are then poured more tea, and each time you drain it you smell the cup and notice the intensity and fragrance of the tea as it plumps and takes in more water at each soaking. Notice how it deepens and intensifies, how the flavour begins to alter.

After the very grassy, asparagus-y new tea, you might try florally teas like rosehip, jasmine or chrysanthemum flower. You can place entire chrysanthemum buds in your teacup and watch them open into a magnificent bloom. Afterwards, you might like to get adventurous and try the patchouli smokiness of barley tea or the fat-stripping *pu-erh*.

Then, lastly, comes the oolong. The most expensive tea in the world is in the oolong family. It has a distinctive taste and its myriad varieties have spawned an entire world of tea connoisseurs who sample and rate their brews like the finest wines.

Alas, my tongue isn't sophisticated enough to tell the difference between a moderately priced and outrageously expensive oolong, so we went for the cheapest available and bought a small amount on leaving — along with jasmine, rose, barley and a few cases of delicious, traditional tea snacks.

It may be the caffeine talking, but I'm totally hooked.

The Board Game Trap

It's a mousetrap all right

I was well prepared for indoor boredom issues before we left Australia, and firmly set down in my mind that this was a) temporary and b) we knew what we were in for and would just have to find ways to cope with it. If an incalculable percentage of the world's kids can spend their lives in apartments, we can surely spend four years doing the same.

And so when we left Australia, along with our eight million books, I packed the entire Parker Brothers and Hasbro range of board games, every card game ever shuffled, and a massive supply of arts and crafts, educational products and anything that even vaguely resembled a capacity for indoor sports (like tennis balls on elastic bands, whereupon they cannot smash things *too* easily).

According to chapter nine, subclause 38 of Murphy's Parental Law, when a parent spends either a lot of money or a lot of time acquiring something, kids develop a violent aversion to it. Even more so if you cart it to the other side of the world and have limited storage in your apartment. Consequently, neither of my kids will bat an eyelid at the fabulous, pro-endorsed automatic golfball putting returner we lugged over to Beijing. And other than Twister, the board games still pretty much remain untouched, ditto the ridiculously expensive set of educational products from the Early Learning Centre.

Curses.

Interesting that our kids won't hesitate to smash twelve eggs in order to obtain urgent use of a crappy old egg carton to make Noah an ark, or whine for eight hours straight until I burn a thumb and ruin a pot making homemade playdough.

Incidentally, said homemade playdough is now a weekly occurrence and is met with squeals of delight when the last of the blue food colouring has been agonisingly kneaded through with my playdough-

kneading-RSI-stricken-Smurf-blue hands. It is then liberally rolled, cut and moulded for about 28.7 seconds before being left to dry into a cement-like cowpat, never to be used again.

Sigh. The parenting perils continue no matter *where* you are in the world.

The Wall

Surreal moments in time

We've actually not been in a hurry to see the Great Wall of China. I mean, 2000 years have already passed; it's probably not going anywhere in a hurry. And we figure we'll be sick of seeing the thing by the time we take all our potential visitors for a gander.

But when ANZA (the Australia/New Zealand network in Beijing) provided the chance to attend a black-tie dinner on the Wall recently, we absolutely couldn't resist. The Wall might be the Wall, but the Wall with a frock, tux, champagne flute and dancing for 80? Come on. It had to be done.

So we did it.

Xiansheng had the tuxedo handmade, including pin-tucked shirt and classic bow tie, by our new tailor Xiao Fei. He looked exquisite, might I just say. And I wore a black and pink silk creation with a pair of vintage heels (by vintage I mean old and skanky) and both the tux and the dress and all associated paraphernalia cost less than a pair of decent shoes would at home. Nice.

Ayi babysat and 80 of us piled into a couple of buses, armed with sparkling wine and plastic cups, and I spent the last part of the journey with my nose glued to the window, anxiously anticipating that first Great glimpse.

Tears sprang to my eyes when I first saw it through the dimming light and misty fog. It struck me how tall it was. I mean, it went *up*. I was

expecting it to sort of undulate like a snake when in fact it scaled heights like a leaping tiger. One point was so high, scaling those steps would have taken six months off your heart muscle. Really. We avoided it. We were in silk frocks and heels, after all.

Following the long bus ride and copious fluids by mouth, many of us were anxious to find a bathroom upon arrival. Call it what you will but it wasn't really a bathroom. Yes, they were squat toilets, which I'm okay with mostly, but let's just say these were the type that tested your mettle.

I took a deep breath, ran in, hoisted up that dress, straddled those stilettos either side of the pan and went on full jet power. I then stood, kicked the flush button with my foot and watched in horror as the entire contents of that toilet rose up out of the bowl … and all over my shoes.

Oh yes, I screamed. Then I somehow got out, hobbled across the car park and tried to erase this horrendous experience for the rest of the evening — not an easy accomplishment with Eau de Sewer wafting up from one's feet.

But the setting on the Wall soon erased even the greatest pong. It was truly divine.

A wide, curved part of the Wall had been transformed into a James Bond movie set. Waiters in white coats toted silver trays with old-fashioned champagne bowls, glinting in the red light of dozens of Chinese lanterns. Men in black tuxedos and smelling of cologne flirted with women in gorgeous gowns and baubles as the night descended. Music hummed gently while the red-hemmed buffet groaned under delicious delicacies and, above us all, the Great Wall loomed high, draped up the hillside silently.

The evening was quite surreal, really. Eating dinner was surreal, laughing with guests was surreal, phoning home to brag to family and friends — 'Guesh where we are? *Hic!*' — was surreal. The sudden rain shower and brolly-popping was surreal and then the most surreal part of all was when the music pumped up after dinner, and the DJ spun some dance tracks and we got on that Wall in our stinky heels and boogied the night away.

There is a Chinese saying that you are not a great man until you have walked on the Great Wall of China. We created another that night: you are not a great woman until you have *danced* on the Great Wall of China. And so we did. And as hits from the '70s, '80s and '90s spewed across the valley, I can imagine that wise, ancient structure sighing to itself, '*Sheesh*. And so it comes to this. In my day …'

If only we could hear what it had to say.

The Bai Jiu Thing

Bingeing on rocket fuel fires up expat *tai tais*

Have you heard about *bai jiu*? Let me tell you a little something about it, but fasten your seatbelt.

Literally 'white alcohol', *bai jiu* is a rice-based cousin of methylated spirits, and is a nightmare for any *tai tai* who would actually like her Xiansheng to keep on living. It's not the actual spirit that has the potential to kill you — it's the quantities it's imbibed in.

I detest the stuff. Not only does it taste like liquid crapola, it comes with a certain unsaid machismo that I suppose can only be matched by Australian beer guzzlers on a heavy pub-razing binge. Its rash consumption is honestly quite ridiculous and I'll never understand it so long as my goody-two-shoes sensibilities allow.

I do enjoy alcohol, don't get me wrong. Bubbles are my tipple of choice but I also enjoy wine and a cocktail or aperitif or two. Margaritas are my serious poison, but at least they taste great for goodness sake, and you can savour and enjoy them. Not so with *bai jiu*.

Bai jiu is used for the sole purpose of proving how much 'ocean capacity' you have for drink. When you drink it, no matter how large

the serving, it must be drained in one gulp — *gan bei* or 'dry glass'. If it's done in sips, you're a girl.

Many *bai jiu* sessions are work-related. Participants eat dinner and begin an endless round of toasting, starting with the most senior person in the party, and continuing on down to the minions. Everyone must be toasted, and it's even better if you toast someone several times, especially your host.

Xiansheng accepts these sessions as an important building block in his work with the Chinese and he does it well and with gusto, but it terrifies me to see him *bai jiu*-pickled. Peeling a pickled husband off the floor has given me and plenty of other *tai tai* much cause for alarm. It's not easy, but like many things in China, I don't have to understand it — I just have to try to accept it. Hell, I've even participated. And I did Xiansheng proud.

It was a party of around fifteen and I was toasted very deliberately on several occasions. Every eye lingered on my glass, awaiting an upside down slam onto the table (if a drop of liquid falls, your glass is not 'dry'). Usually, women are not expected to *gan bei*, but I wanted to show support for Xiansheng and I knew the importance of making an effort. So I drained glass after glass. And when the *bai jiu* ran dry and the beer came out, I also drained every glass of amber ale.

The Chinese were stunned. I almost literally had eyeballs on the bottom of every glass I touched, and when I was suitably blathered and had rightfully impressed Xiansheng's colleagues, I was released from the bounds of alcohol poisoning, but only after much carousing on how, as a *woman*, I was able to perform such a feat.

The Australians around the table simply smiled. I guess these *bai jiu* skolling pros had never taken on an Aussie sheila before.

'Nuff said.

The Great Indoors

It's an inner battle

When Ella started full-time school recently, I had the Herculean task of occupying the mind and body of a small boy who was used to spending the majority of his waking hours in a large, flat backyard with shady trees, purple flowers, a splash pool, all manner of outdoorsy toys (including sheets billowing on the clothesline), squeaky clean air and the soft pop of tennis balls.

When we were entrapped in our Beijing apartment on Night One, my first order of business for Riley was to rule out the no-jumping/climbing-on-furniture rule. I mean, how hellish would life be if a two-year-old had to actually *stand on the floor*, walking around chairs and sofas all night and day? Hellish. Riley has therefore been allowed to climb, scale, balance, jump, bound and leap to his heart's content. Yes, even on the beds. And obstacle courses and cubby houses have been encouraged daily.

My only exception is standing on the roomy windowsills, mainly because it invariably comes with the hammering of little fists on plate glass windows. At 26 floors high and with questionable sealing holding these giant windows in place … well, it is forbidden (and, of course, as a result, it's where he wants to climb the most).

I've tried to get Riley into the Great Beijing Outdoors when I can. It ain't no Aussie backyard but I really put an effort into finding fun haunts for him. There is photographic proof of trips to Chaoyang Park, Ritan and Ditan parks, to the sandpit downstairs in our building *(what was I thinking?)*, to the Worker's Stadium, to the little strip of walking track behind our complex, to friends' yards, to the Chinese workout station on the street … I really made an effort. But this effort has gradually worn me down.

Was it the hacking, hocking and spitting that did it? Was it the

cloying pollution? The dog poop and cigarette butts poking out of the dusty grass? The jagged pieces of metal and rusting holes in the play equipment? The 'don't walk on the grass' signs in every park when my son is aching to tread on soft green blades or even roll and press his ribs into them?

After a few short months, the outings have all but stopped. Only on pristinely clear days is Riley allowed outside, and that's never. The poor kid pulls at the front door like our apartment is a prison and he's doing Life. He begs to go outside but mostly he begs to go to the beach. A lot.

I've tried to do the playgroup thing and make friends with the kids of other mums — through my husband's work, through Ella's school, through neighbours, through the fellow *laowai* met on the streets ... but this is often difficult. Sometimes it's language and cultural barriers. Sometimes it's timing. Sometimes it's the fact that we live too far away from each other or that nap times clash — different cultures, different nap times. And is Australia the only country in the world where kids wake early and go to bed early? Many is a time we are invited for play dates at seven in the evening, just when our kids are settling down for sleepy-byes.

But the biggest issue for securing play dates for our son is the transitory nature of expat life in Beijing. People are already leaving and we've only been here five months. The good ones go quickly; they charm you and then they leave. This would surely stick in your craw after a while. I can see why some long-term expats have stopped 'caring' about people because, after a time, you just have to clear your craw.

So, darling little Riley makes best friends with all the kids who either leave pretty much soon after meeting, or who are planning on going away for twelve weeks over summer. Not us, alas. We are here this summer — oh Lord, we are *here*. And as for the kids who *won't* be going away and are available to play ... well, Riley either refuses to play with them or they're little shits or their mothers drive me bonkers.

Such is Beijing life.

Bu Xie

No need to thank

There's a phrase in China that essentially means 'no problem' or 'you're welcome' or 'don't mention it'. It's *bu xie* (pronounced 'boo shee-eh' and meaning literally: don't thank).

Due to its no-nonsense, somewhat abridged use, Mandarin doesn't frequently feature the word 'please'. One *does* say 'thank you', but it's not cloyingly over-used in the general vernacular as it is in the West, where its impact is often rendered meaningless.

In China, kids don't thank their parents for passing the soy sauce. It's not because they're rude, it's because their parents don't expect to be thanked. It's *normal* for them to pass the sauce; no expectations for thanks — it's the least they could do, it's only sauce after all. Friends see this similarly: the more you have to thank someone, the less important you are to them. Friends really don't need to thank, it's that simple.

Just before we left Australia, our Mandarin teacher, Ping, took us to lunch (on a very meagre student income) to thank us for all we had done for her during our mutual time living in Adelaide. It was a wonderful lunch. She brought along a Chinese colleague and we feasted and drank and toasted each other as is the true Chinese way, and at the end of the meal, I thanked Ping in front of her friend.

A short time later, I thanked her again, and she brushed this second thank you off with a nervous smile. The next time I thanked her, she became clearly uncomfortable, and by the fourth time, she pulled me aside to tell me my endless thanks made our friendship appear less valuable, especially in front of her Chinese colleague, and could I stop it right now please.

In a way, her reaction makes a lot of sense, but I still can't stop the thanking habit — it's that socially entrenched. At first I thought I

should drop it while in China, but it really is something Xiansheng and I feel strongly about … and we'll therefore continue to teach it to our children, China or no China.

So, despite the ceaseless requests *not* to thank — from everyone I thank — we'll continue with the over thanking. Whenever I thank Ayi for dinner or for doing something miniscule, she continues to say '*bu xie*' each time, yet I still thank. It's sort of like a little tug of war. And do you know what? I'm noticing she actually doesn't mind it now. She actually appears to appreciate the thanks. Just as I'm growing used to the Mandarin way, she too seems to be growing used to the Aussie way.

Isn't that understanding what multiculturalism is all about?

The Foodie House of Horrors

Do people really eat this stuff?

Okay, I am officially intrigued by this whole Chinese food delicacy thing. Since arriving in the capital, we have had some interesting experiences with the insides and outside of various entities that have either crawled, hopped or slithered in their previous incarnation.

Our first experience was the restaurant across from our house. A joint frequented nightly by Party members in black Audis, we were keen to see what the fuss was all about. We got frocked up, asked Ayi to babysit the kids, and trotted off across the road.

It was a lovely restaurant. Great service, beautiful décor, even quite busy — that solid indicator of good food. I guess we should have sensed something might go awry when I asked for wine (*pu tao jiu*). The girl stared at me like I'd just asked for marshmallow curry. Xiansheng and I settled for beer; not such a big deal.

When we were presented with the food menu, however, things kind of plummeted into the bowels of a horror film. Do you recall those times in life when you feel like you've entered the Haunted House at a carnival? You wonder if you're dreaming somehow, but then it dawns on you with mounting horror, that this is *real*. Well, running my eyes over this menu was one of those times.

I flicked those pages. I flicked and flicked and found nothing but carnage. Nothing but the dismembered corpses of non-specific living beings, from sea slugs to cows.

Sure, they say these foods are meant to be delicacies, but forgive me, eating something that not long ago siphoned pig poo is not my idea of delicacy. Let me just run through a small sample of the mouth-watering menu items on offer:

boiled duck blood with pickled red pepper

scalding chicken kidneys

duck claw with pickled vegetables

sliced pig's ear

crystal duck's tongue

white fungus with fruit sauce

flavoured bullfrog

shredded bowel with garlic

snakehead slices

and the pièce de résistance — braised beef penis, kidney and bowel (*mm-mmm*, a tantalising blend).

To be fair, they did have some 'regular' dishes, too — and I would have gone for chicken, but after seeing a picture of a whole, charred chook complete with claws and head, floating in a bowl of grey soup, I suspected even an innocent breast fillet would come stuffed with blanched gizzards.

Feeling brave, Xiansheng ordered a plate of sliced duck, which arrived slimy, pimply and done to an appetising shade of puce. It was surrounded by pale, throat-clutchingly dry dumplings and three mysterious sauces that could well have been any of the above menu items, shoved in a blender and whizzed.

Of all the items on the menu, I could only stomach asking for two: salmon sashimi and lobster pieces with noodles. You can imagine my horror when the waitress said both dishes were not available that night.

'*Mei you.*' Don't have.

Oh *mei you, mei you!* I could write a tome about this phrase, so oft repeated and so oft scratching to my ears. It seems to be *mei you* bloody everything in this town.

Faced with a despairing and nauseated stomach, I scanned that little book of horrors again and finally settled on a plate of broccoli and a plate of pumpkin. How bad could that be? So I pointed to the broccoli and said 'one of these' and then to the pumpkin, and said 'one of these'.

Then the confusion began.

How so much confusion can be created over 'one of these' and 'one of these', complete with pointing finger, remains completely mystifying to me. Perhaps the waitress was wondering why someone would order two plates of vegetables for dinner. *Hello!* Just take one look at the abattoir floor you're serving for dinner!

So. After much to-ing and fro-ing, the broccoli arrived, bunched into the shape of a brain and covered in a shiny sauce of lard mixed with Gravox. And the pumpkin. My God. How can pumpkin be so tortured? Boiled, pale, stringy, sad — laying in a bowl of used dishwater with a handful of pimply red berries scattered on top (marinated chicken testicles, perhaps?).

It was when I sampled the pumpkin and the bile rose into my throat that I knew our time was up in the Little Shop of Horrors. Two minutes later we were paid, on the street, across the road and straight into Subway, where I struggled to choke down a vegetarian sandwich.

For a country with such a rich variety of exquisite food, why oh why is scraping the abattoir floor considered a delicacy? Yet another intriguing mystery of the Middle Kingdom.

Mei You

Holy Toledo! Bugger! Darn it and damnation!

Okay, I have to elaborate a little more on the *mei you* thing because it's really driving me loop de loop.

Mei you, pronounced 'may yo', is pretty much the shopper's equivalent of all-sold-out. It means 'don't have' and is blurted with frustrating regularity in this town, but not just at markets. It also happens habitually in restaurants, especially in restaurants where the only menu choice is braised beef bowel or chicken nuts (and I don't mean legumes). Let me clarify here that this *mei you* term won't ever apply to the beef bowel or chicken nuts themselves. It will only apply to anything remotely edible or to whatever size you happen to wear or to anything you need urgently and can't find anywhere else. Or all of the above.

It's like Confucian Law (move over Murphy) and its recurrence is truly one of the marvels of life in China.

The other intriguing thing about this *mei you* phenomenon is that it's said to you when it isn't necessarily true. Sometimes it's said when the person can't be bothered looking for something for you. Or if your price is too low. Or if they don't like you. Or if they just don't *know* whether or not they have it. This applies with exasperating regularity because, in China, no one wants to appear as if they *don't know*. They'd rather lie than utter those very simple, basic words of 'Actually … I don't know.' Or God forbid, 'I don't know, *but why don't I find out for you?*'

Having said that, you just have to bide your time. If China teaches you anything, it's patience — and the fact that anything can be done and anything can be found and anything can be for sale. If you bide your time, the *mei you* phenomenon will evaporate like a plate of hot pork dumplings on a street corner, and you'll once again be grinning from ear to ear, extolling the magical land of China, where anything is possible.

If you can wait.

Alas — for me — patience? *Mei you!*

The Jolly Green Giant

My feet are like Goofy shoes

In Australia, my feet are a size nine (a European 40). This size is relatively normal in our country — perhaps on the larger size of normal but then I am 174 centimetres tall so I need *some* kind of counterbalance down below. Anyway, the point is this: at home, I can buy size nine shoes at every store in town, unless they are sold out to the myriad other size-nine shoe shoppers.

Here in Beijing, my feet are *not* normal. They are bordering on gargantuan. Now I know how Goofy, Minnie and Mickey Mouse feel, poor buggers. They, too, would have a tough time finding shoes for those plates of meat, although I'm sure a kindly illustrator could whip some up in a pinch. Me, I'm not so lucky.

As I came to Beijing with quite literally two or three pairs of shoes, I have been on the shoe hunt pretty much consistently since arriving. What a low blow this shoe shopping experience has been. I mean, really low — like, foot level.

Sheesh. I mean, they're not *that* huge but in the eyes of the shoe stores of Beijing, it seems I have been endowed with clown shoes for feet. Snow shoes. Skis. Surfboards. After trawling the shoe shops of Wangfujing Street in search of anything even remotely worthy of my enormous clodhoppers, I had the crestfallen experience of being rejected from shop after shop like a banished podiatry heathen. I mean, for goodness sake, I'm surprised I could even get my feet in the door, they were that enormous. I kept tripping over and knocking things from shelves 2 metres away if I so much as twinkled a toe.

I'll never forget walking into one last shoe shop, bright-eyed and unabashedly hopeful that perhaps *this* one would have something greater than a size 39. *Mei you, mei you* and *mei you.*

I'll tell you what you can do with your bloody *mei you.*

But more than the *mei you* humiliation was the looks I got. This last girl, upon my announcement that I was searching for a size 40 shoe, took one look at my face, then unhinged her eyeballs and slowly, ever so steadily, rolled them down my body, over my chin, down my neck, over the lumps of my boobs, down my stomach, over each thigh, my knees and ankles to my feet — two massive, flapping platters with nothing but two straps of red leather strung between my colossal Moses-tablet toes.

I followed her eyes myself and looked down at those forlorn sandal-clad, almost-naked slabs, and I honestly don't think I've seen anything so enormous in my life. Tears sprang to my eyes, I was so horrified.

I smiled weakly, fired up my 'reverse mode' warning beep and backed out of the store. Then I went home and very quickly logged onto www.humungousclodhoppers.com and ordered me some shoes.

More on the Jolly Green Giant

You could show Chinese cartoons on my arse

Like my feet, I'm not petite: a size twelve in Australia, a size eight in the United States. In Australia, I'm quite slim and trim. Here, in China, you could show cartoons on my arse, it's so enormous. You could land jumbo jets on my thighs and don't even mention my acres of love handles and bowlful of jelly belly. Olympians could swim laps in it.

When I sift through the dolls clothes on the racks in Beijing's clothing stores for women, I take my five-year-old daughter with me, and many of them would fit her. These are some *teensy* women. I could span the upper chest of many a Chinese woman with one hand and she'd be completely covered. I once tried on a Chinese bra. It fit around my chest, but my boobs were pushed so far together, I could have jammed a bunch of lilies in there (bear in mind that cleavage is not usual for me).

And forget about knickers. In fact, forget about anything that involves encasing my drive-in-movie-screen derrière. I've found A-line skirts that gape around the waist, but as soon as hips or thighs want to get involved, you can forget it. The Chinese feature a race of women built like ten-year-old boys — a shape highly envied in the West, which is jam-packed with curvy bums, hips, thighs, bellies and boobs.

Truth be told, the size thing in Beijing can get mighty depressing after a while. Not only because you can't find any clothes to fit, but also because your self-perception becomes distorted. After all, isn't life about comparisons? How else could I feel somewhat slim in Australia but like a sumo wrestler in China?

It was with much celebration, then, that I found some jeans at Ya Show market that were big enough to encase my rear end, let alone my thighs (admittedly, they *are* stretch jeans). Once again I had the China problem — gaping waistband and skin-tight thighs, but this was nothing a small adjustment couldn't fix, and the fact that I could even get my thighs into them was cause for much leaping about. I bought eight pairs on the spot.

Thank God for Lycra — the best friend of Jolly Green Giants all over China.

Xiao Fei

Jolly green giant sympathiser

Right. *That's it!*

I've decided that if I can't find anything to cover my movie-screen rear end, I'll rustle up some queen size bed sheets and head to a tailor to see if she can fashion something large enough to swathe my behind.

I've never had any clothes made before. Sooo exciting! When I first arrived here with my ten-year-old pair of jolly green giant-sized jeans, it didn't even occur to me that I would be indulging in tailor-made clothing. Such a luxurious thought would have fit in my skull like a square peg in a round hole. But it's true, it's true, it's true! I'm having some clothes made. The thought of it not only clunks around in my head awkwardly, it also pulls the corners of my mouth upward and makes my eyeballs water.

Who'd have ever dreamed I could have ten silk dresses and five wool suits made for the price of one custom-made polyester suit at home? This is a fashionista's Nirvana. A *tai tai's* trance. A style maven's studio of delight.

I met with our tailor — the one who made Xiansheng's tux for the Great Wall event — Xiao Fei. She's lovely and obviously talented. She has minimal English but does know the words for 'button, seam, long, short, zip, sleeve, wool, silk, cotton, cashmere, skirt and dress' — a vocabulary that, combined with plenty of sign language, could easily produce a solid working relationship.

Clothes know no language barrier!

So, I've ordered two lime-green skirt suits and a powder-pink pea coat and two Chanel-style cropped, bouclé jackets. Chanel style! I mean, come on — this is madness, Jackie O! This is coming from a woman who has spent the last two years in tracksuit pants from Big W and colours her own hair with boxes from the supermarket.

I'm gagging with try-it-on-quick desire. I can't wait for the fitting, which is only a week away. She works fast this woman, and that is good because I'm going to drive everyone bananas in the waiting. Jackets? I have jackets! And suits! A *tai tai's* dream.

Please don't wake me up.

Princess Diana Moments

People are doing good things in this town

Sometimes life throws Princess Diana Moments at you. These are moments where something happens and you're not quite sure it should be you experiencing them or whether it should really be Princess Diana (or any other princess you fancy).

I recently met a man involved in the opening of Beijing's first scholarship vocational school for underprivileged teens (and I mean really underprivileged). I was so intrigued and impressed by the school, the man asked if I would like to attend the opening ceremony and present teachers with certificates. Sure. Why not? I can put on a suit and grin and I'm very good at handing people things and shaking hands. Princess Diana, I am not — but I *can* do this.

So, on the day of the school opening, I frocked up in one of my new lime-green Xiao Fei suits, put a très sophisticated French roll in my hair, slung some baubles around my neck and dusted off my fake Hermès handbag.

When we got to the school, I was greeted by some directors and led through the centre of a line-up of about 60 teenagers, who all broke into applause the moment I walked through. It was an intensely moving moment. These are kids from families who earn less than 50 bucks a month, who have probably never tasted chocolate and have one set of clothes, for goodness sake. And they were applauding *me*. It was *them*

who needed the applause, so I clapped right back. While trying not to cry. This school was a ticket to bigger and better things for these kids; the thrill of it was overwhelming.

Following a quick tour of the school, the opening ceremony began with singers, dancers, speeches and heart-rending words from one of the students' grateful mothers, who had just beaten cancer only to find out her husband was now stricken. Talk about being handed more than your share.

The ceremony experience was wonderful. I handed out certificates to a few people bearing megawatt grins, then I presented a short talk to these glorious young students on the youth of Australia, their schooling, work and lifestyle. Featuring a slideshow of houses, beaches, windsurfers, teens, fashion and Aussie food, it didn't dawn on me until later that these kids were probably seeing such things for the first time ever. Windsurfers? What the? No wonder they sat in stunned silence. I may as well have made a presentation to Plutonians on Pluto; this was so like another planet to them.

Good Lord. How I wanted to snatch these young people and hold them to my heart and squeeze them and take them home with me. Every single one of them. How I wanted to take them around the world to witness the wonder that is our Earth — its people, its cultures, its joys and horrors. We all need this. We all need to see this. It's horrifying to me that these kids have no idea what exists outside their own shanty town.

This experience was a heartbreaking, enlightening and beautiful one. These are the people who will be creating China's future, and to see the determination and strength and hope in their eyes … it was a moment in life I won't soon forget.

Princess Diana, eat your heart out.

Summer in the Jing Sucks

It's a cesspit hellhole

I will never understand people who say they love summer. I don't get it. Perhaps people see mangoes, icy poles, surfing and outdoor BBQs when they think of summer. I do, too, but I also see sticky hands, sand in your swimmers, sunburn and stinking hot nights, unable to sleep because you a) don't have an air-conditioner, or b) you don't want to turn it on and make a bigger hole in the ozone layer.

Sure, I'd love summer too if I could sail to Corsica on a yacht wearing a bikini on a supermodel body while sipping cool bubbles and absconding to an air-conditioned house to sleep under a mosquito net, lulled to sleep by the lapping ocean.

Back to reality.

The reality of summer in Beijing is that we're stuck inside and if we do go outside, we melt instantly or choke on the pollution that bakes and gets even more foul under the blistering summer sun. There's no cooling sea breeze, no seafood and fresh summer fruit on the beach, and no swinging in lazy hammocks under the shade of a coconut tree here, no no.

There's warm beer, flies on meat at the wet market, ponging stinks from the gutters, overheating taxis spewing black smoke, and the highly offensive, burning fingers of an overheated sun, poking you right in the skin. We went to Chaoyang Park the other day, and I swear to God, I felt like a lobster being plunged alive into a boiling pot of water; we were dripping wet when we got home. No wonder the Chinese carry umbrellas to shield them from the sun. At first I thought it was daggy; they won't wear sunglasses or hats but they'll tote that daggy brolly. Now, of course, I think it's a very, very cool idea.

Lord knows how we're going to skirt around this achingly long summer holiday period. We've not been here long enough to justify a holiday on the beach and Xiansheng is too busy with work, anyway. We're stuck in the middle of a lava-filled pit and the heat is rising.

God help us all.

Missing You

The honeymoon period may be over

Just before leaving Australia for Beijing, we were told about the process of transition and settlement we'd experience as expats.

It would start out with much excitement and exuberance — this would last about three months. After this would come the shock period — What Have We Done? — which lasts about another three months. From there, it's the I Want To Go Home period — a time where nothing is working, everything is frustrating, comfort zones have been tested one too many times, the click of the light switch sounds irritating, the ground is too bumpy for your shoes and you're just, well ... *over it.*

Yes, this latter part is usually around the six-month mark, and it's pretty much spot-on. Some people get weepy, angry, confused, walking around in a daze; others just experience mild annoyance. We experienced the latter. It wasn't too bad, but it was definitely there. It didn't last too long, and mostly, it was just missing people, so it's fortuitous that very soon my mother-in-law will arrive in Beijing — our very first visitor. She could well be the very thing we need to give us a dose of home comfort.

In the meantime, we'll just continue to draw on our dwindling stock of comfort items like Aussie chocolate and wine (that always helps). And my mother-in-law (MIL) will bring a restock of sugary treats and even some Aussie magazines and Freddo frogs, which we're *so* excited

about. She'll also bring aerosol deodorant, which is non-existent here. We don't want to pong or go without chocolate frogs for *too* long now, do we?

Surprisingly, we're not missing too much else from home. We're adventurous enough with food but it's probably just those special little Australian treats we miss the most. And perhaps television. There are a few English language channels here but mostly the choice of programs is dire. We seem to be relying on DVDs and there's always plenty of those to go around — the kids have it all from *Thomas the Tank Engine* to Barbie movies. I even found *Dallas* seasons one to three the other day. I was leaping around the DVD shop like a mad crazed soap-addict with big hair and gargantuan shoulder pads.

We're also missing — well I am, anyway — being able to jump in a car and go straight to a shopping centre with everything under one roof, where I don't have to dodge rain or sandstorms or potholes or potentially rabid dogs or poop/whiz/lurgies. I so miss wheeling my trolley full of groceries onto smooth bitumen, packing them in the car, driving home in temperature-controlled comfort and unpacking them straight into my refrigerator. That doesn't happen here, oh no.

If I want to get the best prices and quality, I have to go to Chaoyangmenwai Dajie for bread, I have to go to Liangma for flowers, I have to go to expat supermarket Jenny Lou's for yoghurt and cheese, the local Jingkelong supermarket for Chinese candy, Xin Yuan Li wet market for fruit and vegetables and nuts, Pacific Century Place shopping centre for fish, Watsons chemist for face masques, creams and toothbrushes. It's a right royal pain and although it all seems 'charming' at the start, it soon soon soon wears thin.

Nevertheless. Half the fun is in the challenges, is it not? And there's plenty of those to keep us on our toes. How long until we tire of challenges is uncertain, but you can bet your life you'll be reading about it here soon enough.

The Matriarch

She has arrived

I'm a very fortunate woman. I have the most wonderful mother-in-law (MIL) in the world. Seriously. This is particularly helpful to my soul because I lost my own dear mum many years ago when she was far too young, and MIL is as close to helping ease that loss as anyone possibly could.

I was actually ecstatic when MIL said she would come to visit us in Beijing and, of course, I was ecstatic for the kids. To have their Granny here is a major treat for all of us, sharing with her this surreal Beijing experience. But how do you decide where to take visitors in China's capital, especially those people who really mean something to you? There is so much to see and do, it's easy to stand on the spot and spin with panic about fitting it all in.

The first thing we've done with MIL is feed her. Food is big here. It's so big, it's like Italy or something. So we strap on our feedbags and we eat out lots and she loves it. We've even taken her to the night market off Wangfujing Street where you can see the reproductive organs of farm animals speared on skewers and grilled on an open flame. *Mmmm* — delish. And if this isn't your thing, you could opt for a crunchy centipede or two, a scorpion, a skinned snake or a sea anemone, plugged onto the end of a stick like a briny lollipop.

MIL passed on eating at the night market but she loved the stomach-turning spectacle. In fact, at first I wondered if this barrage of skewered horror is produced solely for touristic shock value, but when you see the Chinese voraciously nibbling little black parcels with crunchy legs sticking out of their mouths, you soon realise this is the real deal.

So, despite passing on a skewered seahorse or two, MIL is loving it in Beijing and this brings me much personal satisfaction. Not only

because I love her and so appreciate her being within squeezing distance of my children, but also because half the fun of this China adventure is in the sharing. Truly. I mean, it's all great, but when you can share it with someone you love … nothing beats that.

The most precious thing of all when she arrived, was when we sat up til the wee hours chatting on the couch and she kept saying, 'I can't believe I'm in China, I can't believe I'm in China.'

Strange. That's exactly how I feel. Even after six months in the capital. It usually hits me when I'm standing on the 26th floor looking down at a grey-veiled cityscape, but also when I wipe the white dust from the television or when a vendor splits open a pomelo at the wet market. These are the small moments I'll truly remember here.

And I hope in my heart of hearts that MIL can take home these special moments, too.

Mid-Autumn Festival

And the illustrious mooncake

I don't want to talk about summer. It was a horror. Thank goodness autumn is finally tumbling from the trees.

My mother-in-law has arrived at a wonderful time of year. In early autumn, the weather is divine: the heat of summer starts to curl away and the days end with goose-bumping evenings that are a joy to stroll through. The pollution has cleared and things are blue-skied and fresh. Leaves are yellowing and dropping and floating on breezes, and we're draping light scarves, tied loosely at the neck. The Mid-Autumn Festival is here, too. It's a joyful time.

While Chinese New Year is the Christmas of the Chinese people, Mid-Autumn Festival is probably the closest equivalent to an American Thanksgiving — an excuse to gather, to celebrate a bountiful harvest

and to spend time sharing and feasting with family and friends.

If you have ever tried a Mid-Autumn Festival mooncake, you'll know they're an acquired taste. Me, I could stuff my cheeks with them for the long cold winter. Cloyingly thick and subtly sweet, these ancient cakes are packed with fruit and lotus seed pastes. The outer pastry is cake-like and stamped with traditional Chinese characters or designs, and oftentimes you'll find a yellow egg yolk inside, representing the full autumn moon.

The history of the mooncake is rather special. The cakes were used by the Chinese during the Yuan Dynasty (1200–1368AD) to smuggle secret notes of revolt past the non-mooncake-eating Mongols. These sweet little cakes quickly and effectively spread news of the revolt — to be staged on the fifteenth day of the eighth moon, the same day the festival is held in modern times.

Today's modern mooncakes are a flavour bonanza. You can find raspberry, mango, rose petal, vanilla and even chocolate ice-cream cakes by Häagen-Dazs. They're a wonderful treat, and encompass a delicious time of year here in Beijing.

Oh, simple are the joys of sharing in these wonderful local traditions. When things get lousy in Beijing, these are the things we treasure most.

Big Boy School

How did my little baby become a real-life boy?

You hear about those mothers who clutch at the waft of air left behind when their children head off to school for the first time. They lament, cry and wander the empty halls, unable to know what to do with themselves.

This is just not me. Sorry. School has always made me leaping-

around-ecstatic for more reasons than can be contained here, but the main one being that school opens my children's heads like a can of magic beans and stuffs wonderful things in there. Both my kids love and thrive at school. How could I be happier?

But magic beans aside, there's another reason we wanted to start Riley at school at the ripe old age of two-and-a-half. It's because he isn't speaking. Well, I mean, he *can* speak, he just doesn't do it often and doesn't do it well for his age average. And trust me, plenty of people have an opinion on what comprises 'average'.

Even if we refuse to listen to opinion, we are still a little worried. Probably more than a little worried. Don't we all want our kids to have an advantage in life, wherever possible?

We've already consulted a Western speech therapist who assessed Riley and told us he has a 'speech deficit' that could compromise his future development — whatever that means. Even after a comprehensive explanation, I still have no idea. Needless to say, the anguish Xiansheng and I have gone through over this diagnosis is unparalleled. Have we failed him? Have we caused this terrible problem by talking too much or too little? Was bringing him to China where English saturation is so compromised a vast mistake? What does this mean for his future? His intelligence? His education? This has been a terrifying time for us, a time when nothing but the worst struck-dumb scenario seems foremost in our minds.

So, at the recommendation of the therapist, Riley has just started in pre-nursery at the British School of Beijing because he needs to be saturated with the English language via his *peers*. Dad, a nattering mum and chattering big sister don't seem to be enough, unbelievably, so perhaps school will help.

And yes, I've been ecstatic for him starting pre-nursery because he just loves it, but it's been interesting to note my own feelings of trepidation — something I didn't feel with Ella. There was some heart-pulling emotion when Riley donned his Big Boy uniform and school shoes for the first time. It kind of didn't feel right. He just seemed too … little. Like a little lamb in a big wolf suit.

Is it a youngest-child thing? Is it the fact that he still fits baby-sized undies? Or is it that watching him enter this milestone experience hauls up the harsh reality that I'm now well past procreation, and no more babes will be emerging from this womb? If that isn't a slap in the face of my own mortality, I don't know what is.

Whatever the case, I was surprised to actually worry about Riley a little when he headed off to school with his Mickey Mouse backpack and his teensy little legs sticking out of those shorts and that fuzzy head reflected in the school bus window.

And those worries? Our son came home clutching a paper snake with sand under his fingernails and a grin plastered from ear to ear. And he's been skipping merrily to school ever since.

I may still be a little heartbroken, but my Big Boy has made the grade.

Those Special Moments

Jingshan Park delivers

Those special moments in life often sneak up on us when we least expect them. It's when we turn a corner and suddenly, it's there — something a little breathtaking. Or a lot breathtaking. The ironic thing about stinky, polluted Beijing is that it has a habit of providing lots of breathtaking moments.

Sometimes it can be something someone did. Sometimes it can be a view. Sometimes it can be Ella's piano teacher, the gorgeous Lily, clapping along playfully to my daughter's tunes. Sometimes it can be the ambience of a place, that certain something that fills a space with spirit. And this is what Jingshan Park did for us.

We took a cab to this illustrious park (located just north of the Forbidden City) early in the morning because Riley is starting his days pre-5 a.m. at the moment, and we'd already been up for hours and

hours. It was about 8.15 a.m. when we arrived yet the place was already alive with people — a feat for Beijing where everybody seems to enjoy a daily sleep-in and nothing gets moving til 10 or 11 a.m.

As we entered the eastern gate, the first thing that struck us was the colour of the garden. Bathed in early morning light and rich with that European-masters-antique colour that washes over things at the onset of autumn, everything seemed golden. Along with the turning leaves — orange, gold, brilliant yellow — it was truly like a Monet masterpiece, a palette of captured light.

As we meandered into the park, we were also struck by the people. Mostly elderly, they were actively participating in any manner of physical activity from badminton to fan dancing to *tai chi* or simple stretching. There were women with long, bright ribbons, twirling them in great looping swirls, luminescent in the sunlight. There were blokes in caps kicking be-feathered hackysacks. There were grandmothers pushing dozy kids in strollers or carting them around enfolded in arms, their eyes bright in the morning sun.

The most elderly and infirm were gathered near a hillside, planting their feet on slabs of rock, swinging their arms, clapping, chanting and singing old songs from the Cultural Revolution in a perfectly enunciated Mandarin rhythm that took my breath away. The kids stood mesmerised. I wept, it was so beautiful, and Ella watched me cry with great curiosity.

We then began the climb to the top of the hillside, and on the way up we took meandering paths through petrified wood and rocky outcrops and each turn presented a new and delightful surprise — a man singing tenor against a small enclave in the rock face, a woman sawing a homemade bow against a lute-type instrument, or *er hu*. A kid whizzing in the middle of the footpath. It's *all* wonderful (especially if you side-step the whiz).

From the top of Coal Hill, which was created from the earth dredged to make the moat around the Forbidden City, we stopped for a breather and gazed at the view of Beijing over the ochre rooftops of the Forbidden City, which stretches forever. It's a remarkable view —

a spot where one can sit and only begin to ponder the extraordinary world that was once so central to China and its people. The centre of the world. The concubines, the eunuchs, the minions and the officials, all busily scurrying and liaising and creating a unique and total world for a single Emperor, the king of the Middle Kingdom.

We loved our Jingshan Park experience and we'll be sending visitors back there whenever they visit. There may not be screaming kiddie rides, jumping castles and a kiosk on every footpath, but there is a spirit there that makes your heart melt and pulls you back inside another time.

And for our family, that's what being in China is all about.

Up in Smoke

Does every single lung in China smoke?

Sheesh, will I ever find a café without inhaling smouldering cancer? I'm really getting over it. It's not charming in that Parisian-café sort of way anymore. It's offensive.

It's especially offensive because smokers in China don't just smoke, they *chain smoke*. They butt-light the next stick without so much as a rattling gasp betwixt, and they huff and they puff and they huff and they puff like the big bad wolf. It's like this: they sit down and light up. Sometimes they light up before their bums have even hit the seat. And then they burn these cancerous sticks like they're incense and they're Buddha sitting in the centre of their own smoky temple.

Being a country where people don't seem to like wind or any kind of cool or fresh air, many Chinese venues are overheated and stuffy to start with. Imagine, then, the oppression of an 80 to 90 per cent smoke rate wherever you go, with nary a whisper of breeze in sight.

I'm over it. I go to a café, hook up the laptop, get stuck into my work,

and within minutes my eyes are burning and my throat is choking shut. This morning, I packed up my laptop moments after a patron arrived, sat right next to me and proceeded to blow smoke directly into my face.

I was livid.

I stood, I glared at him. Typically, he had absolutely *no* idea what I was glaring about. So I glared harder and most particularly at the cigarette, like my eyeballs had unhinged and were prodding it firmly. Still no clue; he just continued to stare at me blankly then started chatting with his friends, who all lit up as well.

With frustration levels peaking, I decided to make it really obvious how inconvenienced and annoyed I was at having to leave the café. So I fanned the air and clutched at my chest and coughed and hacked and caused a right scene. Then I looked pointedly at his cigarette, rolled my eyes and walked out. Such a drama queen, me.

His response? Laughter. His friends laughed, too. And then began a running commentary on what I'd just done and why I did it. I didn't care; at least they finally (and perhaps ineffectively) *got it*. And if I have to resort to slapstick to get my message across then I guess that's just what I'll have to do.

Meanwhile, Old Smoky and his mates will be dining out on this story for a month.

Dongxi

Navigating Mandarin

My Mandarin is a poor shade of basic. After a year of slacko study in Adelaide and six months of saturation in Beijing, it's still an off shade, but at least I can get by. 'Me speak good Chinese and me likey your shoes of big pink, where you buy and how much you pay?' would probably most accurately represent the way I speak Mandarin.

Xiansheng calls it 'street Chinese'. If I need to shop, eat, ask directions or argue with someone, I'm pretty much covered, though my vocabulary is so poor, I've been known to insert the word *dongxi* ('thing', pronounced doong-shee) several times in a single sentence. You know: 'I love that red *dongxi* with the *dongxi* on top which you can use for eating slippery *dongxi*' kind of statements.

Coupled with pointing, gesticulating, using complicated facial cues and loads of onomatopoeia (crash, whoosh, tinkle, splat), you can get surprisingly far in Mandarin. The Chinese love it when you try, and they'll go out of their way to tell you how well you speak the language, regardless of the incomprehensible crap tumbling from your mouth (the complete opposite of the French, who will exasperatingly point out even the slightest accent slip).

Basically, if you have the confidence to give it a go and don't really care how stupid you sound, you can learn Mandarin almost solely on just 'giving it a go'. That's how I've done it. I'm not saying you will speak it *well*, but you will definitely learn to speak more than enough to get by and give local Chinese a smile, to boot.

In a verbal sense, Mandarin is intensely complex yet has an unexpected simplicity in its everyday vernacular. If I jump in a cab in Australia, I say something like: 'Hi, how's it going? I just want to go to the Sydney Harbour Bridge, please. The north side, near that gorgeous park. Lovely day, isn't it? Have you been driving a taxi long?'

In China, communications are kept to the point, so it's not considered rude to just get in a cab, state your destination then 'stop here' without so much as a hello, goodbye, please or thank you. Not rude at all.

So, when I take a taxi, I jump in and say, 'Tian'anmen Square.' If I add, 'Hello. How are you? Nice, clean taxi. Is the pineapple on the back windowsill yours or did your wife put it there to keep things fresh, as my Lordy Lord you stink to high heaven — that stale smoke, garlic and *bai jiu* fumes are making my eyes water,' the driver will turn around slowly and give me a 'get out of my cab, you deranged maniac' stare. Either that, or he'll just say '*Shenme?*' (what?).

When my *ayi* wants cash to buy the groceries, she says to me, 'Madam, give me 200 *kuai*' (*kuai* is slang for money). I remember the first time she said it, I was sort of like, 'What do you saaaay?' It was hard to hear her effectively *demand* money, but over time my understanding of the abridged use of Mandarin has deepened, and the tone of the language coupled with the spirit it's said in somehow allows this rather clipped vernacular leeway. It just works.

Perhaps it's the fact that the Chinese have to fight 1.3 billion other people for anything and everything they want in life that makes them operate with such succinct communiqués.

When I began studying French in my late teens, I was convinced it was the most romantic language in the world, yet there is something about Mandarin that's also lucidly romantic. There is a certain poetry, despite its often officious discourse. There is meaning and content in single words that English could never conjure. Take the word *hao* (good), for example. It can conjure entire fairytales of meaning, depending on the context and tone used. Add it to certain other words and it becomes intensely rich in verbal imagery.

In a bid to understand more, I did start formal Mandarin lessons with a cute Chinese chick with a Ming Dynasty haircut, back in Month Three. I knew it was going to be a challenge when her first words to me were *giggle giggle giggle giggle giggle giggle giggle*.

My second clue was when she spent the first three lessons having me sound out Chinese vowels like I was a tone deaf mute (and in front of a café audience, no less). 'No — louder!' she'd say, 'No — it's *ooeui* not *ooeui!* Try again!' So I'd reluctantly oblige, much to the stares and frustration of my fellow café patrons, intent on a peaceful hour while some Australian broad *ooeuid* and *oooahhd* like an unhinged linguistic monk.

I didn't get far with the lessons. I did maybe seven out of the ten I paid for, and the last lesson was the clincher for me; it involved a six-minute (I kid you not, I really kid you not) giggle fit from Cute Chinese Chick that had me initially smiling, then frowning, then staring in horror, then hiding my face in shame.

And what was the laughing fit over? It was when I said a sentence including the word for ten — *shi*. Cute Chick told me I had just said I wanted to pash her. Cute, yes. Funny? Perhaps for a moment or two, however, by the end of six minutes of pealing laughter, my face was stone cold. I kind of never saw her again.

It wasn't because I didn't want to pash her. I'm sure, if I was that way inclined, she would have absolutely been my first choice. She had a cute Ming Dynasty haircut, after all.

Fashion Schmashion

It's bedazzling

When I first saw sequins on the street before lunchtime, it was blinding. I'm sort of used to it now but it still makes me mildly nauseous, as does the studded, tasselled boots and the bedazzled cardigans, not to mention the frills, lace and perms.

Why? Why are local Beijingers caught in an '80s time warp? They are such a gorgeous race of people: slim; divine skin; shiny, swinging hair; lustrous eyes. Why are they committing fashion suicide? One look at the choice inside a clothing market geared towards locals, and I had to run out and breathe into a brown paper stylista bag.

I've met many Westerners here in Beijing who can tell me of the days when *Beijingren* wore a layman uniform of grey button-down shirts and cloth caps. Since the '80s (a coincidence?), I suppose you could say they are branching out. Like a six-year-old let loose in a dress-up box, it may take them a little time to find their fashion rhythm. What they really need is Chinese *Vogue*. Lucky then, that the magazine officially launched here recently. And hallelujah — the clothes on its pages are good. Not a bedazzlement-before-midday in sight.

China, there's now absolutely no excuse. No more perms! No more

spangles! No more rhinestones crocheted into cardigans and no more white vinyl boots! At least not before midnight and not outside a nightclub.

I'll be watching you.

Yours cordially, the self-appointed Fashion Police.

Ayi Envy

Thou shalt not covet thy neighbours' *ayi*

It's shameful, I know, but I am breaking the Eleventh Commandment and coveting my neighbours' *ayi*. Don't get me wrong, my *ayi* does a great job, is efficient, reliable and mostly pleasant. She's just not that likeable.

This would be perfectly okay if I worked full time and didn't have kids, but because we have to share the house most days, we interact frequently, especially because Ayi finds it imperative to fill me in on every domestic move she makes.

'The tomatoes cost five *jiao* (1.6 cents) more today, is that okay or do you want me to wait til tomorrow? *Furen! Furen!* Emergency! I can't fit the waffles in the freezer! Just to let you know I'm down to only 48 garbage bags so I'll get some more tomorrow. I think these leftovers from last Christmas could be thrown out now, *furen*, what do *you* think?'

I've taken to telling her: '*Wo bu yao zhidao*.' I don't want to know. Unless it's life-threatening, I don't want to know. 'You deal with it, Ayi.'

You see, she's a bit of a talker, my *ayi*. I've heard her talk to engineers and reception staff and other *ayis*, even taxi drivers, right in front of me, blabbing about our family and our life. I don't think what she says is malicious — I just don't like the intimacies of our life revealed to all and sundry. When I told her this, she told me she *didn't* do it. I told her I begged to differ.

One time, the reception staff in our building were translating for us

and Ayi began telling them, '*Furen* thinks I talk to people about her family, blah blah blah' and I simply said, 'Well, you're doing it right now.' Ayi stopped dead in her tracks and the realisation hit her like a packet of flying tofu.

Hello!

My other gripe (thanks for listening) with Ayi is that she hoards. And I don't mean useful stuff. Pieces of broken wire, strange plastic or metal objects that once belonged to an unidentifiable object no one ever used. Grimy, used Ziploc bags. Every single tin, container and jar that ever contained anything — ever.

I know and appreciate that this woman came from a generation who recycled the thread from one garment to hem another, mostly out of necessity, but this is also a generation that still burns coal, turns on every light until the house is ablaze, and gushes water down the sink like it's sourced from an endless magical ocean. In fact, Ayi consistently splashes water around like a recalcitrant hose.

I'm teaching Ayi about recycling and saving power and it's like shifting a tablet at Stonehenge. It's tough, especially when she looks at me like I'm a five-year-old brat trying to tell an ancient sage the secrets to the universe. Which brings me to the Attitude Problem.

Sheesh, I'm going to sound like a gripester here, but I have to tell you about the Attitude Problem because it's becoming a real, unexpected issue in our house.

I think I'm a relatively easygoing *furen*. I'm not a witch, not fussy nor pedantic. I'm generous and even quite kind. I frequently let small things go, and trust me, I know plenty of *tai tai* who torture their *ayis* over substandard cleaning. Ayi works in a warm, friendly household, so why she's started with the Attitude Problem is really beyond me.

It actually seems to happen every three to four months. Things can be exactly the same in our house but Ayi gets inexplicably shitty. She grumbles. She slams things. She argues with me when I ask her to do something simple. She huffs, twists her lips together, nods silently as though she's been mortally wounded and shuffles off.

Ayi isn't perfect — she's done a crappy, half-arsed job plenty of

times and I've tolerated it fine. But this Attitude Problem undoes me. I find it infuriating and monumentally stressful. This is *my home*, for goodness sake. Ayi's got it good and it torments me when she does this. In fact, it's so awful, it makes me long for the days of No Ayi, and makes me wonder about the need for an *ayi* at all.

I have three neighbours who have lovely *ayis*. I mean, I know we all have challenges with them — no matter how 'perfect', our cultural differences are just too ingrained — but some *ayis* are easier to handle than others. These three lovely *ayis* are just so sweet and they are *quiet*. They don't get crabby and bang pots. They don't answer back, argue or act miffed. They don't repeatedly commit a housekeeping crime you ask them repeatedly *not* to commit. I pine for an *ayi* like this, I really do.

I also pine for an *ayi* who has true affection for my kids. Not a clingy, heart-breaking obsession (and its associated problems), but a simple affection would be nice. Alas, it's just not there. She sometimes feigns it, but it's not really there, and I guess it's something I'll just have to live with, along with the myriad other things I have to in this town.

Now, excuse me, I'm off to do some more coveting.

Muxiyuan

The elusive fabric market

No doubt most of us have sought a particular Shangri-La in our lifetime. That elusive, otherworldly place we dream of, perhaps hear about, and hope to seek and find. In Beijing, Muxiyuan fabric market has been that place for me (pronounced 'moo-shrr-yoo-ar').

Sure, I had heard about it. I had heard about the endless lanes and infinite rows of fabric: cotton, nylon, rayon, jersey, organza, chiffons, Lycra, tulle, silks in every imaginable variety, even leather and fur — faux and *jian de* (real). I had heard of the mountains of sequins, the

reams of zips, the sheaths of trim from pompom baubles to flapper fringing, the buckles, the thread, the embellishments. I had heard much of this dressmaker Nirvana, with a price tag to make even the most bargain-savvy wholesale tailor weep buttons.

I heard so many delicious tales of this joyous place, but I also heard an equal amount of horror stories — rumours of wannabe seamstresses who sought Muxiyuan but never returned to tell the tale, and instead disappeared into a rayon twilight zone.

Most people take a minimum of three attempts to find Muxiyuan. Being unable to find things is a pretty typical phenomenon in Beijing, however, Muxiyuan is renowned for it — a confusing dichotomy because once you know where it is, it's actually very easy to find (this statement sounds obvious, but that's how bizarre this whole thing is).

Nonetheless, I was determined to make it there First Go. I gathered together an army of like-minded fabric addicts and organised a car. Just to cover myself, I asked Ayi if she happened to know of this elusive place, stacked high with fabric slabs. She did. *Hallelujah!* I enlisted her services, too. We told the driver our general direction, and off we went.

When we arrived at Muxiyuan *da sha* (big building) under direction from Ayi, our excitement was palpable. It wasn't, however, until we hauled our carcasses around stall after stall of parkas, fairy dresses and wigs — with nary a swatch of dressmaking fabric in sight — that things slowly began to dawn on me. Oh yes, it became perfectly clear that Ayi had absolutely no bloody clue where the fabric market was, and had instead made the executive decision that fabric wasn't what we were after. Apparently, a bunch of cheap junk at the Muxiyuan *da sha* would make us *way* more happy.

Had we been looking for a bunch of junk, we would have been ecstatic. As it stood, I was furious. So furious, I would have wrapped Ayi in a bolt of silk and rolled her down a very steep hill — if I could only have *found* some damn silk.

We went home, defeated.

The second attempt to find Muxiyuan was with two friends. We took a taxi and we walked the streets for two hours, pretty much in

circles and mainly because of the Chinese tendency to tell you any old direction rather than admit they don't know where something is. Oh Lord! If only they would say 'I don't know'! During this lengthy trek, we eventually found lurex curtaining and tulle to make tutus. So close, but yet so far. We went home, defeated.

The third time was a charm but we only found it so quickly because we took a friend who had already been to Material Mecca. It ended up being about 50 metres from our attempt number two. You can imagine the frustration, but no matter, we had a wonderland of fabric to navigate, and it was truly a pinnacle Beijing experience.

I've made fluffy kangaroo suits and cheetah catsuits for Ella from fabric at Muxiyuan. Silk ball gowns, cotton kaftans, Chanel copycat suits, chiffon blouses, tweed skirts, pea coats and patterned shirt dresses from fabric at Muxiyuan, plus faux fur rugs and more cushions than pillow heaven. Well, my tailor Xiao Fei made them; I just showed her the pictures.

But nonetheless, they're made and they are worn and enjoyed and it really is overwhelming because when I wear these clothes, I feel like a woman again. How can clothing make someone feel so great? One of the mysterious mysteries of the human condition, no doubt. A mystery only paralleled by the whereabouts of the infamous Muxiyuan.

UN Day

Uniting the Nations

Being a bit of a philanthropic world-hugger, I love the idea of United Nations Day so much that when the kids' school announced its annual celebration, I jumped up in the air a little. Yet another opportunity for my kids to immerse themselves in other cultures? Perfect, but also problematic.

You see, the kids were asked to dress in their national dress. *Hmm.* Australian national dress? What is that? A pair of shorts, a singlet and

some zinc cream on the schnoz? A safari suit and a crocodile? A bikini and a surfboard? Cliché, cliché, cliché.

So I thought outside the Steve Irwin square and I channelled fluffy. Koala, kangaroo, wombat, kookaburra — that sort of thing. I consulted Xiao Fei who took sheets of faux fur from my jaunt to Muxiyuan fabric market and created some animal magic.

The kids were oh-so-cute — Ella resplendent as a blonde kangaroo complete with a little pouch and joey, Riley a mini koala with a fluffy tail and white-fluff-stuffed ears. Adorable.

But best of all was the spectacle they enjoyed while wearing these outfits. They got to see African drumming and do Chinese dancing and sample Japanese food and paint Aboriginal dot paintings and lasso tins in an American grocery rodeo and all those other things one can experience when the whole world descends upon a classroom in Beijing.

I just wish I had been small enough to smuggle myself into a costume to join in the fun. Maybe as a wombat? Instead I manned the Australia table, plugging lamingtons and ANZAC biscuits to voracious Korean princesses, African Zulu warriors, little French soldiers and Mexican dancers.

Wombat suit or no wombat suit, I loved every minute of it.

Eye on the Sky

Our skyline is a-changing

Wow! I mean, I know the Chinese work hard, but this is ridiculous. We've been here six months and already the skyline view from our apartment has turned into Shanghai. It's really quite bizarre. All around us, a jumble of buildings is being stacked by invisible kids with giant Lego blocks. Seemingly overnight, things pop up or fall down. Including *hutong* courtyard houses.

On our first ever bike ride in Beijing, we zipped through the *hutong*

alleyways destined for destruction near Sanlitun Lu. At first we didn't know what the large, white Chinese characters were, painted slap-happily on the brick walls of dusty courtyard houses. Then we realised: these were marked houses, poised to be crumbled and shovelled into a wheelbarrow to make way for a high rise with shiny floors, indoor plumbing and Ikea furniture.

Naturally, we were horrified at the fate of the *hutong* houses at first, but in reality, they are totally impractical. Freezing in winter, stinking in summer, overcrowded and with no indoor plumbing (residents share public bathrooms like we do at a caravan park on the beach), they don't make the most savoury of residences.

Nonetheless, it's a little heartbreaking watching them fall because they *are* beautiful and are so deeply steeped in Beijing's past. A few of the more historic houses will be kept but, for the most part, Beijing is kissing an achingly historical moment goodbye. How fortunate our family is to have experienced and immersed ourselves in these alleyways and seen the people living their daily lives in a courtyard setting, because very soon this will be a far distant thing of the past.

One of our favourite movies of all time is a Chinese film called *Shower* starring Chinese actor Pu Quanxin (whom I happen to have a little crush on). *Shower* is a must-see for anyone who has lived in Beijing and also for those who have not. Set in the midst of this modern day *hutong*-levelling, it traces the fate of a family who own a traditional Chinese bathhouse. I challenge you not to weep into your noodles.

One thing is for sure: we are witnessing history in motion. As our skyline changes and the *hutong* houses crumble, I can already envisage the day I sit in my rocking chair with my hand-knitted knee rug, regaling the great-grandchildren with tales and legends of the great Beijing courtyard houses. What were they really like? Did they really exist? Where did they go?

Well, they went to Progress. And Great-Granny McCartney, with tissues clutched in hand, will be there to tell them all about it. First hand.

Boo!

A haunting Halloween

Our family does Christmas big. We also do an impressive Easter but Christmas is really *it* for us — the whole shebang. It's full-on from the 1 December Christmas tree to the soaked fruit for the Christmas cake and the mulled wine aromas drifting from a pot on the stove, curling around furniture and into every tinselled corner of the house.

So when our first Halloween came along, I was completely unprepared for this strident holiday to almost supersede Santa's reign. Simply put, we had an absolute and very unexpected blast.

It all began with our first pumpkin carving. The kids loved this. We bought the tools and we got digging, and that fresh pumpkin smell and piles of slippery seeds were so tactile that we got totally caught up in things. Very soon we had our first Jack-O-Lantern.

Then we decorated the house in sheaths of black organza from Liangma flower market and we strung up garlands of snowy paper bones and burnt orange pumpkin lanterns and faux cabbages and onions and other harvest goodies. We dotted red-eyed, cackling witches around the house, put black cats across our path, and strung snatches of cobwebs from crooked twig branches.

Ayi freaked out a little but we just loved it. We got so caught up in the hoo-ha, a neighbour and I organised a trick or treat for 78 kids in our building, starting with nibbles (meringue bones, witch finger cookies and fizzing blood-red sodas) in our apartment. Little pirates, wizards, princesses and ghosts haunted our building with their treating shenanigans, tearing from apartment to apartment with bellies full of sugar and mouths full of yelling.

It was some of the most fun we've ever had and the kids are totally hooked. We love the games, the spooking, the way adults become possessed with the eerie fun of it, donning capes, blacking out teeth and

bamboozling children, or making them scream with that delicious blend of excitement and terror they so adore.

Yes, we'll be taking this festival home to Australia with us and single-handedly starting up a Halloween party tradition to knock the socks off unsuspecting ghouls everywhere.

Beware, Australia, beware! *Mwa ha ha!*

Constant Niggles

Does anything work in this place?

We may be living a luxe expat life but we're often reminded it's being lived smack-bang in the middle of an Eastern country. It seems we are consistently slapped with little dramas and an unending need for repairs and upgrades. It really doesn't stop. Every day something breaks or works in a substandard fashion and it's very frustrating, especially given the explanations on offer.

Take the air-conditioning, for example.

Every few months, our apartment's air-conditioners start blowing warm, leaving us suffocating in an airless tank, unable to open the windows because of the pollution outside, and unable to get that breath of faux fresh air the air-cons so generously provide. Even during winter, we are using the air-conditioners at night because the Chinese overheat their buildings and by the time the heat rises to our high-storey apartment, we're baking like scones.

In fact, the air in our apartment is a delicate balancing act. We need the air-conditioners on to cool the air, then we use purifiers to clean this recycled, air-conditioned air. Then we have the humidifiers on to re-humidify this cooled, recycled and cleaned air. It's like a carefully balanced symphony of softly humming appliances, just to make our air space liveable.

So. I called the engineers to tell them our air-cons are blowing warm. When they arrived, they failed to just get on with the job and clean the filters (as was the need) but instead fussed around and told me that when the temperature is colder outside than *inside* the building, the air-conditioners will not work.

What the … ?

Try telling an engineer they are wrong. Of course, after wasting half an hour of my life arguing with them, I eventually won. They cleaned the filters and left, and the air-cons blew cold again.

But air-cons are not the only issue. We were also recently told, by said engineers, that our refrigerator was not cooling effectively because we had a large bag of Japanese candy on top of it. Riiiight. I wonder if it's because the candy was *Japanese*.

Another one: your dishwasher is not working because you are using X brand of dishwasher powder. Honest to God. So it wouldn't be because the dishwasher is a crappy old claptrap that needs replacing immediately then?

Yes, things keep breaking and obscure reasons keeping piling up high. The floor drain in our bathroom frequently pongs to high heaven, and the excuse for this one is that we don't pour enough water down it on a regular basis. Oh, right. As you do. And it has nothing to do with the fact that the plumbing in this building has no S-bends. If they did, the stink would be eliminated and tenants wouldn't have to waste their precious hours flooding their bathroom floors with water to keep down the stink.

Before we left Australia, we were coached on how differently the Chinese think compared to the West. We are forthright, they are meandering. We are open, they are guarded. We are focused on the individual, they — the collective. We tell it like it is, they will send you around a labyrinth rather than admit they don't know the right direction.

Neither way is right or wrong, but that doesn't mean it can't bend my Western brain like a pretzel sometimes.

I think it's time for a holiday.

Christmas Factory Fantasy

Tai tai feeding frenzy outside Beijing

O Holy Night and oh my stars. And baubles and sparkles and shimmering glitter. This was a rare human experience. A magical experience, a festive experience — could it be — could it be? Yes it could. Christmas. In a dusty factory one hour outside Beijing.

But before I continue, I have to say that if you, for a single moment, think China cannot deliver on the Christmas thing, being an atheist state and all, then you are very, very wrong. The Chinese know how to celebrate indeed, and it's with much delight (and relief) that I'm watching this magical time of the Western year unfold in parts of Beijing, mainly expat areas, compounds, hotels and, of course, the markets (anything for a quick *kuai*).

We've already seen Halloween come and go, now make way for Santa and his team; and yes, even baby Jesus in a manger can be found. It's a Christmas lover's paradise and no one could be happier than me and my two Christmas-junkie kids, both of whom were *not* happy when I told them about my adventure to the magical Christmas land near Badaling Great Wall.

I suppose it should come as no surprise to find such a factory in China — everything is made here, after all. This particular treasure trove is owned and run by Americans but employs local staff who create and craft dreamlike Christmas baubles of such beauty it's hard not to gawp and clasp your hands under your chin like a small child.

Our tour of the factory began with a visit to the glass-blowing room where men, silhouetted by orange flames, blew and teased runny globules of clear glass that were stamped between metal clamps, and when released — *hey presto!* A gingerbread house. A toy car. A Nordic Santa Claus.

These shapes were then lowered into vats of mercury, emerging shiny like mirrors, then airbrushed with iridescent colour — vibrant reds,

peacock blues, royal yellows, garland greens. Once dry, they were taken to an enormous, sunlit room where women sat in silence, hand-painting row after beautiful row, some of them painting entire scenes on the *inside* of glass baubles via a teensy hole at the top. Remarkable.

Yes, like Charlie and the Chocolate Factory, it was one delicious room after another. And when we finally arrived in the Yes You Can Now Purchase These room, well, we had to contain ourselves lest we bull-in-a-china-shopped our way to glassy smithereens.

There they were, laid out before us: wrens with feathered tails, stars with glittery trails, telephone boxes, and gifts with bows. There were teardrops filled with powdery glitter and lanterns dusted with snow and even clear glass icicles you can drip from every branch of your tree.

Gently, carefully, agonisingly, we tried to contain ourselves as we politely scrabbled for the goodies. There were plenty of 'no, no, you take that one' — a credit to our lovely group of *tai tai* who were clearly gagging to rugby tackle each other and descend into a major fracas to get to the icicles first.

Call me a Christmas ornament addict, but one of my most memorable Beijing hours was unpacking that Santa sack of sparkle when we got home. I gathered the kids and sat them on the floor (Xiansheng really didn't need to be there — his financial blood pressure was high enough), then I quietly informed the kids that what I was about to reveal would just about knock their little cotton socks off.

They loved it. They wanted to touch, of course. And all credit to them: they held those pieces like baby bunny rabbits, gently, tenderly, carefully cradling, petting and admiring and cooing. It was a wonderful hour we shared together. And now those sparklers have been nestled back in their tissue and are patiently awaiting the Tree. Yes, we'll need a new one to contain all this. Our straggly green muppet from Australia just won't make the grade after the arrival of this impressive stash.

Bring on 1 December!

The Silk Market

We will never speak of that experience again

You may have noticed I love the markets in Beijing. Shopping is exhausting but it's also great fun and the thrill of the buy still outweighs every single bargain-induced migraine for me.

For the most part, the Chinese marketeers are great sports. Occasionally you'll come across a shyster, but you do have the option to just walk away. What you don't expect is to be physically attacked.

A recent horror trip to the Silk Market on Jianguomenwai Dajie in the eastern inner 'burbs made it clear to me these particular marketeers are totally spoiled by hyper-inflated tourist prices. I'm talking ten to twenty times what a local will pay and an even greater discrepancy when talking actual face value.

We were nice, we were calm, we had eight months' bartering experience, we knew how to charm the socks off sellers and make them feel good about their sale — but we also knew what price to pay. It didn't dawn on me that recommending these reasonable (i.e. non-tourist) prices to marketeers at the Silk Market would result in mass hysteria.

After being pushed, pulled, pinched, patronised, harried, blocked, shoved, screamed at and seriously insulted (in both Mandarin and English) by more than one salesperson at this market, I now swear to you I will never set foot inside it again. I'd much rather frequent the local and lesser-known spots like Yue Show clothing market on Chaoyangmenwai Dajie. There, you can build a relationship with marketeers that becomes genuine and warm, as well as mutually beneficial. And that *guanxi* (social and business connection) is what living in China is all about.

Me? I'll be leaving the Silk Market for the tourists. God help them.

the Tree

The towering wonder of Christmas

Everything is expensive in Australia, but most especially Christmas trees. In fact, in retrospect, how on earth did we ever afford to live in Australia *any* time of the year?

We bought a fuzzy mop of a faux Christmas tree some years ago and the kids have celebrated four years under this chest-high bush. It's okay, it has done the job and there are happy memories attached to its lopsided branches. But it's time for retirement — for the King of Trees has arrived.

At first we wanted a real tree but the chronically dry Beijing air kills them in a week, and I didn't want a sucked-dry stump and a pile of yellow pine needles holding up the baubles. We opted for a faux tree instead, and what a beauty she is. She stands 8 feet tall and is the girth of ten men. She looks like a *real* spruce pine: that musky mid-green with the merest hint of silver sparkle on the tips of her fluffy branches. She is breathtaking and I sat in wonder, cross-legged on the floor, with myriad ornament boxes around me, just staring at her beauty. Then I began to unpack our decorating bounty.

In our house, our tree decorating always begins with the lights. For our first Beijing tree, we strung 10-metre strands of white dots through the branches from head to toe until the tree was bathed in blinking, blinding white. Then we put on the icicles — slim, spangling droplets of glass. Then it was the silvery and white snowflakes followed by the illustrious glass ornaments from the Christmas factory — Santas, gingerbread houses, baubles and droplets — all in shades of white, red, pale green, silver and clear. It took hours. And that's only the tree.

Then it was the rest of the house — garlands, wreaths, statues, nutcracker soldiers, the whole shebang. We put on Christmas music and we heated up the mulled wine and nibbled slices of my mum's

Christmas cake (which Ella helped me make). The kids drove us bananas with repeat playings of 'Rudolph the Red-Nosed Reindeer'. Then we watched Rudolph in the 1964 TV classic of the same name. Then, we sat and stared at our handiwork and felt that warm, fuzzy glow in our chests that Christmas brings.

No wonder China is jumping on the bandwagon and getting into the Christmas spirit.

Walking on Iceblocks

Winter has arrived!

I've seen a little bit of snow in my time.

I've stood in chest-high snow drifts in the Dolomites in Italy and I've thrown snowballs at my ex-boyfriend near Stonehenge and I've tasted the flavour of London snow on my tongue and seen the wash of pink light on the snow-glazed streets of Paris. My husband is from Belfast, so he has snow in his blood.

Our kids? Well, they are poised for snow. They are ready and waiting. They've heard the stories and they are ready to experience the mush, the slush, and the bite on the fingertips of freshly laid powder. They have their boots, their mittens and their hats by the door, and every single day when they leap from their beds, they race to the window for a glimpse of powder on the rooftops below.

So far, no go.

Some mornings, the city looks so frozen and cold that I shuffle to the early morning window and hallucinate snow on the rooftops. But it's just cold. Cold appears white sometimes. Or maybe it's my brain playing tricks on me because I want it *so* bad.

In lieu of snow, we instead had a wonderful ice experience today. We walked on the frozen canal near Liangma flower market. The kids

thought it was so cool to walk on water and even slip on it in their boots. They grinned like snowmen with puffy-coat-padded tummies. It was so much fun — such a simple thing, but aren't simple things often the most fun?

Our mittens and scarves and boots are still poised by the door. Bring on snow, Beijing, bring it on!

Festive Traditions

I'm dreaming of a white Christmas

Christmas day in Beijing is a bittersweet affair.

It begins with the dawning realisation that Santa really did make it — an enormous relief for any parent intent on coordinating a successful flying visit (address changes take a while to get through to the man in red; he does get awfully busy).

When snug under the fingertips of sleep, there is nothing more lovely than waking to the sound of peeping kids, rustling through their Santa stockings, then dragging said stockings through the early morning house to Mum and Dad's room. *Squeak squeak peep peep!* go the kids, as their Santa treats tumble onto our bed.

Dad sits up to turn on the lamp dimly and we all exclaim and gush over the spanking bounty of fabulous knick-knacks and candy, crackling in its happy cellophane. And after the stockings, there is begging for candy and then cuddles and reading new storybooks and sticking fingers into finger puppets and scribbling on teensy pads of paper with brand new rainbow pencils.

Then, as every year, Mum or Dad shuffles out to turn on the coffee maker, and also flicks on the living room light, where upon they loudly exclaim something along the lines of: 'My goodness, what is all this

shiny new stuff gleaming under the tree?!' After a heartbeat pause, the thundering feet begin and those kids round that corner in a nanosecond and stop short at the floodlit tree, spurting forth its standard tumble of stacked and wrapped presents, but also an extra stash of treasures, artfully arranged by the crafty Santa Claus.

Dad grumbles something about bank statements and then goes to pour the coffee.

After cooing over the stack of bright new toys, we strike up the Christmas carols and Dad and I bring our fat mugs of coffee and we all four sit under the sparkling tree and begin opening presents, one by one. Someone plays elf and distributes each gift, and we must read aloud who it's for and who it's from. We also nibble the cookies Santa leaves in exchange for a glass of beer, and carrots for the reindeer, and read aloud his friendly thank-you note.

Next are the phone calls and Skype with friends and family. We all yak about the pressies and the things we're going to do today and how much we miss each other and we send cuddles across the miles and invariably have a good cry.

Next it's a visit to our colleague's house for Christmas lunch followed by pudding and lots of delicious sticky things and a tipple or two. There are presents exchanged and some rollicking stories and then Riley chucks several wobblies, so while Dad and Ella stay on to continue the feasting, Mum takes Riley home for an afternoon nap then sits in silence under the tree and cries. She puts on a Christmas movie and cries some more.

Dad and Ella come home and Mum cries, and Dad refills her glass of bubbles. Mum and Dad battle with the kids over the bounty of fab new toys and we all play and make puzzles until dinnertime. Then it's bubble baths and sugarplum sleepyhead kids tumbling into bed and then Dad and Mum sit among the landfill of wrapping paper and toast those dear departed and so very missed. We toast our loved ones far away and then we toast ourselves and congratulate each other on getting through our first Beijing Christmas.

On Boxing Day morning, it snows. Mum cries again. It's only a smattering and there's nothing on the ground, but the rooftops are dusted with a tempting skerrick of icing sugar.

And all is good in the world.

Sisters Unite

Life works in mysterious ways

My darling *jie jie* (big sister) arrived in Beijing just after Christmas Day on her first overseas jaunt and much to the joy of our family. Because she had not travelled overseas before, I never dreamed she would settle in so fast and enjoy Beijing as much as she has. It's quite amazing, really (though I suspect the unparalleled shopping experiences have helped). But what's even more amazing about her arrival was her ability to land a job only days after arriving. As you do.

I had taken her to visit the kids' school and as we walked through the foyer, the principal walked by and fate collided. 'Ahh, so you're a teacher, are you?' he said, 'Come into my office [read: educational lair].'

Half an hour later, in a taxi on the way home, Jie Jie told me the principal had all but offered her a job. I fell over; a tough feat considering I was already sitting down. You see, Jie Jie and I haven't lived in the same city since 1986. Bizarre to think that two sisters from a surfing town on the north coast of New South Wales would end up living in Beijing together someday. But that is the way of our now teensy world. She's moving here next July, with her husband Smoothie, to start the new school year, and she'll be teaching at my kids' school.

It's beyond my wildest dreams that I would have family here in Beijing — I'm ecstatic for the kids and thrilled for our sisterhood. And I'm even more in love with Beijing for making the seemingly impossible, possible.

Once again.

Let it Snow

Oh! the fluttering glory

A first, soft snowfall has a way of enchanting people. Things go quiet. The air develops a kind of thick, padded feeling, like a soundproofed room. Then suddenly, like someone has shaken a blossom tree, soft white petals begin to fall from the sky.

It's a phenomenal thing, really. I can't get enough of it. I'm so obsessed with snow, I keep a piece of dark felt at the ready to catch the flakes and study their incredulous, unique, six-pointed designs. The kids go crazy for it. We love to examine every last, totally inimitable flake.

Beijing's first snowfall for the McCartney family happened while eating breakfast at Grandma's Kitchen near Guanghua Lu. We had entered the restaurant via a frozen, grey streetscape, and after an hour of hot coffee, scrambled eggs and berry-studded pancakes, we returned to a street draped in a soft white blanket.

Jie Jie let out a gasp and then a squeak and then she burst into tears. She's a snow virgin. No matter, I also gasped and squealed and burst into tears (yes, I cry a lot — The Jing does that to you). The kids gasped and squeaked then opened their voices and called them out into the falling ice blossoms. The flurry was gentle but thick, and all five of us skipped and pranced and swirled and grinned on the pavement outside Grandma's Kitchen for a very long time, unable to tear ourselves away from it all.

Oh my. Dirty, grey Beijing looks beautiful in a pristine blanket of newly fallen snow.

Caught up in the wintry spirit, we then tore home and put on thick boots and hotfooted it to Hou Hai Lake for a spot of skating. But this ain't no ordinary skating, no no. This is hilarity combined with a fabulous workout and cultural experience bar none, because skating on Hou Hai features everyone. It features expat kiddies with puffing

ayis, it features little old men riding their bikes onto the surface and tying antiquated skates to their feet. It features local kids tearing around on specially rigged bicycles that cut across the ice on blades.

Our choice of transport is the ice chair — a crudely welded double seat (one at the front, one at the back) with scratchy, blunt blades underneath, and two crooked metal sticks used to propel yourself and that cumbersome chair around. Once you get momentum going, it can be fun but try getting started with your own hefty weight onboard (as well as a child), then try steering and turning and, God forbid, stopping. Oh yes, this is hilariously hairy fun.

Like us, there are people who fall over the moment they set foot on the ice, there are people who can straggle around with a decent semblance of balance, and there are people who play ice hockey in a cordoned-off ice patch, like pros. But the one thing we all share is the spirit of fun. From colliding ice chairs to squeals and slips, everyone is smiling and the wintry atmosphere is marvellous.

After a physical workout that left us pink-cheeked and frostbitten on the toes, we headed to Starbucks at the southern end of the lake and thawed out with a warm drink or two. Then we headed back home and prayed to the snow gods like Oliver to the gobsmacked Mr Bumble …

'More, please!'

How We Froze Our Extremities

And left our kids behind

We don't have the kind of *ayi* you could leave your children with while you abscond to the Maldives for a kid-less holiday. I've already told you she's not the most savvy childcare worker, and last week she fell asleep while looking after Riley at the indoor playground upstairs. She nearly copped a sacking for that but I'm a bit of a softie and she managed to use up yet another of her nine, feline lives.

She's not as young as she feigns, our *ayi*, nor is she as interested in my kids as she feigns. This means I have to be a *teensy* bit careful about placing them in her care. In a nutshell, she doesn't exactly ooze kid-friendly charm; leaving them in her care is a bit like leaving them with your perpetually crabby Great Aunt Myrtle who loves them but refuses to give them candy and barks at them to be seen and not heard. Indeed, with Ayi, Riley can't even toss a sock in the air without her roaring, 'No!' — one of the few English words she's managed to adopt, along with 'baby', 'wee wee' and 'poo poo'. I've lost count of the amount of times I've told her to take a chill pill over tossed socks.

Anyway, it wasn't until my sister Jie Jie arrived in Beijing that we even began to consider going away without the kids. Seeing the Harbin Ice and Snow Festival had been something on our list for a long time, and considering the kids whinge and moan about the cold when opening the freezer for an icy pole, we decided it wouldn't be fair on *anyone* if they came along. The winter temperatures in Harbin can easily reach as low as −40°C at night and −30°C in the day and we had no desire to tote frozen kids home in our luggage. We love their warm cuddles far too much.

So, we planned a decadent, kid-free getaway to Harbin, located in far north-eastern China, close to the Russian border. The kids were thrilled to have their Aunt Jie Jie all to themselves, and I must admit, it was a delight to be sent careening back into the Days Before Kids — a long-lost, peaceful and self-indulgent time, where simplicity, calm and silence were the rule of the day.

Harbin was an extraordinary experience, both emotionally and physically. To have your breath freeze on your pashmina, your fingertips burn on contact with open air and your contact lenses begin to solidify if you don't blink often enough … it's challenging but unforgettable.

Xiansheng and I dressed like Michelin men; we could barely button our coats at night we had so many layers stashed beneath, and we *still* froze. Imagine then, the shivers up our spines as we witnessed the unmissable Harbin polar bears swimming in the frozen Songhua River. And no, they're not furry, they're people — most of whom are over the age of 50.

This astounding experience occurs in a large rectangle cut into the iceblock river. The rectangle is continuously scraped around the perimeter with a spade because the water ices over before your very eyes. There are even diving blocks made of ice on the edge of the pool, its water a balmy 0°C (outside: −25°C), and there's also a shanty, shivering building — the place from which the polar bears emerge, shuffling across the ice in their bare feet with their Speedos on and their swimming caps pulled down firmly over frostbitten ears.

The actual plunging is a sight to behold. The polar bears climb onto their icy block and then plunge into that 'warm' pond. Then they swim to the edge, climb out to thunderous, be-gloved applause and cheering, and shuffle back into the shanty to have the ice chiselled from their skin.

But there's more to Harbin than polar bears. The snow sculptures on Sun Island during the day are so silent and so beautiful that they appear to be carved of icing sugar. And the evening event — the International Ice and Snow Festival — is worth every frozen fingertip and breath-snatching moment. These sizeable replicas of famous landmarks, icons and buildings, lit from the inside with powerful coloured lights, are so beautiful they almost manage to take your mind off the biting wind that's stripping the skin from your face and cracking your eyelashes.

What an exhilarating time we had experiencing this physical challenge and visual delight. And yes, even though we were gone just a couple of days, we missed the kids terribly.

And the kids didn't miss us a bit.

Chinese New Year

If you do one thing this lifetime ...

Chinese New Year in Beijing is an unmissable experience. We've had quite a few unmissable experiences so far on our journey, but this is one I wouldn't forgo for all the tea in China.

Our family was very fortunate that our first CNY was also the time the Chinese government lifted their ban on fireworks within the Third Ring Road after a twelve-year hiatus. This meant every man and his dog, cat, canary and cricket were out in the streets setting off crackers.

Noisy? A gross understatement.

Being relatively new to Beijing and still somewhat starry-eyed, we didn't think of gathering a fireworks arsenal ourselves. We instead sat back and enjoyed the frenzy of purchases made by every other living being in the capital. And did they ever buy up big. We couldn't walk along the street beneath our building without running into a sparkling cracker. We were even given some hand-held swirlers by an eight-year-old who borrowed her father's cigarette to light them for us. Ella and Riley screamed their heads off in terror when it began spinning and howling in my fist, and I must admit, I was also a little frozen in terror, yet I couldn't help but think to myself, as I clutched that madly howling disk of light, 'Gee, my kids need to be exposed to firecrackers more often.'

So, it's been a noisy time. The first fireworks began popping about a week ago, from about six in the morning — and they haven't stopped since. Yes, you read it right. Thank goodness we're 26 floors in the sky with relatively noise-blocking windows because the racket has pretty much been ceaseless. All night long, *pop crack fizz* — God knows how anyone near the ground has caught even a wink of sleep. No wonder half the population of Beijing goes away for the New Year, though I suspect nowhere in China would be quiet right now.

The most amazing thing about these fireworks is the sheer bulk of them. Who on earth sets off fireworks during the day when they are totally washed-out against the pall of the white, polluted sky? Everyone, it seems. And as the week wore on, the speed and frequency of crackers — both day and night versions — ceaselessly escalated, becoming louder, bigger, busier and more frenzied, building, swelling, right up to the big night itself … last night — New Year's Eve.

The kids slept through it, quite incredulously. Xiansheng was exhausted from a week of *bai jiu*-fuelled work celebrations and was in bed by 10 p.m. — this man could sleep through a woodpecker attack on the side of his head. Me? I simply couldn't sleep. Not only because of the clamouring noise, but because of the utter thrill of it all.

So, I poured a glass of wine, fired up the video camera and settled in at the windowsill to marvel at the noise rupturing below. It was truly mind-boggling and even quite frightening.

All over the city, for as far as the eye could see, in every pocket, every *hutong*, at the base of every tower and high-rise, splotches of light exploded, ruptured, detonated and *kapow*-ed incessantly, from smackering snakelike crackers spitting along the ground to enormous aerial shells of blue, green, pink and gold. There were tom thumbs, Catherine wheels, Roman candles, starbursts, mines, spinners, rockets and missiles, all erupting, flaring, popping and thundering with such utter power and unrelenting force, I was reduced to gasping out loud. Indeed, I actually wondered if I was sitting on the set of a World War II movie.

And this is the night it really *truly* hit me: we live in Beijing, China. It's only taken a mass barrage of pyrotechnics to really hammer it home.

This morning, Beijing is coated in a haze of post-firework smog, and the city is in the grips of a whopping great cracker hangover. Everyone is walking around clutching their aching heads and groaning from a week of no sleep. Unbelievable, then, that the crackers have *not* stopped popping. I can hear them now, the odd muffled pop or explosion in the streets below, or a small *pfft* of smoke rising a block over.

Will they continue another day, a week, a month? Who knows. After a twelve-year cracker ban, it seems a firework binge was probably inevitable and something anyone worth their salt would happily tolerate.

Xin nian kuai le! Happy New Year!

Our Family's First Snowman

Well, okay ... our pitiful excuse for one

My husband will never let me live down our first ever family snowman. He comes from Belfast, so he's seen snow — baby, oh has he ever, — which gives him the right to call himself a snowman expert.

Me, I have no right to say that. I was born in Tasmania and I vaguely remember smooshing together some slush on the bonnet of our VW halfway up Mount Wellington. It melted and slid off soon after, and that was the extent of my snow experience as a child. When we moved to New South Wales, I spent the rest of my childhood swimming in the warm Pacific Ocean with a chocolate-brown tan. Not much snow in my childhood, no no. Sandcastles yes, snowmen no. And on that note, why don't we build sandpeople at the beach and snowcastles in the snow?

But I digress.

Xiansheng was upstairs for the beginning part of our family's first snowman, so he's probably only got himself to blame, being that he was unavailable to direct us with the architectural planning. As the kids were also new to this and I don't like bending down too far, we decided to build our snowman on a table at the front of our building. We pushed aside the chairs and began plonking handfuls of slush on top (after about fifteen minutes of gleeful ball-throwing).

Very soon we had a wee man about 40 centimetres tall with a cute

belly and a nicely rounded head studded with two silver *jiao* coins for eyes and some little stones for a mouth. We even carefully wedged two short sticks into the body for arms. Cute, cute, cute.

Then Xiansheng came down and shattered our snowy illusion.

'You call that a snowman? That's not a snowman! *Ha ha ha ha ho ho ho!*' he said into our bright-eyed faces, and then promptly flung himself onto the snow-covered lawn nearby and began some serious snow-gathering. Great walloping scoops he made — armfuls of the stuff scraped across the withering wet grass until a large, incongruous pile of mucky slush began to form beneath the bare trees. We all stood watching. Riley sneezed. Ella groaned. Finally, we screwed up our noses, patted the head of our wee snowman and went inside.

'Don't worry!' Xiansheng called after us, 'I'll have it sorted! I'll give you a *real* snowman!'

He didn't last long. Ten minutes later he came through the door grumbling about a pathetic snowfall and went to take a hot shower so he could scrub his cold knees, while we three snowman experts sniggered into our cocoa.

Bring on the next flurry!

The Tooth Fairy Cruises Beijing

Do you believe?

When we left Australia, I was sure to send off change-of-address notes to the VIPs in my children's life — Santa Claus, the Easter Bunny and the Tooth Fairy. I had carefully explained to Ella that these characters don't really visit China and that we would need to let them know our change of address.

Ella, wide-eyed, made sure I didn't forget.

So, when she lost her first baby tooth (*sob!*), the first thing she said to me was: 'Are you sure you gave the Tooth Fairy our change of address?' I reassured her. We prepped the tooth for the Fairy and Ella snuggled in to her first gap-toothed night.

The Tooth Fairy did come; she's an organised fairy, after all. She even left a shimmer of glitter all over the floor and on the nightstand. And not only that — she left a 100 *kuai* ($18) note! Ella was ecstatic. I assured her that this 100 *kuai* thing would be a one-off … first teeth always make the Tooth Fairy extra generous, and Ella had to promise me she wouldn't tell any of her friends about this ridiculous sum (don't want to cause problems with my parent friends or anything).

But money aside, I have to tell you something. Something really disturbing, actually. I have to tell you that some people think this Tooth Fairy hoo-ha is a crock. Can you believe this? And, horror of horrors, some people will even lump the Easter Bunny and Santa Claus in this crock category!

I know you are clutching at your chest right now. It's shocking for me, too. And yes, along with regular fairies in the garden, leprechauns and elves, the illustrious Tooth Fairy is also maligned (most unfairly) in this way.

Imagine. Imagine not having faith in the magic of this world. Imagine presuming that you could possibly know, with 100 per cent certainty, that every tree *doesn't* contain a resident fairy. It's too frightening to me, this presumption, and frightening for children the world over. And frightening for anyone who holds faith in their heart.

If you, God forbid, happen to come across non-believers in this lifetime, remind them of a little girl who wrote to a newspaper editor when her friends told her there was no Santa Claus. The letter is called *Yes Virginia, there is a Santa Claus*. Google it. Print it out and give it to anyone who doesn't believe.

At a 100 *kuai* a tooth, Ella is a true believer.

Bu Yao!

Extending our kids' Mandarin

'Ask Ayi!' is a regular refrain in our house. It's so nice to have someone else to send the kids to (other than Dad), yet every time I tell my kids to 'go ask Ayi', they whine about being unable to speak Mandarin. Suspicions peak, therefore, when I frequently catch them quite suddenly adopting the linguistic capacity to ask for strawberries, Oreos and mango ice cream. *Hmm.*

After a couple of years of daily language lessons at school, I did, however, expect my kids to be able to communicate better in Mandarin. They have an okay vocabulary for their age (colours, days of the week, fruit, extended relatives), their pronunciation is infallible, but their general sentence structure leaves a lot to be desired. Is it just them or is it the way they are taught?

Chinese is typically taught by rote here, even at international schools, with set sentence structure learned by memory. Although this may be effective for learning Chinese characters, I'm not so sure it's effective for absorbing a language kids hear only 5 per cent of their day or less. As it stands, their most oft-used phrase is the simple '*Bu yao!*' — don't want.

Nothing, of course, beats the mother-tongue method, internationally tried and true. I'll never forget meeting an expat mother who, for their family's first six months in Beijing, took her kids out of their international school early every day so they could mix with regular Chinese kids. I would never have been brave enough to do this, and I look upon this woman's decision with enormous, regret-encrusted envy, as both her children are now fluent.

Bit too late for wishing but I suppose there's still time to help the kids' language exposure deepen. Riley constantly asks me, 'How you speak _____ in Chinese?' and I indulge him when I know, but oftentimes I don't.

Maybe I should give Cute Chinese Chick with the Ming Dynasty haircut a call. How you speak 'giggle' in Chinese?

When I Was a Kid ...

Educationally, our kids have got it good

I am frequently dazed by the international school education our children are receiving here in Beijing. Just when I think they've got it good, I realise they've got it even better.

Every time my kids come home from the British School spouting another brain-augmenting day, I can't help but repeat that same phrase over and over in my mind: 'When I was a kid ...' (also tempting to follow it with the classic '... had to walk 10 miles in the snow with no shoes and a bag full of books on my back').

When I was a kid, we didn't have access to interactive whiteboards or a bottomless internet that could flood any project with detailed information at the push of a button. No no. We had to wade through 24 hefty encyclopaedias (for those too young to remember, encyclopaedias are information-packed books) and if the info couldn't be found there, we'd have to — gasp! — make a trip to the local library.

When I was a kid, we didn't make short films using plasticine figurines and digital blue screen technology (in grade three!). We didn't create entire planets in our classroom and spend a week designing and reporting on the flora, fauna and social infrastructure of Planet Zim Zum. We didn't hold weekly assemblies demonstrating how Egyptian mummies had their brains pulled out through their noses. We didn't have access to 100 bongos and an African drumming display that sends chills up your spine or whacky scientists who make volcanoes out of bicarb soda. We didn't read at a grade-two level when we were only four years old. It just didn't happen.

Could it be that I am a little jealous?

Yes. Yes I am. I want to play, too. I want to pull brains out through noses and make short films with blue screen technology! Alas, it all seems too late for me. I will never have the early exposure to the world our kids are having here. The cultural saturation. The language skills. The mind-stretching challenges. These things are restructuring the very composition of our children's brains. It's prepping them for life in unparalleled ways — ways they're unlikely to achieve at home.

Our children will not receive this kind of education in Australia. While our education system is impressive and our teachers are marvellous, government schools suffer typical lack-of-fund-itis, endemic to most countries of the world, I suppose. Unless we want to pay for a school that costs more than a small island (ain't gonna happen), our kids will attend a public school when they go home — with one teacher, a class size double those in Beijing, a quarter of the resources, and no teacher's aide, oh no.

It worries me. Will my kids' brains languish if they aren't exposed to the level of intellectual stimulation they've experienced in Beijing? Will we be compromising their very future? Have we set them on an educational trajectory that will forever remain unparalleled?

Until we go home and find out, I'll be delighting in every British School drop-off, and so will my children. Lucky ducks.

Crowning Glory

Western hair/Chinese hair — not same thing!

The difference between Chinese hair and Caucasian hair is vast. Coarse versus fine, shiny versus arid, straight versus loopy, thick versus sparse, liquid versus fluffy. A generalisation maybe, but this is the ultimate difference between what a hairdresser will find growing on the head of a

Beijing native and that found on the head of a several-generations-Caucasian–Australian, especially one who has fairy floss for hair. Like me.

It actually took me months to muster the courage to walk into my first Beijing salon, mainly because I feared they would completely fluff my fine, arid fluff. What struck me when I first went into the salon, however, was not the hairdressing itself. It was the staring. The being inspected, assessed and blatantly gawped at like a Parisian *haute couture* shop assistant, only without the hoity attitude, just childlike curiosity.

They look at your hands and the rings on your hands. They look at your nails, your watch, your clothes, shoes, bag, skin, hair and finally your face, which they will stare at as though caught in a hypnotic swirl. Persons with low self-esteem, paranoia or agoraphobia enter at own risk.

To dodge the stares, I usually read, which I'm convinced is considered the height of rudeness because I have *never* seen *Beijingren* do this. Ever. They just sit there, patiently, for hours and hours — even under the perming machine — staring. Amazing. Who's got time to do *that*?

I also buck the system when it comes to the handbag handover. It's not paranoia, I just want it with me — it contains my phone, my magazine, my vital bottle of water; it stays with me. Each time, nonetheless, I am asked for it and each time I politely refuse. But God forbid if I place it on the floor. 'No! *Tai zang le!* Too dirty!' they will cry and my bag will be offered its own chair, like a pet. I'm sure they would shampoo it if they could.

Speaking of shampooing, there is nothing like a Chinese head-washing. *Nothing.* They're onto something, these people. There's none of this sitting upright and twisting your neck into yoga contortions before wedging it into a headache-inducing basin, no no. You get to *lie down,* yes, you do. And you have a hot towel for the back of your neck and your head rests on something soft but firm in the basin, so there's no strain at all. Why didn't the West think of this?

Then comes the water, then the deliciously fragrant shampoo … then the fingertips. Oh Lord. The hair-washing mistress begins by pressing into scalp pressure points that make you release little whispers

of delight. She then launches into strong, sweeping, skin-shifting tingles all over your head and down your neck, where the sides will be compressed and kneaded along with the slippery aid of conditioner. I challenge any goosebump to lay flat during this experience.

She will then use her nails to vigorously scratch the scalp, then pull hair by the roots, sending blood rushing to the skin, and the grand finale will be an earlobe massage that really belongs in a parlour of things far less savoury, for its tendency to curl toes and flush faces pink.

I love a Chinese head-washing so much, I'm even over the 'staring' thing. Every eyelash, every freckle, every stray dot of mascara, every open pore is under intense scrutiny. When under the fingertips of my master head-masseuse, my face — upside down to their point of view — must surely resemble the Swiss Alps — white and angular, all mountains and valleys, peaks of cheeks and troughs of deep-set eyes, high ridges of nose bridges and temple plains, with my Roman schnoz rising clear and proud like the Matterhorn.

But I let it all go for this singularly otherworldly experience. When the washing and kneading is done, my neck and ears are lovingly dried and then my head is wrapped, Smurf-like, in a tight towel with my ears sticking out like those of a four-year-old boy. I'm then kindly escorted, in a semi-delirious state, to a waiting chair and if my stylist is not ready, I'm given a hand, arm or shoulder massage.

On top of all this (if you can believe there could possibly be more), a Chinese blow-dry is truly something to behold. My regular doyen is such a perfectionist, he's been known to finalise my blow-dry with a ten-minute fine-tooth-combing — coaxing, quite literally, each strand into place. By the time he's done, I look like my hair has been cast in a blonde mould, a Polly Pocket plastic dome. I absolutely forbid him to hairspray, lest it never move again.

Then, when I finally stand and flick my head, that plastic dome separates like the strands on a fringed lampshade and falls into a flickable sheath that weighs onto my shoulders softly, like silk tassels. Sleek, shiny, frizz-free, gorgeous hair on a head that is usually inhabited by a brillo pad.

That's right, nothing beats a Chinese blow-dry, especially when it costs around three dollars from first rinse to head-flick. When I return to Australia, I honestly don't know what I'll do with my frizzy mop. I guess I'll be able to get a job as a toilet brush.

Good hair. It's a Chinese thing.

The Rabbit Finds Beijing

Easter in the capital

Santa Claus has it all pegged out. He has his high-tech, computerised *Naughty or Nice* list churning out statistics on an hourly basis, slotting kids worldwide into categories that ultimately determine their ranking on the big-gift/small-gift/lump-of-coal scale.

The Easter Bunny isn't that sophisticated.

I don't know much about the elusive Mr Rabbit, but I imagine he is a simple fellow, living in a sunny dale somewhere near the Lake District in England, secreted under a hill of lime-green grass and pink daisies. I imagine he wakes each morning, pops on his denim overalls, perches bifocals on his twitching nose and sets his worker bunnies to smelting great slabs of chocolate in the labyrinth of his underground empire.

Afterwards, he more than likely has a cup of tea and a piece of carrot cake then hops off over the dales for an afternoon lollop in the sunshine.

Come Easter Sunday, I imagine Mr Rabbit puts on his jet-powered, super-sonic, land-bounding hopping shoes, then slings his never-ending choc-egg supply onto his back and bounds off on his egg-delivering route. You see, Easter-egg-hungry kids are *everywhere* nowadays. Even Beijing.

I must admit, Ella in particular was worried whether the Easter Bunny would make it to Beijing. She expressed this concern more than

a few times, as did the kids of some neighbours. So, my Halloween-buddy neighbour and I decided we needed to help Mr Rabbit find our kids and make things chocolate-coated and pastel for them.

It took a lot of liaising with the Bunny. There were heavy discussions about the logistics of importing his eggs, as good ones are either scarce or horrendously expensive in the Chinese capital. But we did it. We got the goods and organised an egg hunt and games for the kids in our building. We dotted the bushes downstairs with pastel ribbon, hid straw bunnies in the grass and perched foil-wrapped choc eggs in surreptitious places, where only kiddliwinks dare to tread. We had 50 kids trailing baskets through the grass, scurrying and peeping with delight.

The great Bunny didn't let us down.

Like all Western festivals, it was a surreal experience celebrating Easter in Beijing. The only outward clue Easter had arrived was the mass selection of chicks, bunnies and hand-painted eggs at Liangma flower market. What a bonanza. It seems that every Western festival comes up trumps in the sales departments of China (surprise, surprise).

In the meantime, Ella and Riley have not only dipped themselves in melted chocolate, they have also experienced a renewed faith in the Easter Bunny and in the knowledge that celebrating an important festival like Easter is something you bring with you no matter *where* you live in the world.

Fu huo jie kuai le! Happy Easter!

Baubles and Bling

Tai Tai bedecked

When my sister Jie Jie first came to visit us in Beijing, I took her to buy baubles and she promptly laid down and had conniptions on the floor. Then she stood up and fossicked and left the store with her body weight in bling.

Let me explain.

When we first arrived in the capital, I wasn't interested in baubles; I had never really been into them. Handbags and shoes? Yes. Baubles and bling? No. I had my engagement ring and wedding band, some Swarovski crystal earrings and a few heirloom pieces, and that was always enough for me.

Things rapidly changed, however, especially after an hour or two at Ling Ling — a local jeweller who has cornered the higher-class bauble market here in Beijing, making friends with many an expat and offering a vast collection of bling from 10 *kuai* novelty bracelets to rare Tahitian pearls worth thousands of dollars.

Unlike a regular tatty market stall, Ling Ling has always offered the *tai tai* dream in her slick store on the fourth floor of the legendary Hongqiao market (the Pearl Market to tourists). When I first went there, I stayed four hours. I bought ropes of pearls, rose quartz, Swarovski crystal, onyx, turquoise, topaz, smoky quartz, citrine, jade-stone and agate for the price of one piece of designer costume jewellery in Australia (and it would probably be *plastic* costume jewellery, to boot). *One piece.*

I remember feeling a little stunned when I walked out of the store, dragging what felt like bags of lead but instead actually contained semi-precious treasure. Owning these baubles was beyond my wildest dreams, and considering most of these gems cost around 5 per cent of their value at home, you could say I had a rather large Princess Diana moment.

I may not be dripping in diamonds, sapphires and emeralds like Princess Di, but this semi-precious bling is still enormously valuable to me because I adore each piece. And isn't real value held in how much you love something, not what price it would fetch at auction?

What a treasure trove we are living in.

Market Fatigue

Could I be getting over it?

I know this is hard to believe, because I can hardly believe it myself. In fact, I don't even know if I want to write it aloud, but here goes:

I think I'm getting tired of Beijing's markets. There. I said it.

Market shopping in Beijing is a true shopper's Nirvana. In classic market shopping-style, the pattern goes like this: you arrive in Beijing and buy everything, and one in every colour, too. You even buy rubbish you don't need, including lots of kitsch Beijing knickknacks like little mirrors, magnets, cards and danglies for your mobile phone and the mobile phone of everyone you know.

After a certain period, you start to get more discerning. You still buy a hell of a lot, but you stop buying the handbags because they're so cheap and start buying ones you really actually like, even if they cost a bit more. You also start looking for more interesting items like 'antiques' at Panjiayuan dirt market, artwork and good quality clothing and fabric, like real silk and real cashmere.

A certain period after this, you kind of get tired of buying altogether. Firstly, your house gets too full of junk; and secondly, you're sick of the mental and emotional exhaustion of a market trip. The thrill of the hunt is still there but the marketeers are starting to get stuck in your craw.

You are over the intense strain of the bargaining process. You are

over the tiresome sales pitches spun into some sticky, touristy web. You are over the drain on your time. You are over the ridiculous start prices and the claptrap that comes along with them. You're over the drama, the conning, the duping, the shoddy products and the whole sorry business. You are more experienced, you *know* the price, you're not a tourist and you're sick to death of repeating this, ad infinitum.

So you just — *sharp intake of breath* — stop shopping. And if you actually *need* to shop, you wait until you have an endless list, then you strap on your skates and tear through that market like a *tai tai* tornado.

That's where I am now. I'm a hurricane. *'Mei you shi jian, mei you shi jian!'* I cry, as I twirl through five floors of copy handbags and 'cashmere' pashminas. 'I don't have time! I don't have time!' And I don't. And, ironically, it seems to be a great bargaining strategy. The pressure of the sale becomes intense when your time is limited, and everyone wins because they get a quick sale and I get to zoom in and out of that market in the time it takes to order a cappuccino.

Put it this way: I never thought I'd tire of the market experience, but I have. And exhaustion is not the only reason, for I now have more wonderful things to focus on. I'm writing again. *Really* writing.

And if this keeps me away from the markets, it can only be a very good thing.

Hair Horrors

White/bleached hair looks bald

I have already spoken of hair in Beijing, but alas, not all hair stories are happy princess-ending ones. Hair lovers, get ready for a horror story.

Firstly, here's some advice. No matter how many times they insist they can colour your mousey hair, never ever trust the Chinese to lighten unless they have had twenty years' experience in London or Melbourne. No exceptions.

So, when I recently became sick of that fetching yellow glow that comes with too many home bleachings, I succumbed to a local hair stylist's insistence that he could make me Marilyn Monroe platinum proud. Like a fool, I was led into the peroxide lair. This stylist is such a sweetie, after all, and foolish me tends to trust sweet.

Chinese hair needs eleven parts bleach to twenty parts peroxide and four hours to lighten even a whisker of a shade. Western hair, especially lint like mine, needs one part bleach to no peroxide, and three-and-a-half minutes — total.

That considered, when this lovely stylist and his two helpers began streaking my hair with foils, all seemed to be going well, if not a tad slowly. After almost 40 minutes of agonising application, my troupe disbanded, leaving me with a band of hair around my face, untouched by bleach. I hesitated. I stewed. Then I just had to say something. I told the stylist he needed to put colour around my hairline otherwise I would end up looking like an inverted skunk.

He acquiesced and used a small brush to paint tiny stripes all the way around the hairline. I should have known better. I should have called him on it because my hair takes to peroxide like vodka to the liver.

But I trusted. Oh, the blonde fool.

You know that feeling when ants are crawling under your skin? For 25 minutes I itched, I pulled at my hairline, I scratched away the colour. It went from orange to butter yellow almost instantly. I was panicked. I squirmed until I was pink in the face. Then I begged for a wash and tore to the basin and revelled in the bleach schlooping down the drain. I prayed to all the hair gods, I begged and pleaded.

It was all in vain.

When I approached the mirror and my Smurf turban was uncoiled, I clutched at my gaping mouth. Oh, horrors of horrors. Tress terror *horribilis*. Revealed was an adequately blonde head all right, but all the way along my hairline was a one-inch band of hair so bleached, so translucent, it was like there existed no hair at all. I was Queen Elizabeth I incarnate. All I needed was a powdered face, a concertina collar and a crown.

I left. I got up and I left. I was polite about it. I said I could fix it at home (I couldn't), I said I would be okay (I wasn't) and I pretended it was all good (far from it). I got up from that seat and I ran home. I ran. I cried. Pathetically. Then I put on a hat and I spent five-and-a-half hours in cabs, scouring Beijing for any box of hair colour other than Black, Ink, Charcoal, Onyx, Ebony, Soot, Slate, Raven, Pitch or Jet.

Of course, I failed.

I bewailed to the heavens somewhere near Sanlitun Lu: 'Where is the blonde, the butter, the champagne and beige? Where is the ash, the caramel, the honey?' Even the local expat supermarket had nothing lighter than Magenta. I was horrified.

At 6 p.m., I trailed back into the salon and begged them to fix it. '*Zai zhe, wo mei you tofa,*' I said. 'I have no hair here.' They agreed. They dyed the whole lot brown, including my Elizabethan strip.

I'm no longer blonde, and we shall never speak of this incident again.

Star Day

The wondrous mechanics of multiculturalism

The great thing about being an expat in Beijing is that you're not only exposed to China when you live here. Things are not only Chinese. Things are Japanese, Korean, American and French. Things are Spanish and Greek and South African. It's multiculturalicious. If you want a worldwide culture bender, all you need to do is live as an expat in Beijing.

Since arriving in the capital, our family has celebrated a traditional North American Thanksgiving, enjoyed an Argentinean birthday celebration, worn demon masks during Japanese Setsubun, trick or treated for candy in our first ever Halloween, decked ourselves in green

for Ireland's St Patrick's Day, cheered on horses during Australia's Melbourne Cup, queued for traditional Christmas candles at the German Embassy, and sampled a global symphony of authentically cooked feasts courtesy of neighbours and friends from all over the world.

It's been a multicultural joy and I can't imagine going home to Australia one day without taking many of these wondrous celebrations along with us. Especially Star Day.

Celebrated on the seventh day of the seventh month, this beautiful Japanese tradition — Tanabata — was introduced to us by our very dear friends from Tokyo. It involves a bamboo tree and lots of beautiful paper decorations and colourful tags to dangle from the tree, just like Christmas, only on these tags you write poems and wishes that you want to come true. A real-life wishing tree!

The kids were agog at Tanabata. They loved the paper-making, the folding, the tinsel and pretty paper. They loved thinking up fandangled wishes (Ella wished for a kangaroo, Riley wished for candy) and writing them neatly on their tags. They loved decorating the bamboo by stringing curling swirls all over its lime-green branches. And they loved placing the bamboo by the window where the moon would see the tags and transport all the carefully scribed wishes to heaven.

There's something inherently wonderful about tradition. There's a familiarity in it, yes, but there's also magic. When my Japanese friend told me she wished for a maid during Tanabata two years before arriving in Beijing, it was with a goosebumping gasp that I turned and looked at her *ayi*, stirring the pot for dinner. Two years on, she had received her wish.

Quickly, I rushed over to the tree and put another tag on the branch. My first tag had said: 'I wish my family health, happiness and success, always.' On the second tag, I wrote: 'I want to be a successful author.'

Fingers crossed!

On Writing

Dragging it out and dusting it off

Speaking of writing, I began a children's book this week. Actually, I began three children's books because I have three separate story ideas and I can't decide which one to do first.

You see, I adore children's books. Always have. And having my own kids has given me so much inspiration — daily inspiration, in fact, and a constant supply of tales from funny to fantastical. I just couldn't resist penning the tales, and Xiansheng even enjoyed them, though he did say the ending of the third one, called *All the Tea in China*, didn't quite cut it.

It annoys me when something doesn't quite cut it, so I dropped the manuscript, which is pretty typical of me. My entire writing life has been like this, in fact. I go full force and achieve quasi success, then give up if the going gets prickly. This has left great walloping writing holes in my résumé, usually filled with flight attending or marketing or desktop publishing. Then when I start writing again, I'm starting from the back of the field. Call it fear, call it a lack of confidence, call it what you will — I know this about myself and I'm frustrated enough to admit it.

So, I've dropped *All the Tea in China* but I'll work on the other two manuscripts instead. Living in Beijing and having access to home help and hence so much extra time, I'd be crazy not to do more of what I love. I need to write like I need to breathe, so why haven't I been breathing?

I just wish the markets and lunches and coffee and mahjong and visits to obscure places with my girlfriends didn't get in the way. It seems the more I do these things, the more I realise how decadent they are. Wonderful, sure, but also indulgent and a little bit time-wasting.

And does anyone really have the luxury of wasting time?

Potential Psychos Are Everywhere

Are our kids as safe as Beijing houses?

Living in Beijing is like having access to a safe house. I don't think I've felt more comfortable anywhere in the world, and with a society that reveres kids and collectively fights to protect them from a comparably low level of predators, things also look good for our children here. Indeed, inhaling too much dust or being skittled by a wayward vehicle is probably the biggest worry our kids face on any Beijing street.

As a result, the freedom you can give small children in this town is probably a little more lax than other places on the planet. But there are still limits. Dumping a toddler in a café for fifteen minutes while you nick off shopping is probably not the wisest decision. You can imagine my horror, then, when I recently witnessed an expat woman do just that.

After a pointed finger and some whispered instructions, said woman disappeared, leaving her small daughter on a café couch, halfway between me and a Chinese woman. The mother had obviously gone to get a coffee and a toddler treat, but after five long minutes, the eyebrows of the Chinese woman rose into her hairline to match the position of my own.

I turned and scanned the café. Then I asked a nearby waitress why the child's mother was taking so long to get her coffee, but the waitress simply scratched her head and said, '*Mama? Mei you mama.*' No mum.

The Chinese patron and I stared at each other. Then we started asking pointless questions that, of course, no one could answer, least of all a two-year-old who spoke a language neither one of us could put a dent in. '*Hui shuo Zhongwen ma?*' we cautiously asked the child, '*Parles-tu français?* Speak English? *Deutsch? Parlo italiano?*' All pulled blank stares.

My Chinese compatriot and I were stumped. Then the child started getting restless and began rolling around on the floor under the table. We continued to quiz her *and* the wait-staff, but alas, no one knew where Negligent Mama had gone.

This went on for another ten minutes before Mama finally breezed back into the coffee shop. The Chinese woman and I looked at each other pointedly then busied ourselves with our work, but my cheeks were flushed. My throat was constricting so tight around a massive lump of expletives and parenting opinion that my ears were turning purple.

How could I *not* say anything? China or no China, relatively safe or not, how could this woman disband her toddler and rely on the kindness of strangers to take responsibility for her baby while she nipped off for a spot of bartering? Who reasons in this way? Who? *Psychos?*

Being unable to focus on my work, me and my bulging throat and puce ears decided to leave. I packed up my things and edged past Neglectful Mama's table, but not without bending cleanly from the waist and hissing some pointed but very calm observations about her parenting skills. She stared at me as though I was a vigilante psycho.

Then I straightened and left. I slipped into a cab and I shook so hard, my teeth rattled. Was it from the adrenaline rush of giving her a serve? Was it because of the totally negligent position she had placed her daughter in? No. It was the numb reaction she gave me — almost a shrug, a half-smile and an 'oh well' look. Let's just hope my comments reminded her that no matter where you are in the world, potential psychos are everywhere.

Even *vigilante* psychos.

Problem Ayi

Furen gets narky

Golly gee, am I possibly the most intolerant *furen* in Beijing? Am I the only *tai tai* who doesn't really like her *ayi*?

I know the cultural differences — goodness knows I live with them each and every day. I know the hot/cold thing. I just nod with numb tolerance when Ayi says it's blowing an Arctic gale in the kitchen when it's really just blowing a smooth ribbon of cool that gets all but lost in the suffocating heat of our steaming kitchen.

I know the 'I didn't do it' thing where Ayi will blame a recent glass breakage on a visiting neighbour or a mysterious gust of wind rather than cop the rap on the chin. (I have repeatedly told her that breakages are fine with me, whereas weaselling out of responsibility faster than a rat on a bagel is NOT.)

I know the discrepancies in thought patterns between the East and the West. I know it all. Doesn't mean I understand it. Doesn't mean I have to like it. I tolerate it, sure, but sometimes it gets to me. And sometimes it *really* gets to me.

The bottom line is, this is my home. *Our* home. It is the place we can strip off our layers and reveal our inner skins, our foibles, our flaws, our warts. It's where we can let down our guard and totally relax and enjoy the freedom of having things *our* way.

The moment we step outside our front door, no matter where we live in the world or what culture we live in, we have to fit in. We have to compromise and empathise and consider those around us, lest we desire anarchy. In our home, we can eat dinner in our underwear, stick our fingers up our noses to the knuckle, forget to flush the toilet (highly anarchistic) and stare at cartoons all day long if we really want to. We don't even need to speak, let alone try to ingratiate or charm anyone.

In our home, we live a life that is comfortable for *our family*. We

have our traditions, our needs, our likes and dislikes, firmly established over decades of sharing. We like fresh air and cool nights. We like sunny windows and soft music. Sometimes we even like pumping music to boogie to. We like Disney movies and sofas pulled close to the TV and a plate drainer sitting on the sink. We don't like to hoard junk, we like to recycle, we detest stuffy rooms and we don't tolerate neighbourly pop-ins very well. We like water with ice in it and only one type of meat at dinnertime and icy poles in winter.

That is our family.

When someone comes into that highly personal, tightly configured sanctuary and tampers with it — nay, *deliberately attempts* to upset the balance to suit their own desires … well, one begins to get narky.

I have a tamperer, and I'm getting *very* narky.

And the worst of it is that the tampering is so *unnecessary*. Ayi is only in our house a few hours a day, in a lovely, temperate, safe apartment. Why she feels the need to cause unrest and strain is really beyond me. It's really screwing with me and pushing me to the outer limits of forbearance.

Tolerance. I know. I'm deepening my capacity for it every day and if there's anywhere in the world to learn it, it's Beijing.

Coins with Legs

Our salmonella experience

There's no way I'm the type of mum who needs to keep up with the Joneses. I march to my own accomplishment drum, that's for sure, but when our neighbours showed us their button-like turtles recently, scrabbling around in a glass bowl like coins with legs … well, we just had to get some.

So cute!

I have to tell you, I'm not an animal person. I really do think they're incredible and adorable and amazing and I do like and appreciate them and stand up for their rights, but I'm probably like your average grandmother: she fawns over the grandbabies but also relishes handing them back at the end of the day. That's me (in a four-legged critter, non-grandma sense).

So, suffice to say that despite their coin-like cuteness, little penny turtles fall into that giving-back-baby category. I had hoped it would be different. I had hoped turtles would be easy-care and not very demanding, but it's amazing how much care two little coins and their legs need.

Firstly, I wanted their bowl to be clean. Permanently. But alas, turtles poop and whiz and spit out their food with alarming regularity. Water doesn't stay crystal clear for long under those conditions, so I became obsessed with cleaning the bowl the moment it became cloudy. This turned out to be several times a day.

Then there's the guilt over the bowl thing. These guys need exercise. I hate that they're trapped in that circular prison for hours on end, so I get the kids to pop them in the bottom of the shower for a play after school each day. This, of course, needs constant supervision (it is an excitable time, after all) and there are always lengthy protests from the kids when I want to wrap it up for the evening.

Then there's the salmonella thing. I didn't know about it until post-purchase. I didn't know that turtles (like all reptiles) carry salmonella at considerably higher rates than other animals. In fact, health departments don't recommend turtles in the homes of children under five, as their immune systems are still tightening up and can be prone to more serious infection.

Although I realise these facts are probably on the border of scaremongering, it still unnerved me. Maybe I just needed an excuse not to have a pet in the house. Whatever the case, it wasn't long into our period of turtle ownership, when the entire family came down with a bad case of the runs (a symptom of mild salmonella poisoning), that I made the executive decision to set our little coins free.

I talked to the kids. At first they protested but then I explained how the turtles needed friends and room to grow and move, and what a better life they would have if they could switch their glass bowl and shower excursions for a life of freedom in the pond at the base of our building. One look at that pond — a turtle wonderland — and the kids were convinced. Those turtles slipped into that dark green water and took off like a shot. It was a lovely sight to see, and best of all, our diarrhoea cleared up faster than you could say 'turtle soup'.

The kids coped well. Just the mere mention of ice cream made everything all right again, and our little friends have never been mentioned since.

My Love Affair with the Wall

Jinshanling steals my heart

Sure, I'd seen it before.

Mutianyu was lovely and sent me roses; I still see it occasionally. Badaling? *Myeh*; was kinda glad when it didn't call the next day. But Jinshanling Great Wall. Oh, Jinshanling. Oriental dreams are made of you. How you broke my heart.

We had taken the Jingcheng Expressway to Chengde (north of Beijing) for the weekend and on the way home, we stopped for a peek at the Jinshanling section of the Great Wall, almost as an afterthought.

It was your regular chair-lift ride with the standard bushland view and the usual landing platform on a cemented hilltop. But when my feet landed on that cement and I turned around, all typical expectations dissolved. My heart stopped. My breath caught. Tears sprang. And there it was — draped over the wandering hills like a cashmere serpent,

rolling, reclining and basking in my eyes; a bewitching lothario.

I was love-struck.

The Wall had never looked like this. It went forever. It rose, it plummeted, it coiled around and flung itself wide. It peaked and troughed and meandered and teased. It trailed away skinny into far-off Simitai and scooped around powerfully under my feet to hold me close.

I gasped, clutched at my hands and rested my head against its grey stones, watching the sun cast itself bronze over the hilltops. This was a life-altering moment for me. This is how the Wall should make you feel. This is it. I never wanted to leave.

Our previous day in Chengde had also been spent on a high. We had explored the summer retreat of Empress Dowager Cixi on glorified golf buggies and wandered the Eight Outer Temples in awe. All are UNESCO World Heritage sites and their charm and spirit are a wonder to behold, especially the Qing Dynasty resort where we found it hard to believe we were walking where emperors and empresses once strolled, their yellow robes resplendent in the sunlight. Luscious and massive, its temples, pavilions, lakes, weeping willows, peacocks and horse-riding plain are hemmed in by 10 kilometres of scaled-down Wall. You could have called it the Medium-Sized Wall.

Xiansheng and I loved it, and what surprised me a lot about this trip was how much the kids enjoyed it, too. This ain't no Club Med resort with a pale blue swimming pool, that's for sure, so it was interesting to see the kids run and climb and spin prayer wheels and explore more than happily. It was also wonderful to see them drenched in the history and culture of China.

We actually left Chengde quite reluctantly, but little did we know we had the Jinshanling Great Wall power moment to look forward to. The beauty of the Wall, however, wasn't the only thing that would remain forever ingrained in my head. Or *on* my head.

At the base of the Jinshanling hillside is a car park and shop and toilet block. Prepping for our long drive home, we all popped in to the 'toilet' for a wee before hitting the road. Ella, at only just six years of age, is not world-weary enough to enter a Chinese public toilet without

batting an eyelid. She still finds them 'icky' and a bad squat toilet is enough to render her bladder inoperative. Nonetheless, I took her in and calmly talked her through it.

Because half the contents of this toilet were actually sprayed all over the floor and around the sides of the sunken toilet bowl, I lifted Ella and held her above the bowl so that her feet wouldn't need to touch the floor. I had my back to the toilet door, leaning far enough over to ensure anything she managed to release would hit the target (unlike certain other patrons before us).

This leaning forward, with back strained, holding onto a six-year-old with a mental bladder-lock is a precarious position to be in. Especially when the floor is covered in whiz and other unpleasant waste.

I remember the moment my feet began to slip.

It was imperceptible at first, just sort of an unbalanced feeling. Then Ella sensed the shift in gravity and grabbed my beanie, pulling it down over my eyes. That's when I became really discombobulated and started yelling for her to wee — fast. She couldn't. She clutched. I yelled some more. She panicked and clutched harder, pulling my centre of gravity even further forward and thus causing my sneakers to go into a serious backward slide.

In the moments before the top of my head crashed into the cement wall behind the toilet, I knew I had two choices: put my hands up to stop myself falling and thus drop my pink, spotless daughter into the cesspit below, *or* hold on tight and take the full force of a crushing fall on the crown.

Well, I mean, which would *you* choose? The pain was so fierce, I'm sure I blacked out for a split second. The impact reverberated in a contracting wave from my skull, down my neck and back to my putrid sneakers. There were tidal waves in the fluid of my eyeballs, I swear to God. Then those cartoon stars appeared, dancing around my head.

I couldn't open my eyes at first. Ella clutched at me like a baby sloth to the underbelly of its mum, and I begged her not to move while I passed through the pain and pondered how to extricate myself.

Basically, I was in the downward-dog yoga position — legs splayed out straight, bum in the air, head down and implanted into the wall — only I had a six-year-old sloth clutching my belly.

I couldn't even call out for Xiansheng; my lungs had all but collapsed. Ella remained stock-still but somehow we extricated ourselves and Ella ran out calling for Dad as a stumbling, pain-intoxicated mother trailed behind, muttering to the pink elephants dancing around her head.

Amazingly, I didn't cry; it must have been the concussion. I got in the car and we began our long drive home. But wait, there's more.

Ella (with bladder full) began whining that the sun was in her eyes, so I grabbed a towel, undid my seatbelt and stretched into the back seat to reach the power button on her window, lowering it a crack. I then stuffed the end of the towel part way through the window crack and instructed Ella to push the button upward on the count of three, to wedge the towel in place.

'Okay, when I say go …' I said, and Ella promptly pushed the button. It was the middle finger of my right hand that suffered the excruciating power of that window. When I screamed for her to push the button to release my finger, she pushed it *the wrong way* and my finger was all but crushed.

You could hear my screams in Hong Kong.

It's moments like these that remind us how precarious life can be — how utterly divine one minute, and then skirting the bowels of toilet bowls the next. Many a time, my life flashed before my eyes on this road trip — mainly thanks to the Chinese drivers overtaking cars on hairpin bends, narrowly missing a head-on with us by a cat's whisker. God knows how we survived, quite literally.

Nonetheless, the experience was worth it. Chengde was a very special place — and Jinshanling … well, if you want your heart batted around like a kitten with a ball of yarn, don't miss your chance to be seduced by Jinshanling. Your love affair may be fleeting but the memory will be cast in stone.

Or a cement wall.

Gong Fu Baby

Charles the Genius

Because we're so often trapped indoors, Xiansheng and I are ever on the lookout for ways to keep our three-year-old son physically active. When our neighbour suggested starting a *gong fu* (kung fu) group for littlies, we were very, verrry interested.

Within hours, we gathered together a small group of three- to five-year-olds in the gym downstairs but alas, as suspected, the teacher found it near impossible to hold the boys' attention. Not surprisingly, little kids actually struggle to stand in *gong fu* poses and deliver a well-timed series of punches to the solar plexus of their opponent. This teacher just didn't get the fact that his charges were small, uncoordinated and far more interested in running around clocking each other over the head with *gong fu* sticks than they were in bowing to *laoshi* (teacher).

The session lasted ten minutes and we disbanded, all but giving up on the idea. Until Charles came along, that is.

A friend of a Western neighbour, Charles is a martial arts expert who has many feathers in his *gong fu* cap. He also teaches yoga, meditation and creative crafts from his workshop in Shunyi (the outer 'burbs of The Jing). He speaks enough English to engage the children, but what he also has is that super magic touch — a complete understanding of what little kids are made of.

In fact, I've never seen anything like it in my life. The kids were totally entranced. They flung sticks. They leapt about. They rolled, tumbled and were jammed into little boy sandwiches and thrown over shoulders. They stood on their heads, raced around chairs like crabs and became rabbits, tigers and cranes. They were exhilarated, exercised and totally enraptured in every minute of the hour-long session. Genius, genius, genius. Let's bottle Charles and sell him at Ya Show market and call it Gong Fu Genius.

Yes, there were *gong fu*-esque movements and traditions slipped in, but Charles's programme was purely built on fun. He even had the foresight to know that any good *gong fu* session should be wrapped-up with a rowdy game of Duck Duck Ghost (as opposed to Duck Duck Goose — I didn't have the heart to correct his English).

No matter. It's a great hour out, and Riley is now becoming our little *gong fu* master. Who'd have thought it?

Chinese Santa Claus

There's something not quite right about it

It's hard to believe our second Christmas in Beijing is fast approaching. What's also hard to believe is how rapidly the Festive Season is spreading across the capital and into the hearts of everyone, even those Christmas-non-believers — much more so than last year. Everything seems so rapid in this town, even the adoption of Christian festivals.

I've said it before and I'll say it again, if the Chinese do anything well, it's celebration. They sure know how to put on a spectacle and each year it seems the sparkle of Christmas is more blinding than the last. In fact, I feel like I'm standing on Regent Street in London on 24 December. Well, maybe not quite Regent Street. But I did feel like I was in New York yesterday, because Santas are starting to pop up on street corners like it's the Big Apple or more aptly, the Big Crab Apple. And when Santas start popping up on the streets of Beijing, that's when you truly know you're in the midst of a world-class city, fully embracing the long-ignored traditions of the Rest of the World.

I'll never forget seeing my first Chinese Santa. Dark-eyed, swarthy and in desperate need of a feed, his waist was more waspish than Audrey Hepburn. Nonetheless, his smile and warmth was Santa all over and we loved how he managed to capture this vital Christmas spirit. Didn't stop

the kids from laying on a series of heavy Santa questions, though.

'Why is he so skinny, Mama? Why does he have black fluffy bits sticking out of his hat? Why is his suit hot pink?' After a long bout of Christmas shopping, I was too tired to field these questions and hand-balled them to Xiansheng, who groaned in agony before spinning some convoluted Santa-ry tale.

The kids looked subsequently dumbfounded.

We've since spotted Santa at school fairs, in department stores, at bazaars, parties and expat resident get-togethers. Each time he looked a little or a whole lot different than the last one and it was so distracting and confusing for the kids that I finally decided to come clean and reveal all.

Yes, that's right. Don't be horrified, but I did it.

I told them Santa actually can't be everywhere at once and does indeed hire out lackeys to field demand while he busies himself in his workshop at the North Pole. At least the questions abated and the questions over the hot pink suit were easily palmed off as a dodgy Ya Show find.

Like many things in China, I'm sure things will change rapidly. I'm sure by next year that hot pink Chinese Santa will become a long-lost moment in history, and the Santas of Beijing will become as fat and jolly as the St Nick we all know and love.

Odd that I feel sad about that.

The Baby With Only One Arm

How did we walk away?

Yesterday I experienced one of the most poignant times of my life. I don't even know how I can express it to you here, but I will try.

Let me start by saying that a month ago I was talking with a neighbour about doing something positive for the Festive Season, to raise some money for those less fortunate, or something along those lines. My neighbour said

she knew of an orphanage in desperate need of funding. In a country where even the poverty-stricken are poverty-stricken, my friend and I felt compelled to put together a plan.

A short time later, four eager *tai tai* sat in the office of the head nun of an orphanage two hours from Beijing. A warm, intelligent woman with excellent English, the nun clasped our hands in hers and welcomed us to her foster home. Soon after, she ushered us into a room to meet her kids.

When the door to the room opened, the first thing I noticed was the railings. Then the purpose-built tables with the therapeutic toys, welded tight to the surface so flailing hands couldn't knock them crashing to the floor. The third thing I noticed was the people. There were lots of people. Carers. Young carers, like uni students or something. And so many of them — one to every five or so kids. It was really quite amazing, and although the rooms certainly weren't hyper-equipped, they were clean and very well laid out. The bedrooms were tidy and spotless and homey. The kitchens were impeccable, and above all, the atmosphere was Love.

When we entered the room, things were quiet. We were asked to remove our shoes and wash our hands, then we were ushered down the purpose-built ramps to meet the kids. And that's when I saw them. The kids.

The kids.

I don't know how naive I will sound by saying this, but I had no idea these kids would be disabled. And I mean, *all* of them. All of them had cerebral palsy, from mild afflictions to extreme. Here were a bunch of kids, from babies to early teens, encased in bodies that spasmed into twisted coils while their minds beamed freshly from perfectly normal brains. Here they were, in wheelchairs, in rocking chairs, sprawled on the floor, strapped to tables, swiping at bolted down objects, loping across the room with limbs splayed, laughing, smiling, grimacing, with all eyes on us, the foreign *tai tai*.

My breath was stolen from my chest and we four *tai tai* clutched at each other for support. Then, after some moments, we broke free of

each other and began wandering gently among those children and we knelt and we touched and we talked and looked deep into those eyes, trapped in those skulls.

I went straight to the boy strapped into the wheelchair by the window. I've worked with cerebral-palsy kids before, so I understood his physical actions and reactions, yet they nonetheless managed to undo me.

When I first spoke to the boy, in Mandarin, he looked up at me and he wailed an awful, blood-curdling cry. Stricken with quadriplegia cerebral palsy (in spasm from the eyes down), it was his way of speaking, yet even though I knew that, it still unnerved and upset me enormously. I remained calm and spoke as much Mandarin as I knew, but after a few moments, I started to feel distressed. Instead of disbanding him and running like a coward, I instead reached out and took his taught, spasmed hand and I told him he was beautiful. I said it so many times, I felt like an utter fool. Then I walked away and found somewhere private where I could cry.

After spending some time with these wonderful children and staff, we then visited another branch of the orphanage, with younger children of lesser disability. Amazingly, many of them were simply cleft palate kids, post-surgery. Some had other physical afflictions — like the breathtaking six-month-old baby girl, born with one arm. Ironically, she was perfection. When one of our *tai tai* (who has a same-aged baby girl at home) saw this child, it took every ounce of strength to hold her up.

But sweet little baby girl aside, I have to tell you about one wee boy who ran up to me when we arrived. He ran up to *me*, just me. His name was Alan and he was about three years old, post-cleft palate surgery. When he ran towards me, I grabbed that child and I swung him high into the air and he squealed with delight, then proceeded to trail me the whole time we were there. Every time I turned around, his adorable face was there, staring at me, melting me.

I fell in love with that child on sight and if my legs could have run fast enough, I would have lifted that young boy into my arms and I would have opened the door and I would have run like the wind. I

would have taken him and I would have run and I would have snuck him into our family forever.

I will never, ever forget him.

I will not forget his sweet face, I will not forget his black eyes. I will not forget the joy and expectation in his face. To hell with the fact that I am not physically with him and will never be physically with him. To me, he is mine. I didn't tell my husband about him. It doesn't matter — it's just Alan and me.

Later, we did raise funds for the orphanage but the funds we raised pale in comparison to the effect this visit had on our lives as *tai tai*. One day, Alan will be adopted by a loving family and he will never want for love and he will never even remember we met. His heart is not the one that will ache for the rest of his days.

That aching heart will be mine.

Sick

Beijing's physical challenges

Almost without exception, people who arrive in Beijing get sick within the first six months, often repeatedly. Strange and persistent microbes swarm around in the air here, screwing with your body's ecosystem. Diarrhoea, nausea and headaches are common, as are colds, sore throats and feeling just, well, *un*well. This is due to many things including the different food, the high salt and fat content in most dishes, the iffy water, and the filth and airborne viruses that coat the streets and float between people who live in such close proximity. This is why hand-washing is so important and why we have thus developed a catchcry upon entering our home: 'Shoes off, hands washed!'

Another phenomenon is the respiratory ailments. If you're a pollution-triggered asthmatic, it will be a nightmare for you here.

And even if you're not asthmatic, you may experience a tightness in the chest or regular dizziness due to the lack of oxygen in the air. Basically, it's mild suffocation. Delightful.

In winter, the air in Beijing becomes bone dry and brittle — so much so, the house zings with static electricity. Xiansheng and I have actually produced bright blue (and painful!) sparks between our pecking lips on many occasions, and have taken to slapping each other's face gently to earth ourselves before a peck (sometimes not so gently).

I'll never forget the day Ella rolled around on our micro-suede couch and when she stood up, her lengthy hair stuck out from her scalp like Thing One from Dr Seuss's *The Cat in the Hat*. It stood a foot from her head, without a word of a lie, and I have the photos to prove it. I told her she better not touch me lest she zap me to Kingdom Come, and so she proceeded to chase me around the house, squealing. Trust me, I ran.

In this chronically dry air, we use humidifiers and we also use moisturiser galore. Darling Ella has English Rose skin, so we need special cream for her. Her hands become covered in blood-angry patches if she doesn't moisturise ceaselessly. We also drink lots and lots of water (and run to the loo more than we care to).

Small ailments in Beijing can be fiddly to deal with but serious illness is also common, especially among expats whose immune systems are not primed for the China super-bug challenge. I know of many an expat child who has been poised for airlift to Bangkok or Hong Kong, and I can't even imagine the terror experienced by their parents.

Our family has so far escaped more serious sickness in Beijing; that is until I was struck down last week with a mystery virus, just as my mother-in-law (MIL) arrived for her second visit and Ayi took a week off for Chinese New Year.

The luck of it.

It started pretty innocently. I just didn't feel quite 'right'. Then there was a constant low-grade fever and although there were no serious outward symptoms, I just felt *off*. Then MIL arrived and Ayi absconded for her week off, and that very same day I went to the doctor to see

what was the matter. I wasn't at all horrendously sick but after explaining my symptoms, the doctor calmly stood up and said he wanted to admit me.

This was totally surprising and really, really annoying. There's no way I wanted to lie in a hospital bed, but he made me. I had a blood test, chest X-ray and ultrasound, and when the blood results came back it was revealed I had a mass infection, only they couldn't work out where it was. Interesting.

Within hours, I was terribly ill. I had intravenous antibiotics for three days solid and my infection numbers became so high the doctor warned me I would be airlifted to Hong Kong if the numbers didn't drop at the next blood reading. This is when I actually got quite scared, so thank God the numbers dropped the next day — barely and insignificantly, but at least they dropped and I was allowed to stay in Beijing.

By Day Four, the numbers improved rapidly yet I spent the day throwing up from all the antibiotics. I remember saying to Xiansheng, 'Kill me now.' He instead insisted I take a nap, and when I woke up my disabling nausea was completely gone and I got up and went home.

Such is life in China.

In the meantime, poor MIL spent the week cooking, cleaning and kid-minding. What a holiday, poor thing. Riley's birthday, Chinese New Year and my birthday came and went, and I remember sitting at the table, weak as a kitten, attempting to blow out a belated handful of candles on a cake — and giving thanks I had actually made it to another birthday.

Temple Blessings

Anyone can send wishes to heaven

Our family has visited many a Chinese temple. From the faux Potala Palace in Chengde to the Jade Buddha Temple in Shanghai, from the stunning Soul's Retreat in Hangzhou to the famed Lama Temple in Beijing, we've seen many, many a temple. Some have egg-yellow walls, some faded red, some have round gateways, some have ethnic minority influence, some have prayer flags, some have prayer wheels, some even have rooms representing the departments of heaven, complete with life-size replicas of people having their tongues cut out.

But what all of them have in common is incense, or joss sticks, upon which you can send your prayers and wishes to heaven.

How I've longed to send my prayers and wishes to heaven.

I remember the first time I headed straight to the joss-stick seller at a temple and Xiansheng pulled me aside and suggested it might offend the more pious Chinese worshippers if a big blonde Western woman stuck a few sticks into the urn and sent clouds of billowing smoke just to say hi to her mum.

Since then, I've never dared do it. I wouldn't want to offend. It's true, I wouldn't really be praying to the Gods; I would just be sending a cheerio to Mum and to my father-in-law and to others who have left us far too soon.

To be fair, I have been known to pray. Not to a religiously pre-determined bearded man in the sky but to a force I feel watching over us. Just because I can't give it a name doesn't mean it isn't real and I don't have faith in it.

So, when MIL and I wandered the stunning, wintry-cold grounds of the Dongyue Temple in eastern Beijing recently, I didn't even mention the big fat joss sticks for sale at the antiquated little shop at the entrance. The temple was quiet and only a few smoky sticks burned in the

courtyard's central urn. Nonetheless, we were attracted straight to them.

We had been staring at them a long time, inhaling the fragrant white curls, when I turned to MIL and said, 'I want to light some joss sticks.'

'So do I,' she said.

'Then let's do it,' I said. And, without further ado, I looked to the left, looked to the right, and dashed into that little shop where I bought two great whopping bunches of sticks, wrapped in white paper with red Chinese characters on the front. Then I handed MIL a pack and we walked towards the urn and we unwrapped the end of the pack and we held it firmly against the flame.

The bitterly cold air made lighting a task but eventually our sticks began to smoulder and we pushed them into the sand then stood back to bask in the scent. I looked to the left, to the right. A few people wandering around. No one rushing over to question us. No one rolling their eyes in dismay at the two light-haired Western women performing this sacrilegious act. All was calm.

MIL and I linked arms as the joss sticks burned quietly, then suddenly they began billowing cleansing white smoke all around us. And as we watched, we sent our prayers to heaven, via the Gods of All Sorts and into the souls of our loved ones gone.

We cried, we smiled, we paused and we laughed at the simplicity and beauty of it all. After all, who cares what travels on billowing white clouds to heaven? So long as it's love.

Train Shenanigans

Our first clackety overnighter

I remember having the opportunity to chat with the Australian Ambassador to China (another Princess Diana moment) about two weeks after we arrived in Beijing, and one of the first things I asked him

was a China travel recommendation. A highly seasoned Sinophile, the Ambassador said, without hesitation, 'Pingyao.'

It's only taken us three years to go, but we finally went, last weekend. And we loved it.

We took an overnight train to this ancient financial capital, and it may have been exhausting but it was also some of the most fun we've ever had as a family. We boarded the train at around 5 p.m. and settled quickly into our four-berth room with a sliding door and narrow bunk beds with lace-trimmed bedding. The room was clean enough, with a carpeted floor, a mini air-conditioner and a teensy flip-out table beneath the large picture window.

The kids clambered up to the top bunks and proceeded to giggle for hours on end, climbing up and down and scooting around the train like monkeys. Then, of course, they needed to go to the toilet because toilets are like unexplored and fascinating territory for a child, no matter where you are on the planet — even on a rattling, skanky old train.

After an hour or two of challenging toilet trips, we germ-stripped our hands with germ-stripping gel and unearthed our picnic dinner. Xiansheng and the kids began nibbling on sandwiches while I searched fruitlessly for the bottle opener I'd packed for the bottle of Chardonnay clutched in my fist. With dawning horror, as the train clambered its way across the very lengthy Chinese landscape, I knew it would be a long and sorry night if I couldn't numb myself with a much-needed Chardy or two.

Ten minutes later and in total Chardy desperation, I begged Xiansheng to go into the dining car and ask for a bottle opener. My husband looked at me pointedly and then burst out laughing. Frustrated, I initiated a round of bets that the dining car would indeed come up with the goods. Xiansheng argued with me for an appropriately frustrating period of time before reluctantly heading there to check.

When he came back, I held out my hand and he reached out and placed nothing in the centre of my palm. Then he slapped my palm and said: 'Told you!' He then proceeded to tell me that when he got to the

dining car, he found a booze opener all right. The stench of it hit him like an oncoming freight train. There, draped across the very first table of the car, were not only two totally plastered chefs in their grimy chef's hats, but also the train's uniformed policeman, paralytically drunk and clutching a very empty bottle of *bai jiu* in one fist, with a finger from the other fist jammed up his nose to the first knuckle.

The first thing Xiansheng did was take a photo to prove it, then he turned on his heel and left, but halfway back to our cabin, he second-thought his return (knowing I would just turn him around and send him back again) and went back to the drunken dining car. When he politely gathered the attention of the drunks and asked them for a wine bottle opener, they first said, '*Shenme?*' What? Then they said '*Shenme?*' seven more times before finally realising what Xiansheng wanted, and bursting into raucous laughter.

I heard the laughter from our cabin.

When Xiansheng returned, I took one look at him and the invisible bottle opener on my palm and I said: 'Get your car keys.'

Fifteen minutes later, and sweating like a roasted pig, Xiansheng had almost managed to push the cork all the way in with his ignition key. Ella, on the top bunk, flipped herself upside down and regarded his attempts with interest before saying, 'Daddy, why are you trying to start the wine with your car keys?' Obviously thinking that 'Because mummy is a shameless drunk' was not the right answer, Xiansheng instead grunted and glared at *me*. Ha! He didn't complain once that sweet grapey drop seared his tongue.

Ah, this was the life. A careening clickety-clack train, skinny, rock-hard bunks with scratchy lace sheets, two heavily dozing children and a sleepless husband and wife watching China speed past into the night, sipping warm Chardy and spitting out cork crumbs onto the carpet.

A fine introduction to Pingyao, which incidentally, you must put on your travel list immediately. My friend the Ambassador was right. And make sure you take the train there … and *don't forget the bottle opener*. It may not be the Princess Diana way to travel, but it sure is a hoot.

You Got to Have Friends

Or not

Like many expat women in Beijing, I've become a veteran in the art of saying goodbye, of letting friendships go. Gradually, you get over the need for expat friends. Sometimes it's because you find other things that are more important but usually it's because you've become a twisted pile of bitter due to the falling-in-like and subsequent loss scenario. What happens is: you fall in like with several wonderful, incredible people and then they up and leave you. Strand you. Go home.

How dare they!

Most of the expats I've met and lost in Beijing, I didn't want to let go. Some, I was indifferent about and others I was whooping it up like a bling bling cowgirl on Rodeo Drive, more than happy to say *adiós*. Seriously, though, many, if not most friendships in Beijing run their course and would never survive outside this bizarro expat world. It's nothing personal; it's just that everyone is thrown together in a pot that doesn't offer the choice and selectivity we enjoy at home.

And it doesn't help that, over time, you miss your old friends and family back home more than ever before — like really terribly miss them, and realise how blessed you are to have them. Or maybe you've simply decided that if you have to do one more girlie lunch or shopping expedition, you'll implode.

It could also be because you've reached the zenith of your posting and suddenly you find yourself on the downward slide — the homeward stretch. That's when things shift into high gear: so much to think about, so much to plan, so much to do while still in Beijing, and friendships get compromised in the busyness swirl. During this countdown time, what's the point of forging new friendships?

I've said goodbye to two dear Beijing friends recently. One of them a marvellous Aussie heading back to Perth, and the other an

extraordinary Japanese housewife who is truly a jewel-box of treasure and quite possibly could have been a past-life twin of mine.

I'm really surprised how devastating these losses have been. Both these women have left large, very empty holes in my life in Beijing. Since their departure, it's almost by external force that I'm compelled not to get involved with new people. This has been exacerbated by the recent arrival of my sister Jie Jie and her husband Smoothie, who are now living in the capital. Of course, I want to spend a lot of time with them, and my Beijing friends have consequently taken a seat even further back on the priority train.

It's kind of sad, in a way, but I really have no choice. My desire for emotional investment has not only switched off, but my serious desire to write has been switched on, and it's taking up every spare social minute.

Some social acquaintances have taken my sudden inward shift well. Others have taken it personally (it's really *not* personal), and some even stick their noses in the air when I walk by. It's difficult but it's also something I simply *must* do. Beijing is a magical place with magical things happening and I must plan our remaining time very carefully here. I must make sure our family enjoys the most of this extraordinary place, which (of course) we've taken for granted, and which is so rapidly coming to an end. Before we know it, we will be back home to our Normal life. A wonderful life, but nonetheless a Normal life.

And if glorious Beijing is anything, it's *not* Normal.

Holidays in Paradise

Adding Sanya to the five-star list

Since coming to live in China, we've been in the fortunate position to be able to travel. To go on super-dooper holidays further afield than we ever imagined — much further than the outskirts of our local town

or the nearest coastal beach or caravan park, which were the holidays of my childhood.

When I was a kid, we would pack up the car and go camping with tents that were scratchy on the ground — not a single luxe pillow-top mattress in sight. We'd shower in the local caravan park toilet block with plastic thongs on our feet — no bubbling spa bath overlooking a turquoise blue ocean, no no. We'd poop in the bush using fresh leaves for paper — no bidet or heated ceramic toilet seat for our little pink bottoms, thankyouverymuch.

Our kids, on the other hand, are getting a little bit used to luxe. After a week in Sanya on China's Hainan Island (seven days of pure paradise), I fear it will be impossible to get these kids into a sleeping bag ever again. Our trips to Phuket and Langkawi islands were similarly luxe, and subsequent nights in Hong Kong, Bangkok and other world spots have really created emperors and empresses out of our very regular little monkeys.

When I look back at my Australian childhood, going camping and staying in caravans are some of my most joyous memories. We loved it. We loved winding fat damper dough onto sticks and baking them over the campfire before pouring golden syrup into the hole left by the stick. We loved 'hunting' wildlife with little more than a torch and a handful of nervous giggles. We loved curling up gum leaves and trying to make them whistle. We loved dipping into icy cold creeks in our underwear or running headlong into the churning ocean for some body-surfing and a tonne of sand deposits in our gruns (bathing-suit bottoms for non-surfing readers).

What is it about our childhood memories? Why do they swamp us when we become parents? Why do we so dearly love to re-encounter the joys of our past and re-invent them with our own kids? From particular toy brands to old-fashioned games to everyday experiences, it's so rewarding to watch our kids enjoy our own retro past. It conjures memories of the tenderness and rawness of being a child, of being able to appreciate and so fully immerse ourselves in life, unfettered by responsibility and the demands of adulthood.

Watching my kids pop ice blocks from plastic sheaths for the first time sent me soaring back to when I was five, only we had to cut *our* blocks from the plastic sheet with scissors, being careful not to nick the sides and risk the coloured juice leaking out. When I first watched the kids click together Lego bricks, I was cast back to when I was eight, sitting on the moss green carpet of our living room in Tasmania, with the winter sun streaming in and a village of Lego houses spread all around, with red tile roofs and shutters that opened to let the breezes in. Watching my kids roll up beach towels and wear them as turbans on their heads sent me straight back to when I was nine, when we'd sun ourselves on the cement steps near our above-ground swimming pool, rolling up towels to create curtains of long 'hair' for our heads.

Don't we want to give our kids a life of glorious experience and opportunity? Aren't we consistently trying to form fond and beautiful memories for them to revert to when life as an adult becomes challenging? It means everything to watch my children delight in life's experiences — but although watching them doze in the beachside hammocks of a five-star hotel is certainly picture-perfect, I also crave their losing a gumboot in the suction of black farmyard mud, digging out the lumpy stones and pebbles beneath their sleeping bags, and fishing mulligrubs from their holes in the hard-packed earth with long spears of grass.

For now, we'll take the five-star padding while we can, because very soon, tents and gas stoves will probably be our only option. And frankly, I'm looking forward to this more than I ever imagined.

To Write or Not to Write

That is the question

Actually, the real question is this: when am I going to get on my behind and write for a living? As in: a job.

Not such an easy question to answer.

I love to write. I wrote my first novel when I was ten. It was a love story, believe it or not — or more probably a friendship story, as the main characters were only ten years old, after all. My first magazine article was published when I was twenty. It was a glorious feeling. When my first book — *You Name It* — was published in 1995, I leapt around the living room for fifteen minutes straight before collapsing on the floor from exhaustion. Oh yes, that was a Life Moment. When you love doing something that much, the feeling when success elusively arrives is really overwhelming.

Over the years, I've written poetry, plays, workshops and countless manuscripts of varying genres from novels to non-fiction. No style was ever constant, just so long as I could write. But one constant with me has been my powerful ability to give up. One pernickety comment or rejection slip too many, and that's it, I'm off the project, telling myself that maybe writing is not for me. Maybe I'm not meant to do this. Maybe I'm not good enough and should just try something else.

Over the years, I did try something else. I tried being a barmaid, promotional girl, data entry clerk, catwalk model, desktop publisher, teacher, speaker, website designer, craft marketeer, astrologer, executive secretary, eBay seller, personal assistant and flight attendant. I worked in marketing, sales, advertising, businesses big and little. I even took on an incredibly important role as a mother.

Yes, I tried it all. But writing kept calling me back, despite fears that Fate was telling me it wasn't what I was 'meant to do'.

Something strange has happened since we've arrived in Beijing,

however. I've gradually realised that Fate doesn't design our lives. We do. What we do, what we believe, how we act in the world designs our Fate. As the famed artist Edvard Munch once said, 'Thou shalt live thine own life. Thou shalt never regret.'

So, I've decided to write my own life. I've decided to contact a magazine here in Beijing called *tbjkids*. I'm going to write to the editor and I'm going to ask her if she takes freelance work. What have I got to lose? What harm can it do? I know I can do great quality work for them, I just have to take that first Herculean step and ask. What's the worst that can happen? They'll say 'no'?

We shall see. And then we shall never regret.

Expat Man Eats Donkey

Hee-haw!

Oh Lord, this is possibly the grossest thing I've ever had close proximity to. It still turns my stomach, and hearing about it first-hand actually stopped me eating for an entire day (there's a weight-loss plan for you).

You see, Xiansheng recently had the life-altering experience of ingesting the reproductive organs of a donkey. Actually, it was two donkeys — a male and a female, perhaps husband and wife. God rest their procreative souls.

If my husband had told me he was served these donkey parts in a warming, gravy-coated stew, I could have perhaps stomached the idea of it. The fact that he was served cold cuts — I'm talking cold slices of reproductive organs (let your imagination run wild) — really screwed with my gag reflex. I know and appreciate and respect that these parts are considered a delicacy in some Chinese circles, but the gag reflex is involuntary, after all. It wasn't my fault.

It also wasn't my fault that I found it necessary to give Xiansheng a

wide berth for a few days, at least until that feast had worked its way through and completely exited his body. I just couldn't even bear the thought of those donkeys residing in his digestive tract. I had to form distance.

A week later, Xiansheng turned 21 again, and we had a celebration for him — a delicious feast of sushi and sashimi in honour of our upcoming trip to Japan to celebrate this milestone age. Funny that we find it *no* problem to slurp down slimy, raw fish, yet donkey uterus is out of bounds.

Xiansheng loved the raw fish feast, and to finish off the spectacular meal, in honour of his recent culinary exploits Ella presented him with a very special dessert: a stuffed toy donkey on a plate, complete with knife and fork.

To his credit, he didn't flinch. He did laugh. Then he started munching on that poor creature — to the horrified refrain of every donkey-loving person in the house.

Post Office

God help me; what is it with this place?

Today I went to the post office to send off some things. I have to tell you about this small, basic occurrence because it might help you begin to understand how China has quietly driven me to insanity.

Here is what happened.

I placed a letter in a standard white envelope, addressed it to Shanghai and sealed it. I took it to the post office and handed it to the clerk who promptly told me it's not possible to send white envelopes to Shanghai. Only brown ones can be sent. I stared at her. She was absolutely serious.

I re-addressed a brown envelope.

The next thing I wanted to send was some items to a friend in the States — some baby clothes, some teensy toys. The postal clerk insisted these had

to go in a humungous China Post box. I said a padded envelope would do. She said they don't have envelopes big enough and the items must go in a humungous China Post box. I pointed to a pile of padded envelopes behind her, the smallest of which would *easily* fit my items.

They put the items into a padded envelope and off went the parcel.

My last item was a large envelope to Chongqing. I had pasted an address in Chinese characters onto the front of that envelope, then handwrote, in English, the return address in the top left-hand corner, as I have done countless times in China. The letter was rejected for sending because the return address, in fact, had to be on the *bottom right-hand corner* when going to Chongqing and when using an envelope of this size.

Overcome with controlled rage, I snatched the envelope from the clerk and seized a pen. I then circled the address in the top left-hand corner and drew a big fat arrow down and around, pointing to the bottom right-hand corner. Then I crossed my arms and stared at the clerk, my nostrils flaring like a bull.

She sent the bloody envelope.

You're Fired!

I think I want to sack my *ayi*

What she does that drives me into the pits of despair is not what's important here. It's the fact that it's happening more and more frequently and with greater drama that's the issue. And after well over three years of it, I'm at boiling point.

I don't know why I don't sack Ayi. Other *tai tai* have told me they wouldn't hesitate to get rid of her (heartless sods), but then they're the first ones to tell you of the nightmare of changing *ayis*. What if I sack Ayi and then get another one who's even worse? And what about the

hefty challenge of re-training, re-explaining, re-showing, re-guiding, re-hashing things over and over again in a language that's hard enough to navigate without adding specific *instructions* to it.

For all her mental game-playing and intermittent psycho behaviour, Ayi actually does a pretty good job. She needs a bit of a fluff-up every now and then — like when you fluff a doona and it resettles its feathers to be more effective — but overall, she's consistent. Sometimes she shows initiative and sometimes she's phenomenally helpful. I don't think she's evil. She cooks well. She whinges a bit and can be a little slow, but she's not lazy. She's familiar with my knickers and the inside of our toilet bowls and she knows our house, our family, our preferences and how things work.

Changing this could be more trouble than it's worth. On top of that, she's elderly and it would undo me to think that sacking her means she probably wouldn't get a job anywhere else.

Oh, the *ayi* technicalities!

What to do? Sometimes I like her, sometimes I detest her, and things aren't great at the moment. Every time her key turns in the lock, my shoulders rise up and clench into fists. Is this really a healthy way to live? But then, is changing *ayis* also going to give me health problems?

I'll sleep on it, as I always do, and will probably wake up, as I always do, giving Ayi another chance.

Stop the Press!

I'm a real working writer

Sometimes, taking a deep breath and asking pays off. Sometimes taking a risk or being brave comes up trumps. Sometimes believing in yourself (for once) takes you further than you could ever imagine.

It took a lot for me to harness the courage to approach the editor of *tbjkids* magazine about writing for them, and, much to my delight, she

was, well, delighted! She wants me to write for the magazine, and not only that, after writing my first tiny piece for the tidbits section, she's since phoned to ask for a travel piece, an end-page piece, and a feature article on how to throw a gorgeous baby shower.

Oh yes, I'm agog. I feel like a magazine addict at a magazine addict's fair. I've always been a magazine addict, actually, and most especially magazines that involve kids and families. How could this be more perfect? I'll tell you how.

It couldn't be.

I don't know where this is going but I'm squeezing my eyes shut and making a wish and hoping on a star, comet and planet. Oh, and I'm also going to work my guts out, and I'm *not* going to give up.

Watch this space.

My Kingdom for a Rabbit

*Un*convincing a pet-obsessed child

My daughter wants a rabbit. Or a dog, cat, bird, hamster, pony or polar bear, in no particular order.

The problem is that this Want is sticking like a pancake in an unbuttered pan, and won't fade away with the myriad other desires preceding it, like becoming a Chinese acrobat, having the world's largest Pokemon card collection or moving permanently to a bungalow on the beach in Phuket.

It's not that I don't like animals, truly. I become as enamoured with Labrador puppies, freshly hatched chicks and the adorable belly rolls on a seal as much as the next person — I just don't want them inside my house. There are lots of reasons, the very least being that we don't have a grassy backyard, a hen house or an Arctic Ocean in our apartment. It's also the fact that owning a pet in Beijing can be far too

fleeting, is fraught with far too many health issues and, frankly, the desire is just not there.

It's also because I'm a sook. I can't bear the thought of leaving a pet in Beijing, or worse, of losing it to rabies or feline AIDS or simply old age. When our daughter's fish died after a one-night family absence, she was hysterical and I've never forgiven myself. We've tried other fish but they too left us quickly — and I swear I had nothing to do with it. Flushing those bloated little bodies down the loo is not something I relish and I couldn't imagine what we'd do if the pet wasn't flushable.

But there's more than just fear-of-loss involved here. It's pet hair. I'm talking asthmatic lung spasms and chain-linked sneezing and eyeballs turning into itching cesspits of blood-shot damnation. Even if I wasn't so allergic, I'd still have an issue with pet hair in the home. Yes, I know about vacuum cleaners. And yes, yes, I have an *ayi* who just delights in sweeping floors and brushing down furniture, but it's hard enough for her to keep the perpetual haze of dust from every surface without also adding fur balls.

My final argument for Not Getting A Pet is the care factor. Yes, we've heard it all before — 'Mum, I'll feed it, I'll bathe it, I'll take care of it.' Ain't gonna happen. Like the fish before them, any pet that comes to live in our house will be looked after by none other than Me, *Moi*, *Wo*. And you only have to recall the fate of those fish to understand my pet track record.

Not even my own memories of begging for a dog at seven years of age are enough to sway me. All kids do this, so it seems. Even pet-dream-squashing me. My Ella will eventually tire of asking (hopefully) and then maybe one day, when we return to Australia, she can keep something fluffy in a hutch at the end of a very long Aussie backyard, in the shade of a large tree and well away from my furniture, lungs, eyeballs and low desire to care for yet another clan member.

I guess I'll get my comeuppance eventually … Ella assures me she wants to become a vet. In the meantime, she'll just have to rely on her menagerie of stuffed pets.

And don't worry — I haven't taken up taxidermy.

White Shoes

The unending, mind-bending battle with Beijing's dirt

Our son Riley has a white shoe obsession. Nike, Adidas, Puma, Lacoste, Converse (well … designer *copies*). All good, so long as they're white. Blue will not do. Nor will grey. Brown? Forget it. And red? *Ha ha hee hee ha ha ho!*

Now, normally such an obsession wouldn't be a problem in the average family's life, but when you add four-year-old-outdoorsy-boyness to the open slather of grime on Beijing's streets, it's a whole different story for the White Shoe Brigade. The squeaky-clean, blindingly luminescent sneakers I bring home from Ya Show are condemned to a fate worse than dog dander once strapped to those dirt-destined feet. I kid you not — brand new, shiny shoes at 8 a.m. Dog-eaten, shoddy, charcoal-smeared foot sacks by 4 p.m. No wonder the Chinese take off their shoes upon entering the house. Very wise.

I probably manage to stretch these mucky foot sacks to about a month or two before tossing them in the garbage, and trust me, I've tried many different tactics to keep them looking part-way presentable for school, including a risk-laden tumble in the washing machine. I've even eyed off the scrunchy plastic bags Chinese adults slip over their shoes when entering a house … maybe we could start a new trend on the streets of Beijing.

So, yes, I've hunted Beijing and beaten it black and blue for some black and blue shoes my son might deem worthy of his feet. But no. White it is. Oh how I pine for a pair of shoes that might hide the muck for more than a day, for more than a week, for more than a month, or even more! How I pine to drastically shave down my shoe-seeking visits to Ya Show. I'm quite reluctantly a VIP at my kids' shoe supply stall. '*Nin hao! Hui lai le ma?*' they sing sweetly — she's back! *Ker ching ker ching!*

But it's no good. Riley won't bend.

We've tried bribery, trickery and, God forbid, *reasoning* with our son over this crazy shoe thing. We've tried giving him choice. We've tried reverse psychology. We even tried banning white shoes altogether (it was an ugly, ugly time). It's been a distressing, emotional, mind-bending challenge — one that I know I'm not going to win. I guess a four-year-old's obsession is just too tough to crack and a wise mother knows how to pick her battles.

I therefore think it's time to wave the white shoe flag. I'm off to Ya Show. *Ker ching.*

My Mother's Christmas Cake

Love is a cake of mixed fruit

Once again, Christmas is on the horizon of our Beijing life, and with it comes excitement but also a deep sense of melancholy.

This morning, I slid a large glass bowl from the refrigerator. It was brimming with dried fruit — golden Chinese sultanas, currants, raisins, cranberries and candied peel — shiny with cherry brandy. I lifted off the wrap, stuck my nose into the bowl and inhaled deeply. The aroma reached my toes.

I placed the bowl on the kitchen bench where the winter sun made it warm, then slid a large spoon down the side of the bowl, lifting the gleaming fruit up and over, fruit tumbling and rolling, drunken, fat and glistening like a bowl of precious, aromatic jewels. This motion affects my heart.

I then put on Christmas music, tied on an apron, lit some incense and began talking to my mother.

As I do each Christmas, I told her how much I'm missing her — still so terribly, even after almost eighteen years. Then I told her, as I always do, how surprised I am that she never met my children and that

I'll have to spend the rest of my life without her, as though I've only just realised this. Then I told her about the kids and my husband and about our lives, and I talked to her of my ups and downs and successes and losses and I asked her advice, as though she were sitting opposite me, tilting a warm cup of tea to her lips. If I closed my eyes, I could see her sipping.

Then I put the kettle on and made a cup of tea, then my legs gave way and my head slowly lowered until it reached my knees and my heart got crushed from the motion and I wept onto my jeans.

After a while, I stopped and wiped my eyes because Mum's Christmas cake needs joy mixed into it, not sadness. I stood and put my hands on the kitchen bench and the glistening fruit giggled at me in the bowl, still drunk and happy. I eyed off the cherry brandy for a brief moment, then poured myself some tea and stirred the fruit once again.

Next, it was the flour, powdery and light, sifted with allspice, cinnamon and baking soda. I banged the side of the sifter with my hand and watched the flour pouf in white clouds before settling into dust.

In another bowl, the butter had been resting, melty from the sun on the windowpane. I plonked a cup of tightly packed brown sugar into the yellow nest and whipped till creamy, then added eggs, one, two, three, four. Mix, mix, blend, all the time thinking of the end result, the tang on my tongue, the sweetness of the fruit, the roundness of the spice, the fragrance of the brandy — I can still taste my mother's Christmas cake, even decades after my very last mouthful.

I can remember sneaking into the pantry, quietly prising open the big square tin, breathing in the blend of fruity aromas and metal, feeling the tang in my nostrils, the release of saliva under my tongue. Then, peeking around the door to make sure no one was coming, I'd snaffle a small slice with the tiny knife Mum left in there — a small slice so she wouldn't even know a wee cake-nibbling mouse had paid another visit.

It was a joy to me, that cake. It typified my mum and who she was. Always sunny, always warm, always rich and fragrant and smelling of face creams. Feeling that fruitcake spread across my tongue, even just *remembering* that taste, evokes such strong memories of my mother,

coupled with the unforgettable wonder of childhood Christmastime. The memories induced are so strong and so precious, it's like I'm ten again and she's standing right next to me.

Our family will have a slice of The Cake with coffee under the tree on Christmas morning and we'll offer slices to friends and neighbours who have the capacity to truly appreciate what this cake means to me. The kids will snaffle it, too. Both of them devour it, as though it's infused with my mother's spirit. It brings me such joy to see them savour it and treasure it the way I do, especially as my mother died well before they were born.

Life has an entrancing way of blending elements together so that even if we miss each other on this earthly plane, we carry within us the memories, the genes, the instinct of those who have gone before us. Memory comes from scent and thoughts and sights and beliefs and Christmas cakes. They amalgamate. They become one. And this is how a daughter can place so much importance in a Christmas cake — an unparalleled way to hold Mum close, and in this way, keep her alive forever.

I'm off to stand in the kitchen, right near the warmth of the oven, and sniff the fragrant air. Happy Christmas, darling Mum.

All By Ourselves

Our very first solo family Christmas

We've had some fabulous Christmas celebrations in Beijing. We've enjoyed wonderful feasts, glasses of bubbles, Christmas cake, laughter and memories we'll never forget. But we lost a lot this year. Friends, I mean. And although plenty of new people have taken their place, we're feeling a little sore and tender. We're also missing our family and old friends more than ever before.

So we've decided to do it alone. Yes, we are having our first Christmas dinner as a complete, nuclear family (Jie Jie and Smoothie are away). We've got pop-in drinks booked at various houses for the afternoon, but the morning and the roast lunch will be us and us alone. It feels weird, it feels strange. And it also feels absolutely *wonderful*.

I get to do it all. I get to peel spuds, I get to roast, I get to dust the Christmas cake with icing sugar. I get to choose dessert and chill the bubbles and fold the napkins and decorate the table. I get to choose the music and the Christmas movie to chill with post-feasting. I get to smile proudly around the table at this beautiful little family unit Xiansheng and I have created.

I'm also nervous about it. I'm nervous about looking around this carefully decorated Christmas table and seeing the empty chairs. I'm nervous about how quiet it will be. Sure, I'm nervous about the continued absence of Nanny to slice up her Christmas cake and of Granda to top up the wine glasses, but I'm also nervous about craving my mother-in-law's tender turkey joint and love-infused meal. And thumping my brothers-in-law in the arm after a particularly bad joke. And nattering with my sisters-in-law about the Christmas sales and school issues and Jung. And clucking with my gaggle of nieces over their pretty presents.

I'm really nervous about it. Sure, Christmas is all about food and sparkles and pressies, but without sharing, without the people you love … well, it's just all pretty wrapping paper.

May your Christmas Day be peeled of wrapping paper and stuffed with people you love.

Raising Vegetarian Kids

But Mum, I don't like eating fluffy chicks ...

What would you do if your seven-year-old announced they didn't want to eat animals anymore?

Let me set the scene. I don't eat red meat and haven't for over twenty years. It's not an ethical thing (though with the current ecological orbit this planet is on, perhaps it should be), but rather a very personal belief that it's just not good for human bodies. I do eat seafood and occasionally a few shreds of pork or chicken. I'm not a vegetarian and I don't whack other people over the head with a celery stick if I see them munching on a cow patty.

Sure, meals in our house don't ever centre round a sheet of meat or half a carcass in a pot, but my kids *are* consistently exposed to a variety of animal flesh. So, why my daughter recently testified she didn't want to eat animals anymore, I cannot really say. Perhaps it was the large, pink chunk of salmon swimming on her plate that did it. Or could it have been the trip to the Beijing wet markets? The pigs' heads, the pongy fish, the racks of dismembered carcasses? What?

Casting my mind back, I do actually recall the look on Ella's face when she made the connection that bacon is actually slices of pig. And that fish is actually, er ... fish, like those that swim in the ocean, wet and slimy. I have no idea what she thought these were before she made this connection, but I do remember it happening. It also happened with chicken. When she realised exactly what she was eating, she stopped chewing, and I could clearly see the feathery white clucker pecking at the seeds in her mind.

So, I didn't know what to say when Ella made the anti-animal-ingestion announcement. I think I muttered something about salmon being so expensive and that she would just have to finish everything on her plate, young lady. She hasn't brought it up again and I'm hoping

she's forgotten all about it — at least until she can make a more 'educated' decision on why she wants to forgo eating animals. In the meantime, I've started conjuring ways to hide salmon, pork, chicken and other snippets of animal tissue in her meals.

But am I doing the right thing? If I have made the conscious decision to forgo red meat, why shouldn't my daughter skip salmon and other meats of her choice? But she just seems so young …

Recently I had lunch (salmon, actually) with a woman who told me her daughter also announced, at seven years old, that she no longer wanted to eat meat. Instead of deciding this was in the Too Hard Basket, this woman said, 'Okay, darling' and went about finding ways to make this work for a body so young.

I was impressed. And also a little bit ashamed that I hadn't also taken on this Herculean (in my eyes) task for my daughter. So I'm thinking about it. I'm going to wait and see what unfolds and hopefully I'll be better armed to deal with this highly inevitable possibility when Ella brings it up again, probably over a plate of mutilated salmon.

Meanwhile, I'm off to find me some fried chicken. *Cluck!*

More Ayi Problems

I think I want to sack my *ayi* II

I must be a sucker for punishment. Either that, or I'm unbelievably stupid. Or too kind. Probably a blend of all three.

I'm really nice to her. She has a good, easy job. I'm not overly fussy or pedantic. Her duties are light. It's a nice, calm house, without drama or acrimony. She hardly ever has to sit the kids (which is not her favourite thing to do). We've been consistently generous with her. We give her lots of time off. We give her liberal overtime. We explain things clearly to her and I honestly feel we don't ask much.

Yet, my *ayi* continues to repeat the same old, same old misdemeanours that drive me absolutely and totally up the wall. And it's not as if they're inconsequential things, either — they're things that really affect our lives. Like thawing meat on the bench in the stink of summer. Like leaving serious stains on clothes and not treating them as asked, over and over and over, ad infinitum. Like mixing up clothing so we can never find anything and subsequently run late for school or work or very important meetings. Like doing half-arsed cleaning and dusting so that items have become permanently damaged.

Small things, maybe, but when committed repeatedly and then backed up firmly with a stinky, shitty attitude, it's really exasperating. Then there are the lies. The teensy white lies that may be of little consequence to start with, but then escalate and become surprisingly problematic (don't they always?).

Every time I go to sack Ayi and start to look for another, Xiansheng convinces me it will be more trouble than it's worth, and we've only got around a year to go. I tell him I'd rather not *have* an *ayi* than continue to put up with this drama. Xiansheng reminds me that my magazine work is getting even busier and it would be a lousy time to lose an *ayi* now. I tell him I don't care. He nonetheless tells me to sleep on it.

Ayi must have an in-built sacking radar. Either that or the house really is bugged. The very morning I decide I want to get rid of her, for absolute certain this time, she comes in all fabulous and sunny and excels at everything and even does things with initiative. I even tell her off for something and she still smiles and says, '*Mei wenti, furen!*' No problem, Madam!

I baulk. She cooks another great meal. I falter. She cleans out all the cupboards and lines up all the food tins and finds all the long-time-missing school swimming caps and takes out all the dry-cleaning and darns some socks. All without asking. I weaken. I acquiesce.

She's staying.

It's solely the drama of finding a new one that gives this woman 900 lives with our family; another chance she quite simply does *not* deserve. Let me just say this: I'm actually pining for the day I have to scrub the loo myself.

Temple Fair Crush

Our last Chinese New Year

Our favourite time of year in Beijing is wintertime. This is not only because of the 'fresher' air, the snow, the skating and the snuggling, but because of Chinese New Year. It's such a vibrant, exciting time. There's a festivity like Christmas, and coupled with the Olympic Games build-up, it's just such a great time to be here.

We're getting out and about this New Year more than any other year, and our fireworks arsenal is truly mind-boggling. We've even gone in with some friends and neighbours and amassed a really decent stash to set popping come New Year's Eve.

Despite the excitement, no New Year's Eve in China will be like the one we experienced two years ago. Now that the fireworks ban has been lifted and exploited, things have calmed down considerably and new rules have been set in place. There are strict hours and dates for firework cracking and, like the fine citizens they are, the Chinese pretty much obey. So, our hunger for the calamity of this festival has been a little under-fed since that first momentous one.

As a consequence, we decided to risk life and limb by nipping into a Temple Fair at Ditan Park the other day. Xiansheng wasn't in the least bit interested and the kids would have got lost in the mash, so it was just me, Jie Jie and Smoothie that went in the end. And boy, was it worth it. Uncomfortable, sure. At times even a little scary, but so worth it.

I have a bit of a queue phobia. When we pulled up in a taxi and saw the crush of people around the entrance to Ditan Park, I started hyperventilating a little, so we grabbed each other's arms and did the Chinese thing: we charged right on in. And, bizarrely, we got our tickets in a matter of minutes. It seems the crush was just for hanging-out purposes — maybe waiting for other family members, maybe waiting to catch a breath before heading on into the fray, we will never know. But we walked up, got the tickets, smooshed through the crowd and went straight in.

You must go! We loved it all, from the endless strip of stalls selling carnival kitsch to the stages spouting acrobats, singers and dances *en masse*, their brightly coloured costumes popping against the grey sky. We loved the crashing music, the calling marketeers, the clattering bamboo wind catchers and sparkling flags, the crazy carnival rides and processions of faux emperors in yellow robes, toted high above the heads of the thronging crowd.

We loved how we were pressed, bodily, against the next person, like *jiaozi* in a bamboo steamer — so tightly, the laughter was crushed from our lungs. We couldn't move a muscle and if we'd lifted our feet, we would have been carried along in the throng, a thousand-headed swarm of black hair with two blonde heads in the middle (and one grey Smoothie beanie).

We only lasted about an hour and twenty minutes but the buzz lasted for days. We returned home with loudly clacking wind wheels and sunglasses in the shape of 2008, and a bear hat for Riley and a rat baby for Ella (a baby doll dressed unnervingly as a rodent; well, it is the year of the Rat, after all).

What a China experience. These are the moments when you truly understand you're an outsider, that you are a guest clinched in the history of another land. These are the times you rise above the filth and the frustrations and give thanks for your temporary Beijing life.

My Big Girl Birthday

And to think I still feel fifteen

I'm definitely the kind of person who creates fuss and hoo-ha for everyone else. I'm a hoo-ha giver, not a hoo-ha taker. I love to give presents, throw parties, organise special moments for people and make them feel really squishy inside. I do it all for selfish reasons: it makes *me* happy.

So when Xiansheng asked what I wanted to do for my Big Birthday last week, I told him I wanted to go to Paris. When that didn't work out, I told him that if we didn't have the time nor wherewithal to go to Paris, then there was nothing else I really wanted to do. And I really meant it. I wasn't being one of those scratchy *tai tai*, attempting to send a shirty message. I really, really meant it.

So I didn't do anything except a teensy lunch with Jie Jie and a lovely friend on D-Day and then we drank champagne that night (perfect!) and then Xiansheng said, 'Please go and buy yourself that digital SLR camera you've been drooling over for X amount of years and get snapping.' So I did.

And that was my Big, Fabulous Birthday.

I've since been snapping, snapping, snapping. I love taking photos, and it's fun to be able to use them in my work, too. You see, I recently decided now that I'm a big girl that I no longer have any excuses left. I have been writing for local magazines and websites with much success, but I now have to get *completely* off my arse and do more. I *have* to do more.

I have promised Xiansheng that if I'm not in a position to earn a decent full-time wage with my writing by the time we leave Beijing, I will get a job in an office.

Yes, that's right. An office.

Now, let me clarify: there is absolutely nothing wrong with working in an office, and there are many sensational and varied roles undertaken in such spaces. *I* just don't want to do it. Not any more. I've done it for long enough, and now that I have kids and dictionaries of words bursting from my head, I'm determined to make sure I utilise every possible working moment to further my fervent desire to write.

The thought of having to return to an office in Australia has scared me into a self-confidence and drive I never knew I had. I have no excuse; I can't be scared any more. I can't procrastinate. I can't blame my failure on anything other than my total lack of tenacity.

I'm going for it, lock, stock and smoking laptop.

Bagging a Greenie

How large is your eco footprint?

It's not easy being green. Especially when you live in Beijing where everything is grey. This is, however, rapidly changing.

Three years ago, my green fabric shopping bags from Coles drew questionable stares from the locals, as did my Crocs shoes (but that's a whole other story). Sure, they may not be the prettiest, rhinestone-spangled shopping bags on the Beijing block, but they are strong and they hold *a lot*. Many a shopkeeper has oohed and ahhed with envy over these bags.

But the most important thing they do, of course, is eliminate the need for plastic bags, a common blight on our planet's increasingly frail ecosystem. Yes, the world's oceans have become plastic soup and we need to start fishing for shopping bags.

I'm probably not alone when I say I was delighted to see expat supermarkets Jenny Lou and April Gourmet jump on the green bandwagon with their self-promoting sacks. *Olé* Westernised supermarkets have also followed suit, although you do have to purchase your family's body-weight in groceries before you qualify for a free bag (whereupon you'll also receive some kitsch, junky toy to take home and chuck in the bin).

Upgrading to degradable bags are not the only thing that will make Beijing greener. China has a long way to go before turning Green: the environmental atrocities I witness daily have always sort of put the kybosh on making a personal effort. After all, it's 1.3 billion against four. How could one little family create enough of an impact to make a difference here in Beijing, let alone China?

Living a temporary, expat life carries with it a certain dreamlike quality — that you're not living a Real Life and that all the old rules don't necessarily apply. Along with culture changes and major shifts in

the way things are done (a lot of it taken out of our hands), it's easy to forget about Real Life. But with the glut of Going Green programmes surrounding Earth Day on 22 April this year, my guilt levels began to rise. Why wasn't I making an effort any more? Why was I being so slack? Why wasn't I encouraging my children to heed the Green call that I'm so gung-ho about in Australia?

Well, it's time to make a stand. I have procrastinated long enough and this old-time Greenie is back on the wagon. My Green shopping bags are poised by the front door. I no longer accept plastic bags and if I forget my green bags while shopping, I buy a new one and absorb the cost. I turn off lights and remind the kids to the do same. I am blasting the house with a shot of air-con, then turning it off and waiting until it's unbearably warm to repeat the same. The fridge is pulled out from the wall so it runs more efficiently, my microwave is used more than the oven, and the kettle only boils enough water for one or two cups. We have switched to energy-efficient light bulbs, are looking into buying organic, local food, and are trying to eat with the seasons. We are eating less meat, more vegetables. We are buying less, reusing more. We are sorting items into our building's recycling and educating Ayi to do the same.

It's working. My seven-year-old daughter is now reminding *me* to turn off the tap when brushing my teeth. My husband is finally remembering to turn off the energy-efficient light bulbs we've installed. Even my five-year-old son is dumping stuff in the recycle.

And everything feels a lighter shade of green.

Let's Go Fly a Kite

Feng hen da

The Chinese don't seem to like wind (*feng*). Indeed, being such an extreme weather phenomenon, it no doubt causes all manner of physical ailments in China, from flus to mental fatigue to carbuncles. When it's windy, my *ayi* rushes into the house wrapped to the eyeballs like a mummy, fresh from the pashmina grave. If she thinks the soft draught from our crappy air-conditioner is the equivalent of a brisk breeze, then the galloping *feng* outside must surely be a high force gale.

'*Feng hen da!*' she says. Wind really big, really strong.

'I know! Isn't it fabulous?' I want to say back, but I know she will look at me and think the same thing she does most days of our lives together: 'Stupid foreigner. I know you let your children sleep with the air-conditioner on. That's child abuse, you know.'

So I say nothing and instead grab the kids and they slip on their sneakers and we head downstairs (with no coats — *gasp!*) to harness that wind and make the most of every gusting puff. We take kites.

There's something about kites and childhood. They are an idyllic match. Flying a kite encompasses all the skills children do so well — running, jumping, leaping, laughing, bounding, squealing, lifting the arms high above the head and looking skyward. All the movements of a small child fit perfectly into the act of kite-flying, and Ella and Riley are kite-flying masters.

Sure, there are moments when the gusts of wind run out of puff and the kites take a spin or scud across the ground. This is when the complaining begins and I have to unhand my cafe latte and dash over to untangle a string or re-roll it or plunge the kite into a soft air pocket and watch it clutch and climb its way rapidly on high.

It's a fabulous feeling. The kids then unroll the string and stand with their little faces skyward, pulling and tugging and manoeuvring that canvas bird into the clouds. Watching them makes me so so happy.

Here they are in China, spinning kites into a rare blue sky on a bracing but sunny breeze. We're in China. Yes, it *still* hits me every now and then, and memories like these will be stop points for our family, of a time in Beijing that was far too fleeting.

A Compounded Situation

Living life in, on and under the compound

Things that scratch at me: apathy, rudeness, anything half-arsed, unpacking the dishwasher and compound living. You can imagine, then, how I felt way back when we first learned we were coming to China. Family living options: compound living on a compound, compound living in a compounded community, and compound living in a singular compounded building.

Ai yi yi. So many choices — how could we decide? We opted for the latter. It seemed the less compounded of a compounding situation.

Coming to Beijing is like being sucked into a social vortex. Everyone wants to check you out. They want to know your standing, your ranking in the order of things. It's only normal, of course, but after a while it can become a challenge playing the social game — a game of unsaid expectation that you should be part of things, part of the group. Part of the compound.

I don't have a problem with socialising but as most *tai tai* will tell you, one could easily spend 90 per cent of one's time doing coffee, lunching and shopping in Beijing. Easily. While I once relished this freedom, I now find I'm a busy mummy. I have two kids, a husband, an *ayi* to point things out to, family and old friends to keep up-to-date, bodily functions to perform, travel haunts to plan and a thousand books to write.

Love the odd spot of coffee at Comptoirs de France, a lingering trip to

Muxiyuan fabric market and the occasional gossip at Lovely Nails, but how do you fit in the constantly renewing flow of people you meet here (school, my work, Xiansheng's work, the compound, on the street)? How?

And compound living — er ... compounds the problem, because you're surrounded.

If you have anything even scantly incriminating happening in your house (vodka tonics before 5 p.m., DVDs with a single mild expletive, a particularly mess-ridden living room, a shouting session with the kids, a breakfast dish mountain in the sink, no make-up on and hair like a kabushka), a neighbour, or their kid, will ding-dong the doorbell at the precise, acme-embarrassment moment.

If your kids want to play with their neighbour-friends, they will drive you bananas with wanting to move in permanently to their apartment or their friends will want to move permanently into yours. On long stretches of holidays, all the kids your children want to play with will go away and your kids will develop a sudden aversion to playing with all the lovely ones left behind and/or there will be *no* lovely ones left behind.

If you're having a crappy day/fat day/blue day/deadline day/cannot-cope-with-washing-hair day — you're bound to run into the chicest, be-scarfed neighbour on the block who's keen for a 90-minute chit chat by the lift. I mean, it's nice ... but it's *always there*. Like dorm-sharing. No escape. And they just keep coming — as old ones leave, new ones come. Eyeballs at every corner, ears by every door.

Most of them are really, really lovely, but there are also the ones who take intense personal exception to the fact that you can't give up your precious hours to get to know them, that you can't call up God to create another precious weekend to spend with their family, that you don't organise daily play dates with their kids or go on four-hour shopping expeditions together.

These are the ones who greet you in the lift with the tightly pursed mouth, the trace of sarcasm in their voice, the wounded body language and the odd comment about your being so *busy all the time*. This is

incredulous to me. These people I simply cannot explain. Get a life! And funny that they're often the ones I hardly even know. For goodness sake, it's nothing personal.

Compound living. One thing I *won't* be missing when we leave Beijing.

The Beijing Family Challenge

Stretching family boundaries in the capital

It's our three-year anniversary of life in Beijing on 4 May. Clichés aside, yada yada yada — my, how it's flown.

I remember our first night well. I remember the dark Beijing night, the foggy, yellow air and that indefinable, permeating smell of noodles, eggshells and dust. I remember the nervousness but I also remember feeling almost instantly relaxed. People were smiling. They stared, they gawped, but not in a way that said, 'My Lord, your roots need touching up.' In hindsight, that unwanted attention was kind of welcoming, in an unnerving way.

I remember being unable to sleep on those hardwood planks. I remember the sheets felt scratchy, the sunlight cast different shadows, even the water felt different on our skin. I remember trying to push a stroller on the streets outside, where the pavement featured more jagged metal than a giant's mouthful of dodgy dental work.

I remember being shocked that in China there is no such thing as a question that cannot be asked — and we were asked it, my friend. We were prodded and poked and asked how much we paid for anything. We had noses stuck deep into our shopping trolley — and I mean right

down in there, close enough to smell the total price.

After three years, people are still innately curious, but they have also changed. And so have we. No one would *dare* prod me now.

Yes, in only three short years, *Beijingren* have changed — or perhaps my perception of them has changed. Sure, people still hock one up and let it fly, but it's only occasionally now and I haven't slipped on one for a very long time. The permanent, wide-eyed look on our kids' faces is long gone. So is the feeling that everything is overwhelming. We know our way around — we have our favourite spots, our favourite eateries, our favourite weekend jaunts and favourite places we like to take visitors.

We know where and how to shop. We are regulars at Fundazzle, The Bookworm, Ritan Park, Kempi Deli, Din Tai Fung and the inexorable Starbucks chain. We have a pretty solid hold on the language, the culture and the soul-stretching challenges. China has certainly swept us up in its vast, antique arms and held us close.

But while we have absolutely become besotted with Beijing, it's a strange love affair. The love is there but there's also a continuing love/hate element that skims around the outskirts of this union. Life here may be fascinating and fun but it's still not easy. There are certainly times when we want to phone up Beijing and tell it we need some space.

But just when we want to pack it all in and slide quickly down this last leg to home base, we remember that for all its foibles, its frustrations and idiosyncrasies, Beijing has a long, remarkable history of culture and diversity not yet lost within the hardline advancement of the West. We have always known that, for a short time, we were going to be part of it. When the times get tough, we just tough it out. We focus on the wonders this town has to share or we dash off to another country for a quick break, then we come back and we re-immerse and become part of it all again.

And part of it, we now most certainly are.

Life's Mysterious Ways

And why you really *can* do anything

As mentioned previously, now that I'm a Big Girl (read: sitting on the precipice of middle-age, but we will never speak of that again), I've realised there are no more excuses. I have to let go of my fears and do some serious boundary-stretching, and the strange thing is, boundary-stretching often involves the simplest of steps that are never as scary or as stressful as we feared they'd be.

Because my work with *tbjkids* has unexpectedly dropped due to editorial management changes, I made the executive decision that this would *not* become an obstacle for me or my work. So, I stretched open my boundaries, whipped out my tenacity, and contacted *Time Out* magazine here in Beijing about doing some proofreading or sub-editing. Then I contacted *City Weekend* magazine and *Little Star* educational and schools magazine about doing the same.

Within days, I was doing my first sub-edits and proofing. Within weeks, I was writing *Time Out*'s monthly kids preview and events listings, and feature articles for *Little Star*. Within a month, I became *City Weekend*'s Family Matters columnist and bloggist and *Time Out*'s Kids Editor while still continuing to contribute bits and pieces to *tbjkids*. Who'da thunk it?

Like I've said before — what's the worst that can happen if you ask? Someone might say no?

Like all writers, I've had many, many a no, so it feels great to be hearing a yes (or twenty). But what feels even greater is the monster-conquering. That's right. Once you stare the monster straight in the eyeball and show it you're not afraid, it begins to melt. It crumbles and falls away.

As Goethe once said: 'At the moment of commitment, the universe conspires to assist you.' In other words, once you mentally and

emotionally and physically commit, without compromise, things will start to miraculously unfold. They will start to work, no matter the obstacle, no matter the person who grabs at your highest flying leap and hauls you to the ground, no matter the chronically stunted people who can't bear to utter a single word of encouragement or praise, no matter the people who go out of their way to shut you out or complicate things for you or inexplicably ignore, snub or debase you (sometimes right in front of you). Even with these kinds of people all around, you find yourself remaining tall. You find yourself standing strong.

Sure, you may bend a little against the negative force but once you let them slide on by, all the muck and waste drains down the shithole, and there you are — free and clean and embarking on a superlative journey of doing what you love.

Please do what you love. I highly recommend it.

Orgasmic Organic

Oh baby! oh baby ... am I converted!

I have just received my very first order (what took me so long!?) from a local food delivery service, Organic Farm. The bags that arrived were so heavy I could barely lift them to the kitchen. And I only spent 240 *yuan* (around $40).

Hopping around the kitchen like a possessed flea, this was like Christmas on the farm. I slashed open those bags and a nest of luminescent treasures awaited: purple cabbage and onions the colour of king's robes, pale gold and supernaturally smooth ginger, pearlescent soybeans and olive-green mung beans and chalky buckwheat flour (hello, pancakes!), packets of dark green herbs bursting with chlorophyll and pungent on the nose — the basil leaves are so rich and fleshy and abundant, I will be making Italian all weekend.

There is a kilo of Fuji apples possessing that tangy and elusive scent reminiscent of my early years as an apple aficionado in Tasmania — where the best apples in the world are grown, and where you will never know a better crunch against your teeth. There are pale green zucchinis, bumpy cucumbers, cherry tomatoes with tight, shiny, fire-engine skins, and the cleanest, glossiest, firmest potatoes you've ever seen in your life, nestling in an Organic Farm brown paper bag like something from a boutique greengrocer in Greenwich Village. You can just feel your teeth sliding into those potatoes, cut into fat chips and roasted in the oven, sending you soaring back to childhood when potatoes tasted like potatoes.

This is truly veggie bliss in a bag. I'm itching to break open the eggs. Where to start? What to try first? It's all so overwhelming. I think I'll soak the soybeans for the massive pots of vibrant vegetable soup we make every weekend, sometimes studded with flecks of bacon, sometimes swirled with Indian spices, sometimes sprinkled with croutons or grated cheese. Then tomorrow night it will be basil-infused lasagne. And with all those apples — a syrupy apple pie, crusted with brown sugar. Sunday morning will be buckwheat pancakes — the kids' favourite — and a ratatouille seems vital with all those zucchinis and tomatoes. The packet of mint — it's been a long time since my husband and I indulged in a mint julep …

But what's making me happiest of all is the thrill of watching sustainable farming and organics become popular here in China. Along with the elimination of plastic bags in shopping centres, this is a giant step in a very positive planetary direction.

That's It, She's Gone!

I think I want to sack my *ayi* III

You're probably tired of hearing this by now, but ... how can one teensy, elderly woman cause so much hell in one family's life? I am wondering if she's been hired by someone who really wants to push me over Suicide Ledge at the top of Mount Tolerance.

Get ready for the latest.

Last year, we had an air-conditioner installed in our kitchen because in summer it gets so hot you could crack an egg on the floor and fry it without turning on a single gas burner. Ayi gave us a moderate amount of grief over this air-conditioner then, but it's not even the height of summer and she's already started — cracking my head open like said egg.

In our house, Ayi has been told (for over three years now) to *never*, under *any* circumstances, adjust the heating or the air-conditioning. *Ever*. The temperature comfort of our home is at the behest of *our family* — i.e. the people who actually *live* in the home — and *not* at the behest of someone who pops in to iron and cook, and who has such a screwed sense of temperature comfort, it's like we've been borne of totally opposite species, not opposite cultures. Truly.

On a recent roasting day in the kitchen (no, the gas burners weren't even on), Ayi did what she's been asked *never* to do: she adjusted the air-conditioner in the kitchen, either closing the vents or turning it off completely. And she didn't do it once. She did it several times, unashamedly ignoring my requests for her to desist. After years of asking her *not* to do this, I was already poised and ready to mentally implode.

I calmly explained to her, for the umpteenth time, *not* to do this. If she was cold (!?), she should go and put on a cardigan.

Now, let me just explain something to you before I allow this corker of a story to unfold. I know Ayi is elderly. I know Ayi is set in her ways.

I know Ayi has deeply embedded cultural edicts that believe, accurately or not, that air-conditioners are the spawn of the devil and will quite literally strip the skin from your body via a series of pox-like welts, and then will unhinge themselves from the wall and come after your entire family and kill them all.

So, in light of this firmly entrenched belief, I never have the air-conditioner on high, and even if I did, this useless machine could never cool down our kitchen. In fact, its cooling effect is so pathetic that you have to hold a hand beneath the vent to even feel the pale ribbon of air. Nonetheless, being such a nice *furen*, I always adjust the vent so the air flows down the wall instead of directly onto Ayi, who freezes into a block of ice the moment the machine whispers into life.

So, today, after having my tolerance severely compromised by Ayi's flagrant disregard for my 'authority', it was with much amusement (and nausea) that I saw her head to the kitchen to start dinner, but not before hauling up the legs of her pants and wrapping them in plastic bags to protect her shins against the Arctic snowstorm that had become our kitchen floor.

Before you think I'm a monster, I cannot reiterate enough how *not* cold my kitchen was this day. Stinking hot would be a good description. So the plastic bag thing — well, I completely ignored it.

This really pissed Ayi off. After about twenty minutes of her pottering in the kitchen with her crunchy plastic bags, and receiving not an ounce of attention, I began to notice, from my perch in the living room, a change of pace. Maybe it was the plastic bags constricting her movement, but she gradually, ever so slowly, began to hobble, with the occasional glance up at me to see if I was watching.

I wasn't.

So the hobbling got worse. Hobbles became limps. Limps became lopes. Lopes became great hulking lurches across the kitchen, and by the time dinner was served, Ayi's grand performance came to a flourishing finale as she carried a dish of *mi fan* (rice) to the table and promptly clutched at her chest, stumbled sideways and crashed into the wall.

Now, I'm not a completely heartless *furen*. For a split second, I panicked and ran towards her. 'Oh my God,' I thought to myself, 'I've killed her. She's really dying.'

Stupid me.

'Ayi! I'll call an ambulance! What's wrong with you?'

'Oh, nothing *furen*,' she gasped, 'I'm fine, don't worry about it.'

It was when I repeated the same question and she responded with the same answer five or six times that I really started to get angry. And as she recovered herself to reveal to me the source of her sudden and shocking illness, I knew I was dealing with a manipulator more brazen than a chocolate-seeking child.

All I can remember thinking, in the moments before the great reveal, was this: 'If she says it's the air-conditioner, I am going to have to open my front door and pick her up and throw her through it. I will not have any other choice. It will be beyond my physical control.'

So. I watched her recover. I watched her push away from the wall and straighten. I watched her look me brazenly, straight in the eye ... and as I saw her arm straighten and that hand lift from her side ... as I saw her fingers curl into her palm, leaving her index finger pointing straight ... I knew exactly where that finger was headed. It was headed straight for that air-conditioner, and sure enough, that's where it landed.

But before Ayi could even get the words out of her mouth, over three years of sheer frustration rose up and burst out of my voice box with such ferocity that the kids dropped their chopsticks clattering to the floor.

'*Geeet ooout!*' I screamed. 'Get out of my house!' I hollered. 'Get out of our lives, our home, our house! Now! Get out! Get out! *Get out!*'

Well, I've never seen so much back-pedalling in all my life. So much recanting diarrhoea came out of that mouth, the room filled instantly with the stench. But through the haze of blinding rage, through the sheer frustration over why she was doing this to me yet again, I could not even hear what she was saying. I instead flung myself around the kitchen uncontrollably to prevent myself from physically grabbing those scrawny arms, picking her up and throwing her out the door.

But she wouldn't leave. She said she had to clean up the dishes. She pottered. She avoided my eyes. She was totally physically recovered from her stroke/heart attack/seizure and simply got back to work. I trailed her, screaming at the side of her head like a drill sergeant but she still refused to move. I called downstairs and asked security to come and remove her, I was so enraged.

That's when Xiansheng walked through the door and calmed me down.

Ayi indeed went home, but not before insisting she clean up the kitchen. Xiansheng told her to come in tomorrow so we could tell her whether or not she still had a job. What pissed me off the most was that she happily sang out '*Zai jian, furen!*' Goodbye, Madam! when she left, as though fawns and bluebirds were prancing around the living room and I was sitting among a ring of daisies smiling sweetly.

I, in reality, was a ragged wreck, having just taken five years off my life and pushed my pelvic floor 5 centimetres lower from that screaming fit, not to mention the stress and strain of three accumulated years of frustration. For me, every drama Ayi has ever put us through has been totally unwarranted. I have quite literally been reduced to begging her not to give me *mafan* (trouble) because I'm too busy and too much in desire for peace to deal with it. It seems no matter how much I beg this woman to lay off, she couldn't give two shits how her drama terrorises me. It's almost a game to her.

I don't want her here anymore. I really, really don't. I want a happy home not a home governed by this perilous pensioner.

The Nine Hundred Lives of Ayi

Xiansheng talks sense into a frantic *furen*

Well, she has survived another day. You knew she would, didn't you?

Last night, Xiansheng talked some 'sense' into me. He said we only have six months to go, that Ayi's work performance is still good, and that perhaps I could take a different tack. I could tell Ayi that if she continues to give me drama, she will be sent home on the spot and the unworked hours would come out of her pay. Smart move. Money talks. Especially with the Chinese and most especially with *ayis*.

I cannot express the relief this great idea has brought me. My writing has taken off, I'm busier than ever and this is one of the most wonderful times of my life. It's also our final half-year in Beijing — the last thing I want to do is let Ayi ruin that for us. I don't have the time nor wherewithal to find another (potentially worse) *ayi*. So this stupid *furen* is keeping her, and this scurrilous woman continues on in a job she quite simply does not deserve.

Little did I know that very soon a tragedy would occur that would grab small dramas by the throat and really put things into perspective.

China is Still Trembling

Sichuan's earthquake rocks Beijing

The earthquake in Sichuan province has rocked all our lives in some way. Not only am I thankful my children are still alive (many mothers' children are not), I am also thankful they were riding in the school bus and didn't feel a thing when the quake shook this enormous land so deeply. I can

imagine my daughter would never enter our building again if she had been inside when it occurred, and that would have caused all sorts of inconveniences.

I happened to be walking home with a friend when things got rumbly, so we didn't feel a thing, but when I got home, I was greeted by a stark-raving mad *ayi*, maniacally acting out *feng! hen da!* charades, swooshing her arms around our apartment like a bogged helicopter.

'A big wind?' I asked her. 'Inside the apartment?'

'Yes, Madam!' she wailed, making tornado-like gushing sounds, 'Blowing everything from side to side!'

'Did you have the windows open?' I asked with a wink, 'Where do you think the wind came from? Up the lifts and through the front door?' (Please remember, at this stage I had no clue as to the tragedy unfolding 1500 kilometres away.)

'I don't know, Madam, but it was a big wind! The whole building swayed!'

I nodded empathetically, was sorely tempted to make a 'coco loco' sign with my finger, then went to the computer to face a barrage of emails: 'Did you feel that?' 'Did the earth move for you?' 'Am I going mad or did my building just turn on its side?' 'Tan, are you okay?' Turning pale, it didn't take me long to work out what the '*feng, hen da*' was. Alas.

So, when the kids came in minutes later, I was thankful. Not only because they were safe, but because they weren't in a swaying, rocking, 26th floor apartment when the quake happened. Seems overindulgent being so glad about this when parents in Sichuan province are pulling children from the rubble. It's just too heartbreaking.

As one blog-watcher commented: God bless China.

Sibling Rivalry

How a sisterly situation could turn green

My darling Jie Jie has been in Beijing almost a year now and when she first arrived, it was happy happy joy joy. The kids had another bloodline proffering to pounce on and I had someone in town with relationship ties delving into a past greater than two months. We ate, we drank, we scoured Beijing, we shopped, we sighted landmarks, we shared cultural activities and family jokes. It was a glorious time.

It is with regret, however, that I have to reveal that things soon soured.

It was when Jie Jie and Smoothie began to travel. I mean *really* travel. First it was around Beijing. Unfettered by small, demanding children, they woke to endless, vacant weekends, unscathed by soccer practice and ballet recital and music lessons. Great, cavernous holiday weeks lay like puddles at their feet, wailing to be jumped in, with jaunts to Pingyao, Datong and Harbin.

Then they got *really* serious. There were clunking overnight trains and gritty hostels, trekking through lime-green rice fields and facing giant Buddhas on the edges of churning rivers, followed by cable cars to mountaintops and petrified forests topped with monasteries made of matchsticks.

Pretty soon, it stretched to Japan (one of my favourite places on earth) during blossom time (my aching heart), and soon it will be a four-week odyssey through the United States via such places as San Francisco (choke), Vegas (gasp), a helicopter ride over the Grand Canyon (oh, the agony), New Orleans (sob!), overland to Chicago (I can't bear it any longer) and New York (that's it! I'm ruined!), just to round things off.

I put on a happy face. I help them plan. I loan them maps, give them travelling tips (nice ones). But, oh boy, does it *hurt*. I wave them off with a grin akin to the face developed after days of Chinese water torture. I blow kisses through the clenched teeth of an insatiable, travel-lusting

maniac. Then I close the door and slump against the wall, turning a nice shade of lime green.

Ella skips by, flipping her pigtails and says, 'What a pretty green, Mum!' then asks when we're going back to Phuket. The dreaded bikini, five-star beach resort and cocktail hour by the pool *again*??

Bah humbug.

Our Family's Must-See Travel List

Kid-friendly destinations are the only way

When we first came to Beijing, we made a Must-See Travel List, which included, in no particular order, the pandas in Chengdu, the terracotta warriors in Xi'an, the ancient sites of Yunnan, the beach at Beidaihe and a cruise of the Yangtze River to see the three gorges before all was flooded into oblivion. List items ticked so far? Zero. Our family has seen quite a bit of China, yet our original list remains curiously untouched.

Is this because when you get settled in Beijing, your Travel List priorities change? You quickly realise it's not so easy travelling in China with small kids. You also get new entries sneaking in from every side. People start raving about their family-friendly travels and you slowly get sucked into the Highly Recommended vortex. You start poring over maps, flicking through tomes of lime-green tea fields in the south, toothpick temples clinging to cliff faces in the north, seasides from the 1950s in the east, and dust-laden markets reeking of sandalwood in the west. China is full to bursting with so many contrasts, so much beauty — how can one ever decide what to see in the space of a few short years, especially when one has kiddliwinks to consider?

So, now that we've seen a bit of this enormous land, we're

returning, interestingly, to our original list. And, frankly, the thought of leaving China without seeing these original list entries is panicking me a little. We are turning our minds fervently to the retro coast east of Beijing — namely a weekend of sailing with the Beijing Sailing Centre. I'll be pulling memories out of a 30-year-old skill-bank to effect this long-forgotten sporting activity so keep your fingers crossed they don't find a sunburned family of four drifting up on North Korean shores two weeks later.

The three gorges cruise was always on shaky ground thanks to a spate of *mama huhu* (so-so) reports, but, like the pandas, we're wondering if not seeing this will be the mistake of a lifetime (I have romantic notions of my children telling their grandchildren about the day they held a now-extinct — God forbid — giant panda, and sailed the Yangtze before it swallowed half of China's ancient past).

Xi'an is a definite weekend trip (once summer subsides) — so easy to do from Beijing. And, let's face it, how would it really be possible to leave China without eyeballing the real warriors (as opposed to the supposed real warriors shacked up in miniature at Ya Show market)?

Chengdu. A bit harder to talk about. For a while there, we were so overloaded with Olympic mascot Jingjing and other panda-mania, we were kind of avoiding bothering the black and white fuzzballs altogether. Then, just as we decided it was time to make a move and go to Chengdu, then on to the landscape marvels of Jiuzhaigou, the earth decided to tremble and cause terrible tragedy in that God-forsaken place. Now, not only do we feel sick over the calamity that's shaken Sichuan, we also feel an ache that travel may be restricted there for a long time to come.

Yunnan — that's still on the cards. My husband has been lucky enough to see loads more of China than us three stuck-at-home-bodies, and this has been one of his favourite places. Kunming, Dali, Lijiang, Tiger Leaping Gorge, the Tibetan highlands, Shi Lin (Stone Forest), the ethnic minorities — what's not worth seeing in Yunnan?

So, we're plotting. We're trying to carve a trip into our rock-solidly busy Beijing life. By hook or by crook, I'm heavily invested in this before the call of Australia starts echoing across the Pacific Ocean and

into the China Sea. Oh, and add to that original Must-See List some new desires to see Chongqing, Shaolin, Longmen Grottoes, Datong, Suzhou, Tibet, Inner Mongolia, Xinjiang, Macau and Guizhou.

Hmm. I hope I'm not being too ambitious.

The Kids' Fashion Snob

What is it with Beijing's fashion choices for kids?

Oh, the bedazzlement. How overcome I was when I first saw the kids' clothing available in China. The sequins, the lace, the ruffles and frills. The neon, the mesh, the English-language slogans in chronic need of a sober proofreader. And let's not forget the collection of pilfered Disney characters, Bobdog and Hello Kitty emblazoned on pant legs from here to Middle Kingdom Come. Oh, the devastation. I knew kids' clothes were cheap here and sadly, I soon found out why.

You see, I absolutely adore kids' clothing; always have. And like many things in life, the more beautiful, the higher the price tag. When we first came to Beijing, my kids wore expensive designer duds. I was wearing ten-year-old jeans and owned two pairs of shoes but my kids looked like fashion models. Their designer t-shirts alone fetched a price that would have any *tai tai* feigning a faint at Ya Show.

Any sane person knows it's quite ridiculous what real designer clothing costs, yet I happily went without so I could gaze upon my kids in their gorgeous photo-shoot ensembles. Yes, I adored the white clouds of French linen, the trendy patterns, the retro designs. I was, indeed, a kids' clothing aficionado, a wannabe clothing designer for little ones.

Alas, when you go to live in a different country, over time your kids tend to grow and their expensive designer duds become tighter and smaller, and the reality of having to hit the real Beijing clothing world gets closer and closer, and eventually you just have to succumb.

Maybe I succumbed because Beijing taught me how utterly blind-sided we are by clothing prices in the West. Maybe it was actual real-life emergencies like when my daughter had no shoes that fit and her legs stuck out of her pants like Huck Finn. But I did it — I began trawling the markets, the neighbourhood stores, the department stores and slowly, very slowly, among the Garfield tutus, I found some finds.

Happily, things have improved even more in three years, with a spate of gorgeous kids' shops opening in the past twelve months alone, all offering adorable clothing. Nonetheless, I have to admit a part of me has grown somewhat fond of the range of kitsch Chinese kids' clothes. Yes, Ella owns a pair of Betty Boop tracksuit pants and yes, Riley has a few pairs of polyester Chinese pyjamas.

Maybe the clothing snob in me has been taken down a peg or two.

Friendly Superstitious ...

Is the writing on the wall?

Oh, wailing lament! (while clutching at the five adorable stuffed toys lounging on the end of my daughter's bed). Why did it have to be you? How will I tell my daughter the gossipy terrors that have be-stricken you all? Beijing's Olympic mascots — the Friendly Fuwa — is it true?!

Indeed. It seems that superstitions from China's bloggists are at an all-time high in light of recent events supposedly foreshadowed by our fuzzy and very friendly Olympic mascots. Yes, Beijing's gorgeous Friendlies have been indicted in a bloggist smear campaign that is tugging at the heartstrings of my heart. All I can think of is how I must hide this rot from my daughter.

Never been very superstitious, me.

Of all the soft, fluffy toys my children have become enamoured with over their short 7.9 and 5.3 years (respectively), the Beijing Olympic

Friendlies still rate awfully high. The 20-centimetre-high versions of Jingjing, Beibei, Nini, Huanhuan and Yingying (in order of preference — poor Yingying, always holding the wooden spoon) hold high status in the precious real estate on my daughter's bed. Much love and affection has gone into these toys and the whole idea behind their cultural, ethical and welcoming personas, so cleverly crafted by Chinese artist Han Meilin.

Nonetheless, the warm fuzzies surrounding these adorable Fuwa seem to be turning ominous, with online suggestions the Friendlies are indeed harbingers of doom.

Since the beginning of 2008, four disasters have been superstitiously pinned on four of our favourite friendlies — Huanhuan, who represents the Olympic flame, has been indicted in the worldwide protest issues trailing the torch in its international wake.

Nini, the kite-shaped swallow, has been linked to the disastrous train-crash in Shandong, home to Weifang, China's kite-flying capital.

Yingying, the Tibetan antelope, has been paralleled with the recent political unrest facing Tibet.

And lastly, dear Jingjing, the giant panda, has been pinned for the earth-shattering quake in Sichuan province, the home of the panda.

Ridiculous scaremongering? Or a little bit spooky?

With four out of five oddball prophecies already in the bag, this leaves only Beibei, the sturgeon fish, to fulfil its looming disaster somewhere along the Yangtze River, the only place where Chinese sturgeons reside. Adding to the hoo-ha is the fact that all of the above events began or occurred on a date that adds up to the number 8 — Beijing's Olympic year.

While I've never been superstitious, given the seriousness of the issues China has recently faced, I'm off to pray to the Fuwa gods on the end of my daughter's bed.

No — really.

Yabber Yabber Yabber

How a young boy began to speak

You may remember the anguish Xiansheng and I went through over Riley when we first came to Beijing. It was because he didn't talk much. His comprehension also seemed shady, so we hired a Western speech therapist, put him into school early and started him on a year of speech therapy despite Other People saying, 'Don't worry, boys learn to speak more slowly, give him time' and despite our therapist's books being jam-packed with a clientele that was 90 per cent … boys.

During this year of therapy and early schooling, there were minor improvements — most of them actually occurring after a visit to Australia where Riley was surrounded by English-speaking people. We read to him until the pages bled. We flashed flashcards and spoke like Teletubbies. We did everything we could to help our son but his improvement was, nonetheless, slow.

Although we have no doubt this year of therapy had some impact, it did cross my mind more than once that our son was not really 'linguistically compromised'. Perhaps he was just going to be slow on the uptake with speech. Or maybe oration wasn't going to be one of his fortes, like mathematics is not mine or baking mini pavlovas is not Xiansheng's. Riley's physical skill set was highly developed and well above his peers — maybe, just maybe, he was not 'delayed' and was just taking his time with the verbal factor.

It was very much a time of Maybes.

During this horrible Maybe time, my wonderful mother-in-law would intersperse the terror with statements like, 'Oh for goodness sake, leave him alone. He's a boy! He's more focused on mud and footballs. He'll be fine. He will develop at his own pace. Don't rush him. You wait and see — he will be a public speaker or even Prime Minister [of course] one day.'

It's easy to dismiss such wisdom when it comes from someone so biased and someone who so dearly wants the best for her grandson. But I didn't dismiss it. Amid the all-encompassing fear, I did listen to her. I still did what was expected of me as a responsible mother — I did everything in my power to ensure our son had the appropriate stimulation that could help him improve (what other choice did I have?), but I also listened to my mother-in-law. I heard her. And deep, deep down, among the devastation and doubt, I began to believe her.

I consulted my friends and came up with a dozen women who shared similar speech and comprehension fears with their sons. Is it a coincidence that so many boys experience this phenomenon? Is it also a coincidence that so many children (girls included) experience speech delays when exposed to so many languages at once, as is the expat way? I know of many expat children who are consistently exposed to two, three or more languages in their everyday lives. Research tells us that multilingual children often speak later than their peers, as their little minds are so busily sorting through varying linguistic genres.

Well, what a difference three-and-a-half years makes. Our son's speech has blossomed like a flower and although he struggles a little with grammatical structure, he has definitely joined the 'Five Year Old Ceaseless Verbal Diarrhoea Club' that his sister joined at age two. He is also (and I write this with tears of pride), the top reader in his grade. Who'd have thought …

Thank you, Granny.

Acts of Kindness

High-speed rescue on the Second Ring Road

Picture this.

You have just spent a few thousand *kuai* at Hongqiao toy store with two hot, sticky kids aged five and seven, and you are already panicking about the argument you're going to have with your husband over this. It's a 100 degrees outside and you're loaded with four bursting bags, craning your neck (which is plastered with sweat) for a cab, simultaneously trying to grip two very slippery little hands on the ends of two very diva-like bodies.

'It's too hot, Mum!' these bodies wail as you struggle to keep a raging heat headache from rupturing the confines of your skull. Oh, and you also forgot to eat breakfast so your stomach feels like the black pit of despair.

In the misty heat, cab after cab sails by, windows tightly encasing cool, calm, collected air and happily smiling passengers (you're sure you hallucinated several of them popping bottles of champagne). Your heart is sinking lower than Beijing street grime.

Then suddenly, a parking attendant materialises and he smiles a lopsided grin and he gets busy with it on that jam-packed road and from the fluxing waves of heat rising off hot metal cars, a cab slides towards you out of magical nowhere and slips to a stop and the attendant is opening the door and inside there is nothing but cool. You slide those kids into that cool, gasping so hard you might have just run a 10-kilometre marathon.

'*Qu nar?*' Where are you going? he asks and it's the sweetest thing you've heard all day (other than the price of the Nintendo DS you just bought for a song). 'To my freezer in the sky,' you say with a relieved smile.

'*Hao le!*' Great! … and you are zooming off home.

Things go well until you hit the traffic-packed Second Ring Road. *Ugh*. But you're cool, the kids have their toys, you're just happy the rugrats are occupied, and anyway, you have Mickey Mouse lollipops in case of emergency. Clever you.

Nonetheless, after twenty minutes in almost standstill traffic, you feel a surge of relief when things start to flow again, only to be rapidly crushed when out of nowhere the taxi's power suddenly falters. It's not the imminent breakdown that initially worries you. It's the toxic plumes of white smoke billowing from the air-conditioning vents and into the cabin that really send you into a frenzy.

'Stop the car!' you scream, and seconds later, you're hauling two kids and four massive bags out onto the Second Ring Road in the burning heat with cars zooming past at 100 kilometres per hour, and you are in the *centre* lane.

'Oh dear Lord send a miracle fast,' you whimper as you scream at your seven-year-old to plaster herself against the other side of the cab while you grip at your five-year-old in terror and the horrified cab driver runs around flapping his arms like a crane, unsure *what* to do. Thankfully, he pulls himself together quickly and thinks to himself 'stuff the car' and proceeds to protect your kids from the traffic.

Truly, these dire moments seem to take forever. It's probably less than a minute that this drama takes to unfurl on the stinking hot freeway, but it seems like hours of drastic mental anguish — 'How are we going to get out of this?!' — and eyeballing for a vacant taxi (there aren't any, and there *won't* be any).

Then suddenly, an answer materialises before you: a black four-wheel drive and two smiling Chinese faces in the windscreen. It is the fellows who were travelling behind you and got hemmed in by the zooming lanes either side.

The driver winds down the window. 'Get in!' he calls. 'We'll take you home!' Tears spring to your eyes and you bustle the kids into the back seat. The fellows are kind. They flip on the air-conditioner and direct the vents towards you. Then they chit-chat to make you feel comfortable, then they drop you at your building and they drive off

into the pollution-clogged distance and you realise you have just been the recipient of a really lovely act of kindness.

The Chinese will happily let a door slam in your face than hold it open for you, but then will go out of their way to rescue you on a freeway, charm your kids and drop you home.

Thanks, fellas.

Beijing's Monopoly

Those clever marketing minds ...

Isn't it funny what a little bit of sentimentality can do to the opening mechanism of your wallet? 'Exclusive' and 'limited edition' always sell, and when you're an expat with little time left in town, taking the right souvenirs home is tantamount to taking a little bit of Beijing with you.

Despite the new Beijing edition of Monopoly costing almost twice the original version, it has to come home with us, along with a multitude of other inanimate objects that will hopefully enhance and lengthen the most precious souvenirs possible — our memories.

We also have to take Panjiayuan finds like my red and white 'antique' teapot and the stone carvings of Chinese goddesses, not to mention the myriad carved jade-stone from pendants to the entire Chinese zodiac. Then there's the solid marble lion statues (around 150 kilograms each) we sourced near the outer 'burbs of Shunyi, the Mao clocks, the little painting of Chinese farm children from Mutianyu Great Wall, our very kitsch gold Lucky cat and its perpetually waving paw, the tiny bronze statue of the three monkeys — say no evil, hear no evil, see no evil — the exquisite carved wood panel of a deer I found for 50 *kuai* on Liulichang antiques street.

I've even got my sights set on importing a stash of our favourite foods, like Orion pies — chocolate-coated marshmallow sponge-like

cookies — and, of course, Hershey's green tea chocolate, haw chips (sweet, dried discs of haw fruit), and the never-ending selection of green tea.

In the meantime, Beijing Monopoly is still in its shrinkwrap — I have forbidden anyone from opening this until we get home and away from Beijing's dust. And anyway, it will be all the more special when we get home and open it for the first time. It will be so lovely to coo over Sanlitun Lu and Wangfujing Street once again … and plonk houses and hotels thereupon.

A bit like what's happening in real life, actually.

Over It

Enough is enough

I think I officially want to get out of here.

After we'd been living in Beijing for about a year, when our family was still in the honeymoon phase and still quite starry-eyed, I met a couple who were on their way home after four years in the capital. Boy, were they ready to go. In fact, they were simply gagging to get on that aeroplane and leave Beijing in its dust, and I remember not really understanding how they could feel this way. Until now.

Sure, Beijing is amazing, astounding, fabulous and stupendous. But it's also irritating, difficult, frustrating and infuriating. After a particularly bad stretch of infuriating, I'm kinda getting over it.

I want to be able to just say it like it is without mortally wounding or confounding someone. I want to hear things that don't consistently confound *me*. I want to be able to receive a short answer. I want things to be quick and simple, not convoluted and laborious. I want clear understanding, not muffled maybes. I want quality and commitment, not tawdriness and consistent bullshit. I want no more white lies,

meandering truths and sheer and shameless time-wasting. I never again want to meet another person who has Blame on speed-dial or a dictionary of bewildering excuses in a holster on the hip.

I want to strap my kids into their seatbelts and know I can drive from A to B without the constant fear of a bingle or untimely demise. I want good customer service — oh, hang it, I want *great* customer service. I want to know I can ask for something and it will invariably be available to me or someone will make an effort to get it for me. '*Wo bang ni wen yi xia.*' How I ache to hear that consummately elusive phrase — essentially: 'I'll help you by actually opening my bloody mouth and asking someone if it might be possible.'

I want to be able to talk on the phone and understand what is being said to me. I want to receive phone calls without hearing '*Wei? wei?*' repeated, ad nauseum, from the other end. I want to be able to rub an apple against my jeans before giving it to the kids, rather than having to steam and sterilise it. I want to drink water from any tap in the house and I want to be able to go outside and take a deep gasp of fresh air and not have to worry about whether or not I'm ingesting MSG, a litre of oil, a cellar of salt or plastic bags when I eat restaurant food.

I guess I want to be Australian again.

I know, I know — we'll return home and I'll encounter other kinds of frustrations and I'll pine for Beijing within minutes of hitting Aussie turf, but right now I don't care about the mundanity of familiarity. I know I'll miss the challenges and dynamics of Beijing eventually, but right now, I just want the hell out of here.

I want the knots in my shoulders to unhitch without having to be forced by a Chinese masseuse. I want the pink in my kids' lungs to be pinker. I want to hug our extended family and drink margaritas in the sunshine with our friends.

I want to go home.

Hurry Up and Grow Up!

Kids seem to be little for sooo long ...

My son Riley is five-and-a-half years old but he still wakes before 6 a.m. I can hear the groans of empathy as I type — thank you, mums.

Sometimes, just sometimes, he makes it to 7 a.m., and I think maybe once or twice in all his years he's made it past 8 a.m. Those were the times I had to go in and poke him to make sure he was still breathing.

I think the wake-early problem is because he's a light sleeper. Every night before I collapse in an exhausted heap on my pillow, I creep into my kids' rooms, fuss with their blankets, smooth the hair away from their foreheads and give them sleepy sandman kisses on the tips of their noses. Ella sometimes has trouble falling asleep, but once she's under, she lays there like a fallen log, her limbs seemingly filled with sand, sometimes lightly snoring. Xiansheng, indeed, calls her the Log. You could probably hold a clacking mahjong game with some local Chinese grannies on her bedroom floor and she still wouldn't flutter an REM eyelid.

Riley, on the other hand, sits up the moment I soundlessly sneak open his door. He's not quite awake when he does it but he sits up nonetheless, with his head rolling around on top of his shoulders. I gently lay him down again and he fusses a little when I try to land kisses on his face, then I creep out again.

Why am I telling you all this? It's because I like my sleep. I mean, *really* like it. And after around eight years of not getting a solid eight hours, I'm getting kinda tired of it ('scuse the pun). So, when Riley tritt-trotted into our bedroom this morning after my particularly late night, all I could think was, 'Bring on the days when you are sixteen and I have to bang on pots and pans to get you out of bed.' In fact, I think this same thought most mornings. Yes, yes, I actually squeeze my eyes shut and wish my beautiful little boy's life away.

The trouble with wishing is that you might just get what you want. My mother-in-law always tells me not to rush through my children's childhood: '… these are the best years of your life' she oft reminds me. I know, I know — I can hear the laughter from here as you read this, mum of small kids.

Sure, it can be tough, especially when kids are really young or you have three of them under the age of five or have no *ayi* or something mad crazy like that. But isn't it always the way that you can't see the forest for the trees? That it's not until you can look back in cool, calm hindsight that you realise how good you had it? Even now, can't you look back and appreciate the surreal joy of having a newborn baby? (Don't answer this if you have children under two.)

I recently waded through some home videos and sat entranced and weepy at the sight of my daughter watering plants in pink gumboots and a spotted pair of knickers, in the garden of our house in Australia. She was only eighteen months old, chattering away like a ten-year-old. At the time, she was a handful and early motherhood was somewhat chaotic, but looking back with the combined numbing effect of time and sheer affection, MIL was right — it was bliss, and I would trade ten lifetimes to have a single minute with her back then. Where did the time go?

So, this morning, I've thought long and hard about my wishing-life-away, and I've realised that it may be 5.10 a.m. when you receive them, but getting little boy butterfly kisses on your eyelashes beats the empty, echoing hallways of children who have flown the coop, any day.

Now I think I finally understand what MIL means.

Summer Holiday: Day One

The dreaded school-less Olympic period

I've just made homemade playdough. Blue, pink and green.

I know, I know. Desperation levels already. And it's only Day One of nine very looong weeks of summer holidays. We were going to check out the water scene at one of Beijing's parks today, but this strange summer day has put paid to that. Now we are stuck inside with previous plans sullied and spoiled, and four walls and rained-upon windows to stare at.

I was really enthused about these holidays three months ago. 'I can do it,' I thought to myself heartily, partly up for the challenge but mostly just hoping to play tricks on my own mind. I planned so many activities of varying degrees and involvement (with everything from the inside of my kitchen utensil drawer to swathes of school friends also stuck here for the summer) that I was actually getting really excited about how much fun it was going to be. Golly, I'd even convinced myself that it would be a breeze.

Oh foolish woman. I started this last paragraph at 7 a.m. It's now 10 a.m. and this is what has happened in our house so far:

05:55   Five-year-old Riley crawls onto my bed (husband currently overseas)

05:55   Riley sent back to *his* bed

06:27   Riley returns for a repeat performance

06:28   Mother follows through again; Riley retreats

07:03   Scooter wheels begin scuttling across living room floor

07:03   Mother yells at wheels

07:05   Scooter riders scoot into bedroom and beg for breakfast

07:05   Mother groans and doesn't move

07:07   Breakfast posse, led by undeterred seven-year-old Ella, hauls chairs across kitchen tiles to reach cereal boxes perched on top of kitchen cupboard

07:07   Mother cringes in supine position, awaiting the sound of broken crockery, and finally decides that getting up beats sweeping up broken shards of china

07:09   Sprinkle of cereal into bowls as mother enters kitchen and rescues extremely heavy bottle of orange juice from Riley's slippery hands

07:18   Ella begs to use (broken) sewing machine to make clothes for her stuffed toys, Riley begs to go on www.youtube.com (repeat these exact same requests every six minutes until end of this chapter)

07:19   Riley surfs '80s rock bands on www.youtube.com. Ella begins a sudden burst of chores when she realises last week's pocket money has been cut due to low work production levels the previous week

07:28   Both children want snacks; I cut up fruit

08:10   Scooter riding

08:22   Kids' Trivial Pursuit with Ella

08:43   Mouse Trap board game with Riley

09:01   Colouring in

09:10   *Looney Tunes* classics on TV

09:17   Ella has a turn on the computer — www.littlestpetshop.com

09:28   Kids play schools

09:34   Kids play with wooden toys

09:39   Mother makes playdough and ruins another pot

09:48   Kids play with playdough

09:51   Kids start camping game in living room using every sheet and blanket in the house

09:59   Kids come and tell mother they're bored; mother sends them back to fabulous camping game

10:00   Mother calls another mother to inquire about play dates and sleepovers, then heads to computer to finish a paragraph.

But wait. I don't want to stop typing right now. I don't want to go out and look at the lounge room. It's not because of the sheets, blankets

and toys tossed from wall to wall and hanging from the ceiling. It's because I don't want to unhinge the joy I am feeling from the silence right now, interspersed with happy chatting and the kids telling each other what to say next during their camping game. I don't want to go out there because I don't want to break the spell, though I am gagging to rescue the playdough cowpats which will be hardening into paperweights as we speak ...

Total silence now. For at least two minutes ... hmmm. A kitchen cupboard door opens and closes. Should I spoil their fun? I can guarantee both kids will have chipmunk cheeks stuffed with Oreo biscuits ... Should I ruin it for them? More silence. I wait. Then slowly I creep out ... through the lounge room, into the kitchen where I can hear plastic bags rustling ... little monkeys ... what are they into?

They are stuffing their blue, pink and green playdough cowpats into plastic bags to keep them from drying out.

Darling hearts. Maybe the summer hols won't be so bad after all ...

The Harried BJ Housewife

Ayi or not, the housework is never-ending

Okay, this is going to sound like a ranting whinge, and I suppose it is. Maybe you can relate to it, maybe you can't. We shall see.

Everyone — whether they are a full-time *tai tai*, stay-at-home mum, self-employed-dream-job slave, part-time worker, full-time worker, full-time shopper or part-time waster — has their pet-hate housework Thing. For me, it's three things: unpacking the dishwasher, putting clothes away and picking up after everyone. My God, I hate picking up. I really, *really* do. I'd rather iron for twelve hours straight than pick up.

In fact, as of this minute, I don't know if I'm ever going to be able to stoop to collect something from the floor ever again, I hate it *that* much.

I'll do 30 minutes on the treadmill and trample groups of *laowai* tourists at Hongqiao. Don't get me wrong: I'm not lazy. I just hate to stoop down because I've been doing it relatively non-stop for about eleven years and I am, quite frankly, over it to the point of mental incapacity. I've been doing it ever since I met Xiansheng, really. *Hmm.*

Pre-Xiansheng, I didn't need to stoop for anything because, you see, I never threw or dropped anything onto the ground. But my life changed when hubby came along. And it changed even more post-procreation ... because husbands and children have a curious penchant for dropping that is absolutely unparalleled.

Elegantly dumped towels on the bathroom floor. Cracker shards or chips on the kitchen floor or in the creases of the couch. Scooters and bicycles in the doorway, prone or supine, doesn't matter which. Plops of glop (yoghurt, pudding, mashed potato) on the floor under the dining-room table. Specks of Oreo all over the carpet and cushions like sanding sugar on a cookie. Paper. Wrappings. Plastic figurines. Cards. Dice. Toothbrushes. Playdough clods. Clothes clothes clothes. You name it. Dropped dropped dropped right where it belongs — on the floor, of course. Wardrobe? *Ha!* Drawer? *Ho!* Box with a lid? *Titter!* Rubbish bin? *Wa haha ha haaa!*

Sometimes the dropsies are so bad, I can't face them at all. A few times, I've had to quite literally launch myself into a frenzy of picking up, in fast motion, like those time-advance cameras. I wait until Xiansheng takes the kids for a swim or a bike ride, take a deep breath and dart from room to room like a laser beam, toting a large tub of junk, stashing items into their appropriate spots at lightning speed before tearing to the next room. It's wild-crazy but highly effective, not to mention a great workout.

At rare times, I will simply crack it (I'm not a sulker — don't have time; just get straight to point) and the family freak out and tear around making things better for mad, loopy mummy with the wild eyes and flailing arms. Then Xiansheng runs me a nice warm bath with candles and some sweet yellow grapesque liquid in a stemmed glass (there's a tip for you, girls; oh — and remember — drink responsibly).

I know, as you read this, some of you may be thinking: 'Doesn't this woman have an *ayi*, for goodness sake?' Yes (she's still here). But not only is she busy doing other things that I'm happy to relinquish (washing, toilet-scrubbing, mopping, dusting, cooking), she is also quite useless at putting things in the Right Spot, even after three and a bit years. So I just do it myself. Plus, Ayi can't multi-task, nor can she move her tiny carcass at more than 0.2 kilometres per hour.

I guess I have to accept my lot because, honestly, I have many years left of this yet. Despite hefty, daily training in the art of picking up, my three most beloved human beings have still not mastered it.

Am I just flogging a dead clothes horse?

Summer Holiday: Day Fifteen

I'm cracking up

Last week was Week Two of our nine-week *(wail!)* summer holiday debacle and things went pretty smoothly. This week, so far, not so good. And awful to say but true — it's Riley's fault.

Why do boys need the outdoors and sunshine and sports and things to jump on, climb, bash and destroy? *Why?* Why do they need to swim every thirteen seconds? Why do they need to put on superhero suits and fly down outdoor slides, especially in this heat? You try putting a kid in a polyester suit on a red-hot metal slide in the Beijing 'sunshine' and see what happens to the seat of his pants.

Why can't five-year-old boys sit quietly and stare into space dreamily for hours on end, colouring in quietly or watching documentaries on the oceanic life of the Antarctic? Why? And like his dad did when he was a child, why can't my son spend an entire

afternoon lining up little soldiers and cavalrymen until dinnertime? *Why?*

We're not very compatible, me and my son. He likes to leap, I like to bounce lightly. He likes to thunder maple drumsticks on the drum kit, I like to tap a tune on the (computer) keyboard. He likes to spin around the room like the Tasmanian devil, I like to, er — lie down on soft cushions. I'm talking polar opposites here.

Some of my girlfriends who have sons love to wallow in the mud. They get dirty, sweaty, exhausted and appear to enjoy it. I exercise most days but then the rest of the day is dedicated to a variety of placid pursuits like writing, baking and crafts with the kids, films, reading and brain-challenging games; i.e. nothing muscle-stretching, limb-bending, heart-thumping or lung-expanding.

I'm sorry, but I'm just not a roustabout-boy-active kind of mum. I'm the one who's folding eggwhites into passionfruit pulp while they jump on the trampoline, snapping photographs of them as they ride their scooters downstairs at twilight, cataloguing their lives into lusciously fat scrapbooks and taking them on fantastical journeys via the pages of a book.

Yes, the kids get physical. We go swimming … well, *they* do. I stand on the side and take photos or type on my laptop with one eye on the keys and one eye on the splashing. We dance … well, *they* do. I play DJ and laugh my head off at their antics. We go bike riding … well, *they* do. I stand in the shade shouting encouragement with a large skinny latte in one hand and more than likely a camera in the other. We play rumble tumbles … well, Dad does. Isn't rumble-tumbling what dads are for?

Gosh, I sound like a coffee-addicted slug. Right, I'm getting up off my silk cushion to get a latte and supervise some physical exercise for my son.

This Blasted Beijing Heat

Oh, Cat in the Hat, what can we do?
Stuck inside while the sky is blue

We love Beijing in autumn and winter. They are our favourite times of year.

In autumn, there is a thinning but palpable change in the air. Foliage gets crunchy, leaves turn and tumble to the ground, the air temperature drops (surprisingly fast — if you have lived in Beijing more than a year, you'll understand what I mean), jackets and boots are hauled out of mothballs, seasonal fruit and veg shift and change welcomingly, school starts again and the kids are raring to go. The evenings are divine and there are more people on the streets, creating that pre-winter-hibernation buzz. Halloween drops by to give us a creepy jolt, and the heart-warming countdown to the Festive Season begins.

It's just luverly.

In winter, we love the nip in Beijing's air — it has a faux freshness to it. We love the skeleton nakedness of the trees, the bluish white frost of the frozen lakes and canals begging to be slipped on, the knitted beanies and puffy coats, the steamy hotpot restaurants and Sichuan spice, the occasional flutter of snow, and the excuse to escape somewhere tropical for a week to thaw out before returning to make our tragic but awfully charming snowmen, smooshed together from the slush at the bottom of our building.

Summer I don't like so much. Nor spring, as it heralds summer and the thawing of lakes and canals until they become dribbly. The only good thing about spring is the blossoms and magnolia buds that poke their sweet bonnets into the sky like delicately crafted candy, and the gentle release of winter's most icy grip.

I've already ranted about the difficulties of a Beijing summer. There is no beach to escape to. No strong sea breeze. No darkly wooded parks to hide in. There just seems to be no shade. And for a place that can get

so bitterly cold, this town can sure heat up.

The heat of our first Beijing summer actually shocked me, and it seems worse each year. The heat is burning — I mean, a rivers-of-sweat burning that even the old 180-beats-per-minute aerobics class can't provoke. You just can't go outside.

Much of summer is also heavily polluted, but lately we've had a remarkable stretch of blue sky-ish days in Beijing and it's actually quite depressing sitting in our ivory tower, gazing at that blue sky with ice-slushies in hand, pining for a small ocean and a couple of grains of sand, pawing at the windows like puppies at a seaside pound.

We've tried to get out in it, to get our dose of sorely needed Vitamin D. We rush out really early and tear around like maniacs on bicycles and scooters but the descending scalding air almost ruins us, even when toting brollies like all the Chinese Mary Poppinses around town. So, until late August (when we'll have a short, four-day reprieve in Hong Kong), we'll be house-bound. We'll cool it. We'll turn on the air-con and hide.

Praise Buddha, this will be our last Beijing summer.

The Olympic Build-Up

Or lack thereof

What is going on?

There's an odd, vacant, bald feeling in Beijing right now regarding the Olympic Games. It's as though it's not really being held here. Sure, things are being spruced up and spit-polished at a rapid rate, but where is all the celebratory hoo-ha?

Maybe it's because I don't watch or listen to local television and radio, nor read the local rags. Maybe it's because I'm so head-down-bum-up with my writing and all my blog posts for *City Weekend*. Maybe it's because the Olympic movement is so tightly controlled and

hidden behind scaffolding and closed doors. Whatever the case, it feels strangely un-atmospheric.

Today I saw, for the first time, Olympic flags erected along the freeways and main roads in Beijing. I let out such a gasp in the back seat of the taxi, the driver slammed on the brakes. I then smiled really big — finally something that looks Olympicky. There's been such a gradual build-up of expectation, it's kind of nice to see it materialise for all to see — beyond all the Fuwa Friendly stuffed toys, that is.

Of course, all the Olympic venues and sites are still under lock and key. The Bird's Nest Stadium and Water Cube can only be glimpsed from the edge of the Fourth Ring Road, and I'm still not exactly certain where the Olympic Green lies, let alone the Village.

I wonder if we'll get to see these historic venues, but with the city up to its eyeballs in scrupulous security it's unlikely to be soon. I wonder if we'll manage to snaffle some Games tickets. I wonder if I'll run into any athletes in the streets. I wonder if this Olympic thing is really truly happening at all.

Like Beijing life in general, it's yet another Chinese thing that feels somewhat un-real.

My Ayi Doesn't Love My Kids

And why this is a good thing

Recently, one of my friends left Beijing, taking her husband and two small children with her. Her youngest child was raised with two mothers: my friend and my friend's *ayi*. This bi-maternal relationship, while often an enviable situation, is also fraught with Issues.

My friend's second baby was born in Beijing and she was lucky enough to find an *ayi* who was somewhat reserved in her attitude to raising baby the Chinese Way. I've heard of battles greater than Waterloo between mums and *ayis* on the best way to raise baby, and the warring continues all over town, so it was with relief that the *ayi*/newborn experience for my friend was comparably do-able.

The child was raised bilingual. He was toilet-trained the Chinese way and sleep-educated the Western way (i.e. learning to sleep without rocking human arms attached at all times). It was the best of both worlds. The baby thrived. He had a big brother, a loving dad and two devoted mums. The only trouble with this happy family picture was that one of these mums was semi-permanent.

When the family said goodbye to their *ayi*, it was the most heart-rending, distressing, emotional train wreck to be found outside reality television. I saw their *ayi* just the other day and she still has dark circles under her eyes and a hole in her heart. She haunts internet cafés for a glimpse of the toddler by email, and clutches a dog-eared photo of its adorable face. Back home, the toddler was initially a nightmare to settle but is adjusting slowly, still reportedly pining quite badly for Mama Ayi. Re-establishing a completely Western routine has also been a problem.

When we hired our *ayi* well over three years ago, I never expected her to fall in love with my kids. They were old enough to skip that baby-bonding time with her, anyway, and no real relationship has developed since.

Surprisingly, this makes me happy. I used to pine a little that she didn't love my kids, but as we begin our countdown for Home, I've realised Ayi's love disconnection could be a blessing in disguise. This is especially true after witnessing the terror of my friend's *ayi*/baby separation; I'm still not sure that developing a deep, impermanent attachment is the right thing.

It's going to rend my heart in two to leave Beijing. At least I won't have three extra broken hearts to deal with as well.

Let the Games Begin!

So, what did you think?

Of the Opening Ceremony, I mean. Showy enough for you?

Me? I'm not so sure. It started out well. *Loved* the drumming. Just mind-boggling. Loved the Cuisenaire rods jutting up and down in machine-like motion, sucking down like quicksand, rolling in waves and the sudden appearance of ancient Chinese characters. Sooo cool. Xiansheng and I took bets on whether or not there were busy little men beneath the rods, doing all the hard work. What a delight it was to see their smiling faces pop up from the bowels of this contraption when they were done. Beautiful.

China sure has manpower and they used it remarkably, but once the ancient scroll rolled out and those lissom dancers tumbled their way over the canvas, it sort of just plateaued from there — still impressive, but, I don't know … I just wanted to be *wow kapow*-ed.

This is just an opinion. Others might have fallen over from ecstasy, talking in tongues. I just didn't. Maybe I expected too much from China (they're the masters of showmanship, after all). Maybe I expected three gold-dipped emperors entering a vacant arena on horseback to the sound of a single gong. Maybe I was waiting for the Great Wall to emerge from the floor in a cloud of mist. And yes, yes, maybe I expected a Chinese dragon or two. Perhaps a little predictable, a tad clichéd, but my goodness, they are fun, especially when accompanied by those *tsinging* cymbals.

Maybe we just had to *be* there.

Nevertheless, we enjoyed the spectacle from the comfort of our lounge room, and the kids were allowed to stay up *all* night, as a treat. Ella lasted till 9 p.m. before she started groaning from fatigue and Riley's eyes started rolling in his head soon after. By 10.30 p.m. he was asleep on my chest and Ella had already disbanded to bed, miffed that the Australian athletes had not yet made an appearance and that she

had not yet seen the Flame.

Happily, this morning they replayed the Ceremony and she saw the Flame, which was pretty special. Not *kapow*. But pretty special.

What *is* special is the Games coverage on television today. Even though I can only understand 3 per cent of the words, the coverage is pretty darn special. I can flick between about five different channels and get giddy from choice. I have already seen China win its very first gold — Chen Xiexia won first place in the female 48 kilograms weightlifting (now that girl *kapow*-ed me!).

So, we have an exciting two weeks ahead and I'm a very happy *tai tai*. I've even got the kids hepped-up and we have national flags (one Australia, one China) in the most prized place of all: right over the telly.

Aodaliya jia you! Go Australia!

A Fishy Tale

Did he jump or was he pushed?

You should know by now that I'm not the most avid pet-collector. Again, I insist, I like pets very much, I just don't want to own any. Not right now, anyway. We've only just come through the Yes, We Are Absolutely Certain We Want No More Babies stage, so pets don't really factor on the radar, especially while living in Beijing.

So, the reason I'm bringing this up again is because on Friday, Riley came home with an orange goldfish clutched firmly in a suffocating plastic bag. As he and Ella clambered off the Summer Camp bus, they were both buzzing with excitement, regaling me with tales of how one of the other kids' fishes jumped from its plastic bag, and how the children went into a frenzy trying to pick it up from the bus floor.

I cringed, then reassured the kids. 'Those goldfish can't jump that high,' I said, all-knowingly. 'Don't worry.'

Famous last words.

So the fish — unwanted, I might add — found a home in a large, fat vase with pebbles in the bottom, and two pet-hungry pairs of eyes watching his every move. Xiansheng even rode his bike to our local fish store for a good supply of dried bloodworms and a mini air pump. This fish — Mr Fish — was certainly bathed in adoration but he just didn't seem happy in that poor excuse for a home.

Last night, I talked to the kids about how nice it would be to let Mr Fish go; to make some new friends in the pond at the base of our building, with our mates the penny turtles. Once again, they were okay about it but made me promise not to let him go until they returned from Summer Camp this afternoon.

Perfect! I thought. No more daily tank cleanings, no more disdainful glances at that miserable fish, encased in his glass prison. I was looking forward to the release with much excitement. I was going to get Ella to draw a farewell card and Riley to wave him goodbye as he plunged into the limpid deep of fishy freedom.

Alas, not to be. This morning I went out to a meeting and when I returned, I shot a glance at the tank to see how Mr Fish was doing.

Gone.

Gone? *How?* My eyes darted left and right, up to the ceiling and down again, and there he was, stiff as a board in the middle of the living room floor. His tail was even crunchy when I picked him up. It was horrible. Are pets really worth these horrific death scenes?

So, several questions are consuming me right now. What do I tell the kids? Should I tell them it was suicide? Would that distress them? Should I tell them it was an accident? How can a fish have an accident? Should I tell them someone broke in and stole him for their own fishy collection? I'm really stumped on this one.

And the most painful question of all ... *why*, Mr Fish? *Why did you do it?* Were you really that miserable? Was your tank not comfortable enough? And right on the eve of your release into the wild ... such a sad irony. Did you plan to do it while I was not home and could not rescue you? Why, Mr Fish? *Why?*

I guess honesty is the best policy: 'Yes, kids, it looks like goldfish

can jump.' And make calculated decisions about their own fate, too, by the look of things. Mr Fish obviously thought this through, and now I'm not so sure goldfish really do have a three-second memory.

Wish me luck with the kids. And *zai jian*, Mr Fish. Goodbye. I hope things go swimmingly in Guppy Heaven.

In Memoriam.

Bagging a Bargain

Avoiding a touristy trunk full of junk

Being a bit of a seasoned Beijing shopper, the Olympic influx of tourists to our fair capital has got me thinking about the blast they're going to have shopping. There's simply too much to buy in China. Everything is made here, after all, but the sheer volume and variety could see tourists travelling home with a trunk full of junk.

While Beijing certainly has the mother lode when it comes to hokey knick-knacks, there are also some real treasures to be found — some touristy-kitsch and others curiously valuable both in terms of memorabilia and actual preciousness. Forget the watches, stuffed pandas and postcards. Why not think outside the Tian'anmen square?

Instead of an *I Heart BJ* t-shirt, get a retro Chinese print from Plastered T-shirts in the Dongcheng District — the subway ticket and taxi fare prints will make you look like a real local. Teen girls should snaffle a copy of Chinese *Vogue* from street vendors; it represents one of China's fastest growing industries: high fashion.

Panjiayuan 'antiques' market (remember, there are no antiques left in China — none you could afford, anyway; my apologies if you are Bill Gates or the Sultan of Brunei) is an absolute must-see for those who love bric-a-brac. Bargain like a demon but remain calm and friendly and you'll get your price. This is a real treasure-trove of finds, from

original art to stone carvings, bronze statues and clunky baubles for the kids.

Also have a wander along the famous Liulichang 'antiques' street where bric-a-brac treasures like cast-iron clocks, bronze statuettes, carved jade-stone pendants and old coins abound. Also look for traditional paint-brushes for the kids, art books, beautiful writing paper and chops. Kids will love choosing a chop — a small rectangular block of stone which can be carved with their name or a Chinese character; a personalised stamp for life. Don't forget a traditional red-inked stamp pad.

Bargain hard — this is a tourist street, after all. A general rule is to halve a given price, then halve it again. Try to have fun bargaining; it's not a war and a smile will always bring a better price. While you don't want to get ripped off, don't waste precious time and a migraine on bargaining over 5 or 10 *yuan* — these people often don't make much on their wares, so focus on the spirit of the sale, rather than the angst of chasing the rock-bottom deal. Above all else, remember that if you love the item and the price suits you, you've got yourself a true bargain.

If you visit the famed Drum and Bell Tower, be sure to stop off in the small minority shops you'll find in the square. Their wares are nothing like those you'll find at markets — from small drums to wooden toys to handmade, beautifully crafted leather bags and heavily embroidered baby slippers.

Gemstones and precious metals are a must-buy in China, though remember that Chinese jade is either non-existent or will cost you the equivalent of a flight home. Pick up a sterling silver pendant at Ya Show market in a Chinese character — luck, love, happiness — for as little as 20 *yuan*. A stack of fifteen silver bangles lashed together should cost no more than 50 *yuan*. If you have daughters, invest in a good set of pearls. Beijing's authentic, lustrous creations will set you back 5 to 10 per cent of the cost at home; go to Ling Ling on the Pearl Market's (Hongqiao) fourth floor and ask them to show you some genuine quality.

Other market gems, in no particular order: sandalwood fans, quilts, pashminas, woven silk, little Chinese dresses (*qi pao*) and slippers, shoes with flashing lights for toddlers, silk bags with bamboo handles, and

Chinese zodiac animals carved from jade-stone. Don't forget an alarm clock with Chairman Mao waving merrily — an absolute imperative.

And my all-time favourite? Low on class, high on kitsch, our family's prized possession is a Lucky Cat, spray-painted gold and beckoning mountains of fortune into our house with its perpetually waving paw.

When it comes to shopping, I ♥ China.

Olympic Hockeyroos

Our family has scored gold ... Olympic tickets!

Due to my husband's work, my busyness, the kids, the heat, crowds and other unspecified niggles, going into the Olympic ticket bid was a little 'too hard' for our family. Even though I personally *adore* the Games, I wasn't devastated about not going, so my reaction really took me by surprise when Xiansheng came home waving tickets to the women's hockey. I actually jumped up and down, screaming.

Within minutes, my daughter Ella hand-drew and coloured in an Australian flag and I unearthed a batch of flag tattoos and my telephoto lens.

I also began asking all the standard questions I suppose everyone has asked. Can we take cameras (yes), can we take snacks in for the kids (not sure), can we take water (no), can we buy water when we get in there (yes), can we take umbrellas (only fold-up ones), can we arrive earlier or later than our ticket time (mixed reports), can we stay as long as we like (not sure), can we take flags in (small ones), can we retain our tickets (yes), can we jump up and down like monkeys when our team knocks that little ball into the net (oh yes yes *yes!*)?

So, we are officially in the Olympic loop. We even get to go to the Olympic Green, which is just soooo exciting and I'm gagging to take a photo of the Olympic torch atop the Bird's Nest stadium. I want to take photos of *everything*, even the ground and the grass and the signs, and Ella,

having caught the shutterbug from her mother, is also taking her camera.

Can hardly believe we're going. I held our little stack of tickets like a precious gold ingot in my cupped hands and turned them over and over and squeezed them like a Willy Wonka golden ticket. It was a memorable moment. I have hidden them in my house. Hidden from whom, I'm not so sure; probably from my own propensity to put things in that infamous Safe Place — a place where things go to never be found again.

I know it sounds twee, but truly, the most exciting part about this whole ticket thing is that our kids get to go. When the ticket lead-up to the Games first began, I remember hearing lots of queries from parents about taking their kids along. At first, I thought 'But *why?* Heat, queues, crowds, lousy food, long wait times, kids whining to go home as soon as their backsides hit the stalls …'

But now that I'm holding tickets, I've changed my tune. How on earth could we *not* take them? I think they'll love it. And hopefully my stash of lollipops (are lollipops allowed in?) will keep any teensy stretches of sporting boredom at bay.

Whatever happens, this is a special moment in time that I'm enormously grateful for. And those special times absolutely need to be shared with the kids.

Aussie Aussie Aussie — oi oi oi!

Jiminy Cricket!

Are the heavens conspiring against me?

When Riley's goldfish, Mr Fish, topped himself, I knew my pet-keeping fate had been sealed. The kids actually dealt with it well — I told them Mr Fish took a leap for freedom and they just looked at me wide-eyed. No tears. And no, I didn't add that this will teach us for keeping poor oceanic creatures in vases. Hopefully they will cotton on to that fact themselves.

So, the day after the demise of Mr Fish, Ayi came in and set about pottering in the kitchen, when this strange, God-awful screeching noise appeared out of nowhere. Dashing to the kitchen, I was quickly halted when Ayi held up her thumb and forefinger with a dirty great hulking cicada clenched between them, shrieking its head off.

At first I was horrified, but then I realised she was only trying to ease the loss of Mr Fish. She told me lots of Chinese kids keep these things as pets and carry them around in their pockets and under their caps. She said my kids would love him. I told her they'd be terrified of him.

Sure enough, when Ella and Riley came home from Summer Camp and Ayi charged towards them holding this prehistoric creature aloft, both kids ran in the other direction. Curiosity did pull them back eventually, however, and later that night Ella was carrying Mr Cicada (what is it with the 'Mr' title in our house?) around in an enormous plastic tub, taking him for a 'walk'. Riley, however, retained his distance.

That night, Ayi must have taken Mr Cicada home because he wasn't here yesterday and he didn't keep us awake all night last night, as expected. I was going to launch him to freedom from our window, anyway, but it looks like Ayi did that already. Unless she took him home for dinner (do the Chinese eat cicadas)?

But back to yesterday. No Mr Cicada in sight, but Ayi did come in again with *another* surprise. An enormous green grasshopper encased in a miniscule bamboo cage, with barely enough room to stretch his long-jumping legs. A beautiful creature, his teensy prison was stacked with spring onions which he dutifully grazed upon, and whose oniony pong spread throughout the house each and every time he munched.

He is indeed beautiful, and when the kids came home they were intrigued by him. Riley has named him Sam, and when Sam finally felt comfortable enough in our house, he began his chanting call which sent me straight back to the countryside of Australia — in the early evening when the stars begin to pop and the crickets begin trilling their bushland lullaby.

It's now Day Two and I want to crush that lullaby in my fist, along with that critter's bamboo cage.

Sure, at first it was lovely, but by late evening it was irritating. I moved Sam to the enclosed balcony and shut the door. Alas, the balcony fronts onto Riley's room, and Sam's early morning wake-up call had a domino effect on our family. First Sam, then Riley, then Ella, then Mum and Dad wailing their now familiar lament: 'It's too early! Go back to bed!'

Damn Sam.

Today, Sam's chanting lullaby has just about risen to the do-your-head-in level. We were going to let him go today anyway, but it can't be soon enough for me. Not only do I want to save Sam from that cage and the three-day pet curse we have in our house, but boy am I hankering for some cricket-free silence.

So, Sam, it's been just swell. Thanks for stopping by but freedom is imminently yours. The kids will be home any minute now and you'll soon be hopping to freedom in the grass downstairs.

Another one bites the Beijing dust.

The Sportsmanship Games

Can patriotism extend beyond homeland passion?

They say living away from your home country fosters a deeply rooted dose of heart-thumping patriotism. I've experienced this when living away from Australia in the past but living in China has given me a solid re-dose, particularly given the fact that we've come here with children.

Keeping Australia alive and well in our children's minds and hearts has been a given, but it's also been curious to watch our kids pine for their homeland unprompted, and to refer and defer to it consistently, as is their birthright.

Powerful stuff, that birthright; that homeland connection.

Despite falling in love with Beijing and never ever wanting to leave (as at the time of writing this), this homeland connection is calling our family. It's like a siren song, and lately it seems to be getting stronger, lulling us over the waves of the Pacific Ocean, skimming over the Great Barrier Reef, bounding through Papua New Guinea and leaping over the Tropic of Capricorn, glancing off Hong Kong and flooding into the Beijing basin. And we can, of course, hear its call all the more strongly since the commencement of the Olympic Games.

There's nothing much more patriotism-pumping than the Games, no matter where in the world you reside. Watching our Aussie athletes come to Beijing and strive for glory is a wondrous thing, and after seeing our team hover in the top five for the duration of the Games ... well, for a country comprising only 21 million people (roughly the population of Greater Shanghai), that's some pride-inducing feat.

But forgive me my nepotism. The point here is to extend to you, dear reader, that no matter where you're from, watching the Olympics from a foreign country is incredibly eye-opening. Particularly eye-opening for me because it seems the Aussies are not the only ones I'm barracking for.

It's not necessarily China I'm cheering on. It's non-country-specific, actually. It really tends to be whomever I've caught on the telly at that particular moment. It could be a Bulgarian weightlifter, a pair of Spanish synchronised swimmers, a Japanese trampolinist or a pack of rowers from the Old Country (Great Britain to you).

I mean, how could you not gasp, yell, scream with victory and cry out in anguish as these athletes push their bodies beyond normal human capacity? How could you not tear-up at the sight of their faces — devastation, shock, triumph and pure elation — after many years, sometimes an entire lifetime, of training and personal dedication, not to mention pushing their bodies to the brink of human endurance?

While I'm a deeply passionate Aussie team supporter and am first to leap from my seat and scream *Aussie Aussie Aussie!*, does it really matter where we are from when it comes to the thrill of the win? Can

we not extend ourselves beyond the lines of our borders and feel an inner sense of pride for all athletes as they strive for that glint of gold?

The Beijing Olympics is setting a fine example of sportsmanship. Sure, there's been frustration and disappointment for many. Sure, the Chinese are certainly dominating (and this surprises you because … ?), but overall I've been astounded at the all-round sportsmanship displayed at these Games. From the welcoming English-speaking volunteers right up to the gold medalists extending themselves with handshakes and kisses to subordinate winners on the medal dais. It's a fine thing for our children to see.

Sport, whether you're an armchair spectator or semi-professional, is truly something that connects us all. It's something that links us and firmly entrenches us in the human experience — both physically and emotionally. And when it can be celebrated in such a spirit of companionship, this is when the world feels truly at peace — a true embodiment of the Olympic ideology.

And on a final note, in the immortal words of my son: 'Win, Australia! You just *gotta* win!' If only it were that easy …

Chinese Street Gyms

This ain't no high-tech fitness club

Have you heard of the Chinese exercise equipment dotted in pockets along the streets of Beijing? My kids love these things. Elliptical trainers, stationary bikes, StairMasters, lat-pulls, they're all there. It's just that they're made for grannies and everyday *ren*, rather than great hulking chunks of muscle, bulging with testosterone and sweating out steroids.

When we first moved to China, I was scared to let my kids run rampant on these local exercise staples. I felt we didn't 'qualify' to use such an inventive community initiative, really reserved for harried

businessmen on their way to work or elderly *Beijingren* in need of arthritic relief. I felt, well, that we were just too *foreign* and my kids were too small and would totally misuse these exercise options as play equipment or something appalling like that.

How things have changed. Now that we are *lao pengyou de Beijing* — old Beijing friends — our entire family feels far more comfortable stretching our boundaries and stepping into the footprints of the local Chinese. We've now been using this Chinese exercise equipment for around three years and not only are we wholeheartedly welcomed by the locals who use these contraptions to keep fit, we also seem to encourage other Chinese passers-by to join in.

The Chinese have a no-nonsense, admirable approach to health. They shade themselves from the sun, live in synch with the seasons, eat an excellent diet (even if it is a little high in oil and salt), practise an impressively *lao* (old) form of alternative medicine, and believe in keeping physically active and able. Coming from Australia, where few people exercise in public unless they can run like the wind with Olympic track style, pop with muscles while lifting their own bodyweight in barbells or look like a supermodel in a leotard, it was a little cheesy seeing middle-aged women walking backwards on the street in their socks and sandals, let alone ballroom dancing to screechy Cultural Revolution oldies, clapping their hands and chanting in the sunshine, or practising *tai chi* with faux swords under a tree in their pyjamas.

I almost averted my eyes at first. Standing in the middle of the street, slapping their hands together behind their backs like dilapidated flamingos was just, well, *strange* to me. But it soon became an everyday sight in our lives and with it came the understanding that it doesn't matter where you exercise, how you do it or how daft you look, as long as you *do* it, and even better, *enjoy* doing it.

Now I can't live without the grannies at the bottom of my building twirling their wrists around, kicking their legs in the air or performing deep knee bends. I can't get enough of the ballroom dancers, especially the ones who can't find a partner and dance solo, holding an imaginary Fred Astaire. How I've pined to go over and take their hand and swirl

and twirl alongside them. My absolute favourite are the *tai chi* groups who entrance me with their muscle-toning moves, and the granddads who head to the street gym, roll up their singlets and rub their lumbago backs on the big meat-tenderising apparatus next to the joint-loosening contraption.

My personal favourite of these exercise contraptions, often painted bright yellow, blue or green, would have to be the hip-slipping walker. You plant a foot on each pedal and swing your legs like you're running through space, ironing out all the cricks and clicks in any type of hip, especially the crusty hips of an oft-seated writer. I also love the pizza wheels, as my kids call them: flat disks you stand on, grip the handles and twist from side to side like a pony-tail-wearing jivester at a 1950s dance.

My kids' favourites? Everything. They run from piece to piece like mice in a maze, unable to decide what to go on, what to stay on, what to hog. It's a joy watching them enjoy these simple contraptions so much — and for free!

What could be better? I'll tell you what: seeing my kids attract an audience of fellow Chinese sports-enthusiasts to share in the joy.

Summer Holiday: Day 45

We're over halfway through!

Today, I am celebrating. I haven't popped the champagne cork yet; the champagne glass is empty (have to wait until at least 3 p.m., realistically), but I am celebrating nonetheless. This morning, I spoiled myself to a Starbucks non-fat vanilla latte (grande) and even spent an hour chatting with a very intelligent person who was actually older than eight years. This afternoon, I might even have my nails done. Or go long-overdue shopping. Or — *gasp!* — read a magazine in between my regularly scheduled writing. I might even turn on the tele (I never do this in the

day unless the kids are home) and watch some Games. *Ooh la la!* The choice is overwhelming me.

So, today my kids started another two weeks of Summer Camp. And the reason I'm celebrating, above and beyond having personal choice outside playdough, Wii, colouring books, Tonka trucks and Barbies, is that my kids where actually *happy to go*. They were really excited, and this — as many a mother will tell you — is a real feat. Sure, I talked it up, I created infectious enthusiasm, but I honestly do think they enjoy it. Anything that involves swimming, hotdogs and friends is surely enough to keep any kid in rapture.

They had last week at home, and we had a good time. We pottered around and made trips to Jenny Lou's for goodies, and kicked the soccer ball down the corridor into Ayi's room, and coloured in and made ice slushies. Dad even nipped home early to take them both swimming.

But overall, home is rather boring. Sure, Mum likes to play but she still needs to write, shop for food, pick things up off the floor *(groan)* and wash Beijing microbes off her skin and hair occasionally. Boring, I know, but Real — and kids happen to live in a land of make-believe, where fun must gush from a curling Dr Seuss tap. So, it's with relief that they dashed off to Summer Camp at 8.15 a.m. And I have every nerve-cell crossed that they'll return home just as enthused.

The other reason I'm celebrating is that we're halfway through the school holidays. Halfway through! In fact, more than halfway through. More than that, we are also only two and a bit weeks from a trip to Hong Kong for some really really fast R&R — so fast, we'll be jetting back the day the kids were meant to start school *(shhhh)*. We would have gone earlier, only this large International Sporting Event just happened to be happening.

We also have a special reason to go to Hong Kong. We're meeting up with Granny on her way back to Australia from the UK. Any excuse to spend a long weekend in Honkers. The kids will go bananas seeing their Gran, whom they adore. And I'll have someone to take to The Peninsula for High Tea. Again, any excuse (husband and kids never interested — *groan*).

Isn't the world becoming a teensy place? When I was a kid, we'd be lucky to meet up with Granny two suburbs away, let alone popping down to Hong Kong, sweetie darling. I mean, really. It's like the time I watched Riley play in his ClubFootball grand final, and I was particularly impressed by a little five-year-old British boy who scored quite a few goals. I passed on a compliment to the child, and then asked him where he had learned his soccer skills. Expecting him to say 'In Sussex, Ma'am,' he instead confidently announced he had learned his stuff in Singapore. As you do.

Yes, the world is getting smaller and smaller and with that comes ever-increasing reasons to pop a champagne cork. Why, you ask?

Do you really need a reason?

Foodie Culture Shock

Stretching our family's palate in Beijing

I remember one of the first things to rise up and slap us in the face when we first arrived in Beijing was the food. The crumbling toast, the ponging milk and the strange animal parts on offer was disturbing. The Weet-Bix cost the price of a small car and the local Lays chips contained more MSG than even the strongest bowel could tolerate in one, er … sitting.

In our first weeks in the capital, we almost immediately craved food from home. A lot. We craved warm donuts dusted in cinnamon sugar, wobbling tubs of buffalo mozzarella and curling slips of shaved honey ham. We craved yoghurt iceblocks and hunks of nougat that sweet-talked the tongue. We became obsessed with finding wholegrain bread, natural muesli and soy milk. Where to buy Lavazza coffee? How to find fresh barbecued chickens? Is there such a thing as organic in this town? Which way to the gummy-bear store?

This searching consumed me, as the chief hunter and gatherer of food for our family. And securing these finds took months — nay, years. But in the meantime, along with an infinite supply of good restaurants and our *ayi's* cooking talent, something began to shift in our family. It was our palates, sliding sideways like an oral continental drift from Australia to China. Now, after three-and-a-half years, could our mouths have become ... Chinese?

For our family, there is nothing like *gong bao* chicken, Peking duck and the crack of toffee crabapples against the teeth — a favourite with our kids. We crave and adore the scallion pancakes, the marinated tofu, the steaming hotpot cauldrons swimming with sliced lotus root, shaved pork and needle mushrooms. All this is part of us now, along with hole-in-the-wall *baozi* (bread dumplings) and *bing* (egg pancakes).

Although we still indulge in foreign treats, we mostly eat endemic foods now, in parallel with the seasons and fully engaged in the local flavours of China. I've actually been glad to say goodbye to our Australian tongues and I do believe this is the culinary Way while living here. We had to let go of our tongue's security blanket. Immerse. Lap it up. Chow down some chow mien. Suck in a duck. The donuts would always be there when we went home.

And what of our food cravings from home? They haven't actually disappeared. They're not an issue; they're on standby. The only issue now is how we're going to deal with our ravenous food cravings when we return to Australia.

Our cravings for the flavour of China.

Paralympic Meltdown

How can these Games make one woman so pathetic?

Okay, so here's the thing: when it comes to such things as triumph over adversity (and the loss of pets), I'm really pathetic. I become a blubbering mess. And this is also true for the Paralympians.

Don't get me wrong, there's not a shred of self-ingratiating pity in it. It's just sheer and pristine admiration, affection, awe and total respect for people who do whatever they want in life, even if they have no legs or can't see.

I like exercise once I get into it (a bit like certain other pesky physical acts) but for the most part, it's a bit agonising making the daily commitment to work this rear end on the treadmill. I've been known to pull excuses out of nether-regions and stratospheres to kybosh a workout. Sore foot, aching back, headache, tired, new DVD …

Oh, give me a break. If a man can run 5000 metres or score a soccer goal completely blind, then I can ignore a little fatigue and push past it without whining. Surely.

Hmmm. Don't save your sporting admiration for me. Save it for these Paralympians. How can you not shed a tear as talented swimmers, who are severely physically compromised, fling themselves into the deep end of a swimming pool and power through that water with no arms and do it faster than most of us ever could, even when asleep and inside our dreams?

I mean, *come on!* How could you not be completely moved by this? How could you not wail out loud watching China's Wu Chunmiao, winner of the women's 100 metres T11 (blind) sprint, remove her gold medal and drape it gently around the neck of her guide runner?

I really want my kids to see these Paralympic Games and so last night we took Ella (Riley opted out — 'Too rainy, Mum') to the Bird's Nest in torrential rain to see these astounding athletes in action. We saw an

Australian arm amputee win the 200-metre sprint and a blind Chinese 5000-metre runner steal the gold in a last-minute dash. The cataclysmic eruption around the stadium is something I will never forget, so long as I live — it still raises the hairs on my arms. We also enjoyed shot put, javelin, long jump and plenty of wheelchair racing and sprinting.

My only complaint is that I missed a little too much of the action because I spent far too much time watching the reaction on Ella's face. Isn't it real-life moments like these that teach our children more than anything else ever could?

Guest Overload

Everybody's doing it

What is it about September and October? Has Beijing Capital airport crumbled under the weight of an expat family and friend influx or what? Everyone is exhausted and run ragged; everyone is busy beyond any kind of sanity and no one has a spare pillow or blanket to save themselves. Houses are full, beds are chock-a-block and Ya Show market has paid off its mortgage. But the Guest Season in Beijing is almost over and people are finally shipping their last round of visitors out the door.

Not that we should complain. Having people visit is great fun. It gets us off our jaded butts and into the hot spots once again ... who could ever have too much of the Beijing *hutongs* or the Temple of Heaven or the fragrantly smoky forecourt of the Lama Temple?

Most guests are too overwhelmed by this place to just sit on your couch and eat *jiaozi* and fart all day. They are out and about, on tours, buzzing around in taxis, balancing on the edge of the Great Wall, snapping photos of the guards marching like tin soldiers in Tian'anmen Square and sampling all manner of unearthly foodie delights. They are

buying up trinkets, t-shirts and silk. They are bedecking their necks in baubles from the sea, groaning under the skilled hands of a local masseuse and gawping at the provincial throngs power-surging into the Forbidden City.

Having guests gives us an excuse to go along with them, to enjoy Beijing all over again — to feast, to sample, to roll in it and sigh. We get to boast about the kaleidoscope of gorgeousness at our local fruit and veg market. We get to brag about how we swathe ourselves in silk for 90 cents and pluck pearls from stalls like day-old cherries. We can gloat over how we are watching centuries of old China crumble before our very eyes, and are witnessing the construction of a New World.

It is a proud and happy time when guests come to stay. Plus, of course, any excuse to add to the handbag collection. Please don't tell Xiansheng.

So Long Summer

It's been nice knowing you

Ahhh … I can almost feel the change in the air. Almost. It's just about here. I can taste it. And as many a seasoned Beijinger will know, the cold descends in about the same time it takes to grow bamboo. Frighteningly fast.

Exciting.

Exciting because our family is pining for the end of summer. Perhaps it's the vintage blend of the British Isles in our veins but we love the cold. Descendants of lizards are we. Give it all to us: snow, ice, frost, slush, hail, sleet, flurries and blizzards — the lot. Bitter, frozen, icy, freezing, chilly, frosty, wintry, arctic are all good for us. Skating on frozen Hou Hai Lake is one of our favourite family pastimes ever.

We love the numbness of frozen fingertips, the lull of hand-warmers in the pockets, the snugness of a beanie on the head, earmuffs muffling

the ears, thick socks packing boots, soft scarves under the chin, melty lip balm on the lips, warming hot cocoa puffed with marshmallows, huddling by an open fire, bed socks, throw rugs, tearing inside out of the frozen wind while laughing hard with breathlessness, cuddles and Eskimo kisses when the tips of the nose are cold.

We love love love it.

I've been pining for the days when my kids rush in from the school bus without looking like they've been dragged through a wet jungle backwards. I can't wait to see them in their smart school blazers and their snug hats and boots on the weekend. I can't wait to help them shove their feet into snow boots and clump downstairs for a snowball thrashing.

So, goodbye summer — you haven't been too hard on us this year. Have fun in the south … and don't wait up for us.

Publishing a Children's Book in Beijing

Sometimes we have to control our own dreams

Whenever I tell people I'm a writer, they invariably say they'd love to write a book. Indeed, we all have a story to tell, and if you love writing what better thrill than to have a book in print?

I was very fortunate to have a non-fiction book published in Australia some time ago, but it's only recently that I've turned my attention to the children's book genre. Truth be told, I have a wee bit of an obsession with kids' books. I love the pictures. I love the stories that colour in children's brains like an activity book and a box of crayons. I love fun children's books, traditional books, magical books, educational and just plain nonsense books. I even love the smell of them.

What a dream to actually publish a children's picture book. What a dream to see the contents of my head down on paper, flickable. What a dream to entrance and inspire children in any way, shape or form. But how to make this dream a reality?

I've received enough publisher rejection slips to papier mâché the Great Wall. There's been a lot of despair, frustration and tears shed in this writer's lifetime, trust me. But I keep telling myself if *Gone With The Wind* was rejected by more than 30 publishers before becoming one of the world's best-known tales, surely I have a remote chance … Ditto JK Rowling and her little Potter tale — rejected around a dozen times before publication. *A dozen times.* I wouldn't want to be the one responsible for handing out *those* rejection slips. I guess it goes to prove my long-held suspicion that publishing really is a highly subjective thing, and perhaps sometimes quite reliant on luck.

Oh, the frustrations and setbacks.

Interestingly, forging ahead despite setbacks has actually become a lot easier since I started writing in Beijing, but it doesn't mean the setbacks don't disappoint. After completing three children's picture book manuscripts last year and sending them religiously to a long list of publishers in China, Australia and the States, it's been very despairing to watch time slip away, with nary an acceptance letter in sight.

I've had several very encouraging 'We're considering your proposal and will get back to you in eight to twelve weeks' slips in the mail. These slips are the equivalent of a glassed-in bamboo stick to a hungry panda. They're a little tormenting, and the worst of it is that they completely erase a large chunk of your life because most publishers like to be exclusively offered manuscripts. Margaret Mitchell must have been 183 before *Gone With The Wind* was finally put into print.

I'm almost immune to the disappointment now. Almost. It still smarts but at least it doesn't completely swamp and disable me any more. In fact, I'm so immune, I've found a whole new confidence and subsequently decided to revisit my children's book manuscript *All the Tea in China.* I've had to rejig the ending, just as Xiansheng said I should, but I really love this story and I really believe in it. Instead of

tea, though, it's going to involve a sleeping dragon and a little something called the Great Wall. Very exciting.

So, what to do when you're really sold on a story idea, you know it's good and you're just not connecting to the right 'make it happen' person? Well, what you do is you publish it yourself.

So that's what I'm going to do.

I'm not sure I can do it but I'm going to give it a hell of a go. And whatever the case, at least I won't have another sodding rejection slip to groan over.

Exploring Beijing's Ancient Sites

Revisiting the past, kiddie-style

There's a place in Beijing called the Forbidden City. It's a big, flat, grey succession of red-roofed halls stuffed with dusty chairs, dull stone turtles, imposing red doors and the odd big copper pot. Ho hum.

There's also a place in Beijing called Gu Gong. It's an astonishing, ancient city spread across 72 hectares of land that once housed emperors and empresses, warlords and eunuchs. Its pink-washed palaces are stuffed with gold-dipped thrones and 1000-year-old treasures. Its massive copper pots doubled as fire engines, its courtyards were once frequented by concubines toting baskets of pomegranates, and its red, gold-studded gates once hemmed in eye-popping secrets of Ancient China.

But wait — drum roll, please — did you know that these places are one-in-the-same? Yes, Gu Gong is actually the Forbidden City. It just

depends on how you're looking at it. In a city that's crammed with ancient treasures, it's easy to pass over these historical sites because the kids are 'too young'. We love taking the kids to these history-steeped spots in China's capital. You just have to know how to view them, kiddie-style.

For a trip to Tian'anmen Square, we give the kids a video camera to swoop around the panorama of the world's largest city-central square. We tell them about the embalmed body of Chairman Mao and the ancient city walls, and they're soon weaving a movie plot around the mysterious network of hidden tunnels lying beneath their feet.

At Yihe Yuan (the Summer Palace) the kids run themselves ragged on the gentle hills or around the myriad pavilions and halls, ripe for exploring and bouncing around an echo or two. They also love navigating the canals of Suzhou Market Street while Mum and Dad freak out over the lack of barricades to prevent little emperors tossing themselves headlong into the waterways.

For Yonghe Gong (the Lama Temple), they love to light metre-long joss sticks to send their wishes to heaven on billowing fragrant clouds. They adore trailing the gardens, exploring the dark-as-night staircases or clapping their hands against the enormous bell.

For the Wall, their favourite spot is definitely Mutianyu for the super-slick toboggan ride, snaking in a silver ribbon from the top of the Wall to the car park below. We make sure to wait a good few minutes for any grannies to reach the bottom before we go soaring down like a silver bullet. So cool, we want to pay the entry fee twice.

It's easy to do things kiddie-style in Beijing and we're taking full advantage while we still can. We snaffle a crabapple toffee stick, jump on a rickshaw through the *hutongs* around Hou Hai and become once more entranced with this remarkable, historical city. Thank goodness we're not too jaded to thoroughly enjoy these last months in the capital.

The Countdown Has Begun

10, 9, 8, 7, 6, 5, 4, 3, 2, 1 ...

I have avoided this topic for some time now, because, like everything in life, the moment you say it out loud, it tends to become reality. And I'm not sure reality is something I want to deal with right now.

In fifteen weeks, we will be heading back to Australia. That's around three and a bit months — roughly the same time it takes to walk the entire length of the Great Wall and back, or make it to the cash registers at Ikea near the North Third Ring Road.

Fifteen weeks isn't a long time but we've actually been preparing for this reality a lot longer than that. Like, six months or something. It takes that long just to stock up on items at Ya Show and Liangma flower market, not to mention the myriad places we need to experience 'one more time'.

Thankfully, we've just waved goodbye to a month's worth of visitors — some of our dearest friends and family — who created the perfect opportunity to do all that touristy stuff we tend to backlog. It also allowed us to showcase the delicious array of restaurants we enjoy in the capital, and the quirky everyday life that makes Beijing so unique.

Although the next few months will be like walking underwater to a sub-Atlantic Mount Everest then scaling it with cement-filled shoes, I'm still having enough moments of mental clarity to focus on all the things we need to do, see, feel, touch, hear and taste before we leave the East Second Ring Road for the very last time.

We have a life to pack up, a house to sell, a house to buy, a school to locate, books to publish, places to travel to, work to wind up, friends and colleagues to bid farewell and an incredibly lush, culturally rich, deeply emotion-encrusted existence to leave behind. I can't even bear thinking about it. Leaving this place behind ... it's going to be shattering

for our family. We're probably going to need wild horses to drag us to the airport, not a mini van.

Even though we don't feel quite ready, part of us is also excited to be going Home. Australia is a beautiful place to live, despite the fact that a bunch of bananas will cost the same as an entire cart of bok choy at the wet market. It's going to be wonderful to be back in the arms of our homeland, experiencing all the things we hold so close to our hearts.

But now we have another place to hold close, while we still can, and the coming months will be filled with gathering and amassing as much of Beijing as we can fit in a suitcase.

Nevertheless, the fact remains: very soon our family's life will never be the same again.

Embracing the Differences

Where do we all come from and why are we here?

I am a closet busybody. My greatest fantasy is to peek inside everyone's house for a look at the décor and furniture placement. My other fantasy goes a little deeper. It involves peeking inside people's brains — to understand the daily contributions to the complex tapestry that shapes a personality. Why are some of us quiet? Why do some of us like eating bull testicles? How can anyone *really* enjoy motor racing and why do some of us wither like dehydrated daisies the moment summer whispers across the hills?

I love how Beijing is a jumble of differences we'll never experience at home. Not only do we have differing personalities to contend with, we also have differing thought processes. Differing ways of being — culturally, mentally, emotionally, socially, spiritually. It's fascinating to me. So fascinating, I asked three different mothers some questions about motherhood in the hope this would open up my understanding.

My first target is a local Beijing girl, let's call her Sami. She speaks English and is a well-educated customer service manager who has been married six years. Sami has one three-year-old child.

My second is a Shanghai girl and stay-at-home mum, let's call her Pia, who married an American man and has lived in both the States and Japan. They have two children and although she is perfectly Westernised, Pia still holds true to her Chinese roots.

My last ring-in, let's call her Shazza, is an Aussie girl with three children. She is married to an Australian, has been in Beijing for almost three years and works part time.

Let's just see what they have to say.

Nosey-Parker: What do you love most about being a mother?
Sami: I love my son. There is nothing happier than the arrival of a new baby. He is loveable and looks like me. He has come into my life and my blood. It's said that a child is one part meat of the mother's body. I feel so proud.
Pia: Being a mother is the most wonderful thing in life; I can't imagine a more important job or one more satisfying. I get such huge satisfaction from seeing my two boys growing up healthy, curious and with so many interests and talents. Cuddling them, making them feel better when they feel bad, exploring all that's new to them is so wonderful. Being the one person they count on, trust, love and look up to. Yes, being a mother is special.
Shazza: I love the fact that my children love me for being me, no strings attached. I also love that all three of my boys still love giving and getting hugs and kisses.

Nosey-Parker: What is difficult about being a mother?
Sami: It's so difficult to educate a child and teach him good behaviour and manners. I explain to my son what's right and wrong but he often can't resist doing the wrong thing. It's also difficult to balance work and life. I feel I don't have enough time to be with my son, but I have to work.

Pia: While it is not a thankless job, it often feels like a non-stop, no-break occupation, seven days a week, 365 days a year. It can be extremely tiring and it's a challenge not to get upset when you put so much into mothering and the kids so often find ways to be uncooperative.

Shazza: Learning when to let go and letting your children make their own mistakes. Sometimes this is heartbreaking.

Nosey-Parker: Which parent has the most important parental role, you or your husband?

Sami: My husband and I play a two-sided role. In China there is a saying, one of the parents should play 'black face' and the other should play 'red face', which means the couple should balance. Sometimes I'm strong and sometimes my husband is strong. Generally speaking though, my husband plays the most important role. He is patient and tender and plays with my son while I do housework.

Pia: I believe, as a mother, I do, because I'm the one who is with them most of the time. I must set the rules, hand out the discipline, teach, guide and basically take care of them, for the most part. Although we do discuss the parenting rules, my husband follows the rules I've already set forth. We both agree that it's the person who spends the most time with our kids who must play the most important role.

Shazza: I feel both our roles are equally important. The children need both role models to become balanced adults — to learn to respect themselves and others.

Nosey-Parker: How important is Chinese culture and heritage in your children's lives?

Sami: Some Chinese traditional ways are good for the child's physiology and psychology. We prefer traditional Chinese medicine, which is good for the health. I cook Chinese cuisine for my son and never take him to McDonald's or KFC. Chinese family attitude is important in our life. According to local tradition, my husband and I should go to our hometown with our son to visit the grandparents and in-laws during

Chinese New Year and other holidays. We want to let our son know that he is one part of the whole family.

Pia: Teaching our children Chinese culture is very important. It's one of the main reasons we moved to Beijing as it's a bit more traditional than Shanghai, where I'm from. My sons' time here has been filled with celebrating Chinese holidays, eating many of the foods I ate as a child, reading Chinese stories, seeing plays, acrobatics, learning Chinese songs, taking Chinese drawing classes and, of course, learning the wonderful language — speaking as well as reading and writing. My sons have also taken abacus and special Chinese logic classes.

Shazza: It is important to me that my children embrace whatever culture we live in. We are Australians living in China and therefore it's very important for my kids to embrace the culture by speaking Chinese and participating in activities whenever they have the opportunity. My children will be going to bilingual schools in Australia to continue their appreciation of another culture. We are already planning a Chinese New Year dinner in Australia with friends and family.

Nosey-Parker: What kind of role do grandparents and extended family have in your children's lives?

Sami: My mother takes care of my son when my husband and I go to work. She cooks for my son and plays with him, so my mother is also important to my son. Grandparents and extended family often spend money to help us, including buying the house.

Pia: Though my husband's family all live in the US, they are still in touch fairly often, and we take trips in the summer to see them. My family is mostly in Shanghai and we see them two or three times a year. Despite the distance, the boys' grandparents still play a supportive role in their upbringing.

Shazza: Unfortunately, due to my husband's work, our boys don't live near their grandparents or extended family very often. Their grandparents email the kids to their own personal email accounts — this is private time between them, and we, as parents, do not get involved. The kids are building a connection that means they will have

another set of adults to turn to when in need, or simply just for fun. I think this communication is equally important for the grandparents.

Nosey-Parker: What three things do you wish for your children?
Sami: I wish that he is healthy, safe and happy. I wish that he has a good future by receiving a good education and making a great contribution to society. I wish that he has a happy family, with a nice wife and child.
Pia: That they are able to have interests in life that keep them happy. That they are ambitious and strive to do their best. That they find someone they love and are able to have a healthy family.
Shazza: For them all to be happy, safe and successful in whatever they choose to do. And of course — always love their mum.

Differences? Parallels? Does it really matter? For three women embracing three very different lives, this experiment proves that motherhood is both a challenge and a joy, no matter where you come from and no matter your beliefs, needs or creed.

It also proves, once again, that deep inside our ribcages, no matter if our bodies are black, white or yellow, communist, Christian or atheist — a mother's heart beats for her children.

Thumpety-thump.

Self-Publishing in Beijing I

Is my story really marketable?

When I first started thinking about self-publishing my children's book, the thought passed through my mind and almost instantly my head was swamped with an enormous ocean, and there was that original, ambitious thought, bobbing in the centre of that ocean — a teensy speck among the galloping waves.

It was all a little bit overwhelming. Especially in a place where English is a by-product and red tape binds every move you make.

Where to start? *How what when where who?*

Why never entered the picture, which is at least a good thing.

So, first things first. I've written and edited countless manuscripts and I have to say there is nothing more valuable than the opinion of someone you respect. So I've asked some people I respect to read my manuscript and, lucky for me, I've had some great feedback.

I also tested the book on kids and the reaction was also good. Feeling more and more confident — after all, it seems to me it would be quite important to publish a book that kids would actually enjoy.

So now I'm onto researching the market. The target market. I'm not going to print this book in Mandarin (for now), so my only target market is the English-speaking expat community in China and in Australia (and hopefully some other countries in the future ... JK Rowling, look out).

As for the kids I'm aiming the book at — it's definitely the pre- to primary school range, but I'm sure older kids and adults will love it, too; it's just that kinda story. I'm beyond excited about this, especially as there's not much like it on the market (if anything at all).

Even though I'm living in China, I'm going to publish the book in Australia, and this is actually quite easy to do. I've researched ISBNs, barcodes, Cataloguing-in-Publication-Data entries, printers and more. Once you set your mind to it, these things are surprisingly easy to sort (thanks, Google).

The next thing I did was advertise for an illustrator, which I did online. Honestly, I was shocked with the mass response from all over the world (thanks, internet). Out of that batch of talent, I have chosen a very clever fellow who lives in Canada, of all places. Hey, the world is so teensy now, I'm sure we can make this work (*eeep!*).

Will it work? You'll soon find out. Amazing how things fall into place when you know something is right. And when you just don't give up.

Now, there's a novel idea.

The Great Costume Caper

It's a superhero thing

When we left Australia for Beijing, my kids' dress-up box consisted of a stash of second-hand op-shop finds from the bowels of some nanna's knicker drawer. Polyester slips, armpit-length gloves and scratchy lawn bowling hats were just about it.

Since coming to Beijing, this dress-up box looks a *little* bit different. There are Disney princess gowns of velvet and chiffon with matching be-feathered head-dresses. There are luxuriant, scarlet pirate capes trimmed in gold rickrack to complement satiny ruffled shirts and faux boots built into Jolly-Roger pants. There's Narnia knights with injury-proofed foam swords, bedazzled mermaids, pixies, race car drivers, catsuits, black-tulle witches, astronauts, ballerinas and more floaty fairies than you can poke a magic wand at. There's also that kangaroo and koala suit commissioned for UN Day, now apparently called International Day.

Yes, this dress-up box is truly worthy of any Hollywood movie-set, and I am happy to report its contents are one of the few things my kids consistently and gratefully indulge in.

I do, however, have a small worry. It's five-year-old small and consists of a red cape, a blue bodysuit and a large yellow 'S' tattooed on the chest (with built-in muscles, thankyouverymuch). Yes, it's Superman. My son, Superman. My Every Day Every Night Wear to the Shops and Go To Sleep In It son — Superman.

I know it's meant to be 'normal' — I know virtually every boy hits the superhero phase just as sure as he'll hit the monsters-under-the-bed phase (isn't *that* a sleep-sapper?). But can one small boy really surrender himself so totally and unyieldingly to the Superman phenomenon?

When it started, we had every window in our high-storey apartment welded shut. We bought a mini trampoline. We forgave his

kryptonitesque aversion to any food that resembled green. We forbade Ayi to wash the Suit lest it become unavailable for wear in the time it took to whip it off, leap into the bath in a single bound and dry oneself faster than a speeding bullet.

So the Suit is looking a little worse for wear. It's pilling, lumpy and lopsided. It's maybe even a little smelly, but that's okay. It's not the outside that counts, after all, and it's great to know that despite this (hopefully temporary) obsession, inside the Suit is a truly super little man.

Self-Publishing in Beijing II

Challenges and obstacles? Outta my way!

Well, things are going really well. As well as can be expected when you decide you're just going to go ahead and publish a book yourself.

Did I really expect things to go sailingly smooth?

I've had some illustrator niggles, some time issues, some software issues, printer issues and cataloguing issues. Also some computer issues. Our old PC decided to up and die on us last week. It was clutching at its last dying breath when its antiquated carcass (only born in 2004!) finally succumbed. A terrifying event, and one I didn't really need at the time.

Yes, I was backed up but it was still an unwanted drama, especially considering the fact that I'm not only trying to publish this children's book, I'm also trying to finish a book for adults — a compilation of my diaries, magazine columns and blogs (you're reading it! hallelujah! I got it finished!) — all within the next three months.

Along with packing up and leaving Beijing (you should see the troves of ribbon I have to sort through and don't even start me on the handbag and wooden toy collections) and trying to prep a new life in Australia, you could say I'm *mildly* stressed.

Or just daft.

Nonetheless. Challenges and obstacles? Outta my way! My belly is on fire and nothing is going to stop me powering through and getting these awfully large dreams of mine out of La La Land and into Reality. I'll be hauling them out kicking and screaming like a newborn babe.

Don't they say persistence is everything? *Sheesh*. Persistence is tough! But easier to handle when your belly is on fire.

Beijing's Little Quirks

How a little raspberry typifies life in the capital

Let me regale you with a tale about a young girl who was born on the southern tip of an island called Tasmania. This small island lies at the bottom of Australia — a large, red, ancient landmass that fits snugly against Asia's underbelly and has spouted such gems as Mel Gibson, Nicole Kidman and Coopers Ale.

Few know much about this island — Tasmania — but it is a hidden jewel of rugged mountain wilderness, untouched bays, stunning rivers, crisp apple orchards, and the best raspberries in the world. In fact, this little girl spent her first ten years with a permanent raspberry stain around her mouth (like she had got into mummy's red lipstick).

In the north of the island, her grandfather and hero — Bampa — a photographer, journalist, historian and avid gardener, grew lashings of this beaded, celestial fruit. And every time the little girl visited her Bampa, she was treated to an extra special tub: a big fat 2-litre ice-cream tub of the most divine, sweet, rosy, fragrant raspberries any

mouth could possibly imagine. No one was allowed to dive into that tub except that little girl. Bampa even wrote her name across the top of the tub in big, bold letters: TANIA.

You could say I am now a bit of a raspberry aficionado. Yes, yes, if I was stranded on a desert island and could only take one food with me … you guessed it.

So. Today I scooped natural yoghurt, home-baked oats and a sprinkling of roasted almonds and pepitas into my breakfast bowl, and on top, a flourish of fresh Beijing raspberries. As they tumbled into the bowl, my heart fluttered. They're good raspberries. They're not Bampa's raspberries and the seasonal quality only lasts a short while, but they are still good.

In true Beijing style, what I love most about these Beijing raspberries is that they're 'unfinished'. They're not processed to within an inch of their juice. They are fresh from the garden, a little dusty, and some are imperfect. But what strikes me most about these Beijing raspberries is this: some of them still have the *stem attached*.

Now, I'm not joking when I say I've eaten more raspberries than all of you put together. I'll pass up a trip to the movies in favour of a punnet of raspberries in Australia (yes, they cost as much as a movie ticket sometimes). So, you must believe me when I say I've sighted and devoured many a sweet little burgundy jewel.

So how is it that I had to come to Beijing to view my very first be-stemmed raspberry, ever? When I first picked it up and looked at it, the sight kind of got stuck in my eye like a wooden stick. It wouldn't fit. I turned that raspberry over and over and thought 'My God, this has never happened to these eyeballs before. What a marvellous visual treat. How could I have waited so long to see this? *What went wrong with my life?*'

This might seem like a small thing to you, but to me, this raspberry-stem-sighting (and subsequent gentle stem-plucking — oh, how satisfying) typifies Beijing to me.

This is a place where you'll see severed pigs' heads next to your Italian tinned tomatoes at the wet market. This is where you'll see

women in restaurants whizzing with the door open. This is where you'll see cow belly being sliced on an outdoor table next to scorpions on sticks at the night market on Wangfujing. This is where you will see Chinese tots laying a new sewer system on the street. This is where you'll find a greater selection of green vegetables than all the tea in China. This is where you'll see a man blowing snot onto the ground before raking his fingers through freshly cut noodles in a filthy tub in the *hutongs*. This is where you'll see an elderly woman pedalling her frail husband on a three-wheeler bicycle among the streaming vehicles on Dongzhimenwai Dajie.

And this is where you'll find raspberries with stems attached.

How could I ask for a better experience for my children? I'm keeping that damn raspberry and I'm showing it to my children before they get to my ripe old age and miss out.

But seriously, how did this raspberry-stem oversight happen to me? I've thought about it at length and I think I know how.

We grew mulberries in our yard in Tasmania. We grew loganberries, peaches, plums and nectarines, but no raspberries. So, horror of horrors, I've never actually seen them on a bush. And whenever we visited Bampa, his raspberry crop was already harvested — ready and waiting in that big fat ice-cream tub … waiting so long for me, the bottom fruit had turned to a puddle of red.

And where were the stems?

I guess my Bampa had spent countless man-hours shucking every last raspberry so I could scoop them straight from tub to eagerly awaiting mouth.

Now that's love. Miss you, Bampa.

Self-Publishing in Beijing III

I'm juggling and I'm dropping a few balls

Where does time go? Really?

I wrote this children's book nearly two years ago and it's only being published now. This is typical of any writer trying to publish a book; in fact, it normally takes many years from initial concept to sale time and this book has been no exception. But I have a greater issue with time on this one. It's because we'll soon be leaving Beijing and I'm quite literally running out of it.

Now that the process of self-publishing has begun, I've discovered things can most certainly gobble up time. A lot of time. I desperately wish I could claim some of my Beijing years back to fit all this waiting in but I can't. I have to solider on even though I'm seriously down to the wire. Only half my illustrations are done, I still have photographs to take … and my book launch is just weeks away.

Am I barking mad? Yes. Yes I am. But when you love something that much, don't you go crazy for it? I may be on the verge of mental collapse but my body just keeps going, hauling my brain along inside its skull. Nonetheless, today my brain brought me to tears as I was juggling twenty balls in the bathroom. It might be the exhaustion talking, but I seem to be dropping a few balls lately.

Last night, my daughter Ella sat on my lap and wept because she said I was so busy on the weekends that I didn't spend enough time with her. It broke my heart. She has every right to cry; I *have* been busy.

I gently explained to her that the book is almost ready, that I'll soon have more time for her, that this is an amazing, gut-wrenching, life-changing, motherlode of personal passion in the unfolding that I have no choice but to pursue. She just looked at me blankly.

In truth, these kinds of statements are hard for a kid to understand because they look at you and all they see is 'Mum'. They don't see a woman or a person; they only see a mother. They don't realise mothers are people, too — that they have flaws and dreams and needs and desires and passions. And it's absolutely right that all Ella sees is a mother. I wouldn't have it any other way nor expect anything less.

It's just tough sometimes.

I'm absolutely loving this publishing process. I'm in my element and the excitement is building exponentially but it's just a little hard to balance my roles right now. But then, I suppose if anyone can juggle a dozen roles, it's a woman.

Right, sisters?

The Great House Hunt

Buying real estate sight-unseen

Here's a question for you.

How many people have bought a family home 9029 kilometres from Beijing, sight-unseen? Come to think of it, given the nature of this expat life, probably quite a few. But it's our first time. We are sight-unseen real-estate virgins.

Let's just say, thank goodness I'm so busy with my work, wrapping up our lives and pining for our Christmas holiday because if I was somewhat idle, I'd have been committed to a home for nutbags by now.

Last week, we sold our house in Australia. It is the house Xiansheng and I lived in when we were first married. It is the house we brought babies home to and the house first steps were taken in. It's a small house but it was idyllic, in a leafy suburb, with a cubby house out the back and tongue-and-groove feature walls. It had a loving spirit residing within, and it's no wonder it sold within two weeks on the market. It was a beautiful home.

Alas, it's ours no longer. We sold it without even saying goodbye. It hasn't hit me yet. I'm too busy to think about it, but when it does hit me, a tonne of bricks will fall on my heart.

Onward. We now have to find *another* beautiful home to move into. In a different city, in a different Australian state.

We've lived temporarily in this city before but we really don't know much about it. We don't know the schools; we don't know the suburbs; we don't know the good, the bad or the ugly. Thank goodness for angelic friends who have helped fill in the gaps and have spent valuable hours videoing dwellings and sending them by email. What would we have done without them?

Nonetheless, despite the priceless help, this house-hunting via the internet has been an experience I wouldn't wish on many. It's been searching and seeking and pitfalls and highs, followed by excitement, hope, disappointment and disillusionment, overlaid with the uneasy awareness that we'll have to pay a hell of a lot more for a house than we ever dreamed. Like, *a lot* more.

It's been tough. And we haven't even put in a single offer yet.

Tomorrow we may be doing just that. There are two houses we're interested in and they're beautiful but they're going to mean at least two years of baked-bean dinners and no holidays, no no. Will it be worth it? How can we buy a bricks and mortar shell from the other side of the world and move in and make it a home? Isn't a home all about the spirit that resides within; the warmth that descends on you like a rug when you walk in? Doesn't a house really choose *us*?

I have to have faith. I'm putting out the call and hoping it carries far across the Pacific Ocean to our new Aussie dwelling. I'm hoping our house hears us. I'm hoping this house will heartily embrace us and distract us from the angst we'll be feeling over leaving Beijing (which is a whole other issue).

It's a huge life moment for our family.

For goodness sake, will someone please hurry up and invent tele-transportation? I need to beam myself into a kitchen or two. And a shopping centre … and a park … and a school …

Self-Publishing in Beijing IV

I'm ready, baby ...

Since my last, emotional report on self-publishing, I'm officially back to business. I took a chill pill, re-sought my equilibrium, spent some more time with my daughter, and got a little more sleep. I also got some exercise because my body atrophied into the sitting position, with my hands curved into typing claws and my neck permanently craned forward, with a wild, unblinking look in my eye. If you had taken away my chair, I would have been frozen in a sitting position.

How I long to go for an endless, undulating, spine-stretching swim off Nha Trang. Soon enough, my pretties, soon enough. But — to the task at hand ...

I managed to snaffle my last photographs for the book while we had an amazing (short-lived) stretch of gorgeous, clear weather recently. My very tardy illustrator sent in his last piece and I let out a little peep of excitement when I took that artwork, configured it onto its page and clicked the save button on my graphic design software for the very last time.

I started emailing pages to my printer, after checking last week if things were on track, in terms of file size and quality. All good. Then they came to my house, took the files, went away, made a proof, brought it back and showed me.

Yes, there were tears. It looks beautiful. And thank the heavens it looks even better than I had envisaged in my head. How many times does something like *that* ever happen in life? We signed the contract on the spot and, right now, those machines are churning out hundreds of copies of my book.

My book.

I can hardly believe this.

Last week, I managed to garner even more wonderful support for my book launches, I had some advertising material printed, my son Riley gave me official approval on the illustrations for the book, I started prepping goodie bags for the launches and put the sparkling wine in to chill. But the most exciting part of last week was receiving my Cataloguing-in-Publication Data from the National Library of Australia. I ran around like a spinning top screaming when I received this. It looks like real publishing data! Like, with my name and the title and the ISBN and the subject and the edition details and even a Dewey number. I have a Dewey number for goodness sake! *A Dewey number!*

Seeing this Dewey number and all these details — well, it was like the pinnacle of achievement for me. After all the stress and intense hard work of these past few months, it finally made things real. Really real. I felt, well … published.

I am self-published. For those out there who love to write, can you feel how this makes me feel? And so, without further ado, I announce the arrival of my beautiful new baby — a picture book called *Riley and the Sleeping Dragon: A Journey Around Beijing* — a tale featuring black and white photos of Beijing coupled with adorable illustrations by my wonderful collaborator (whom I've never met because he lives in Canada), Mo Qovaizi.

I have to breathe deeply. I have to appreciate this completely. Although I'm existing in a sort of stress/bliss-induced haze, I'm also aware that all this hard work is paying off and I am absolutely, 100 per cent certain that the *reason* it's paying off is because I refused to quit, and because I categorically believed I could do it. This may sound fundamental, but as we all know, these elements are the key to success. That, and the gently dangling tag I placed on the Star Day tree exactly two years ago.

I wrote a wish on that tag to become a successful author and perhaps, just like my gorgeous Japanese girlfriend and her maid, my Tanabata wish is coming true.

A Beijing Thanksgiving

For what we are about to leave, we are truly thankful

Our family is enormously grateful for our time in Beijing. As we pack almost four years of enrichment into sterile boxes, I find my face tipping skyward to give silent thanks for all we have experienced, the amazing people we've met and the gorgeous wares we've hoarded to take home. Trust me, celadon pottery, cashmere coats and silk dresses are something for an average Aussie wife to give thanks for.

As we pack and as we enter the most benevolent and festive time of the Western year, it's dawned on me how important a festival like Thanksgiving is to the human spirit. While Christmas is all about giving, Thanksgiving is a time to appreciate all we've been *given*, and to share in this abundance.

It's been almost 400 years since Governor Bradford of the Plymouth Colony declared the first Thanksgiving day in America. After a particularly harsh winter, the colony's harvest was celebrated with a feast of fish, turkey, geese and deer — a tradition that continues today, although it's the humble gobbler that now takes centre stage.

But why is Thanksgiving only officially celebrated in North America? Well, it's not. Throughout history, people have given thanks for a bountiful harvest. In ancient Egypt and Greece, sacrifices were made to the gods in appreciation of an ongoing bounty, and in modern times, many countries celebrate grateful harvest festivals.

There is Chusok in Korea, the Pongal festival in India, the Yam festival in Nigeria, just to name a few. The Hebrews observe Succoth, and in China, the Mid-Autumn Festival is a time to celebrate abundance and togetherness — a tradition which dates back 3000 years to the Zhou Dynasty.

In Australia, we have harvest festivals of varying kinds, from apples to wheat, but I want more. I don't want to take a lamb to the altar in

Ritan Park but I do want to have a more official excuse to gather with loved ones and stuff pumpkin pie down my turkey gullet. I want the horn of plenty spilling gourds and nuts onto the table and I want to hold hands around the table with evangelistic fervour. I want a North American Thanksgiving. I want it all.

True appreciation resides in the heart, and no matter how we give thanks, where we do it or with whom, just *doing it* is a must.

So — from my heart — thank you, Beijing. For everything.

What Became of Ayi

You reap what you sow

This isn't going to be one of those comeuppance rants that self-righteously chirps with glee over the timely demise or incarceration of the perpetrator and the soaring vindication of the victim; no no, for no one is really a winner in the complex *ayi* game.

Unless someone has spent their life trailed by kowtowing servants or has developed the capacity to completely dismiss the mental, emotional and physical wellbeing of others, I doubt it's easy for anyone to deal with the pits and troughs of hiring home help in China. Of inviting someone into your clan, opening your doors, being kind, generous and accommodating, only to have the recipient take that little rope of kindness and tug it and pull it and unravel it and haul it out and run with it and swing from it, whooping it up like a maniacal freeloader on a meal-ticket bender.

Of course, the consequence of pulling out a lot of rope is that pretty soon you'll have enough to hang yourself. And that's exactly what our *ayi* has done.

Some might call her (and others like her) foolish or even just plain stupid. Even after all this time, I'm not quite sure of my own Ayi

analysis. Perhaps a blend of these coupled with an obvious drive to manipulate, and thought processes deeply embedded with discordant cultural beliefs and peculiarities.

Still, cultural aspects aside, I feel Ayi has, without a doubt, taken every opportunity to wrought and exploit the openness, generosity and kindness of our family. And I'm not alone. Virtually every expat family you meet has a similar *ayi*/cook/driver story to tell, and I suppose it's nice to come to the conclusion that these relationship difficulties just may *not* have been caused by us — the terrible *ayi*-intolerant white devil family from hell.

On an optimistic note, I will say this: for all the emotional and mental drama and strain this small woman has put us through, having her here has also helped afford us a life in Beijing that has been more memorable and successful than we ever dreamed. I do believe that despite its frequent misery, this experience has helped weave the rich tapestry that made our life move forward in a positive direction.

I have learned a lot from Ayi. I have learned deeper levels of tolerance, patience and acceptance, and I have also learned to keep my expectations within realistic bounds. I have learned to open my eyes wider and to stand up and defend myself and my family more ably. I have learned conflict resolution, mediating, and how to compromise and appease. I have developed a deeper sense of our family's identity, its needs, and most of all, I've realised how very blessed we are, how close we are, and how important each precious member of our family unit is. But the best thing I've learned, without a doubt, is that for all our faults, we are kind, generous and forgiving people.

If we can't take the positives from unenviable situations, we are living a very limited life indeed, and so our family is determined to move on and to remember the good times. Having said that, although it's certainly important to forgive, we must also do the right thing in a practical sense, and the right thing to do is to retire Ayi. Forgiving may be divine but ignoring the need for consequence brought on by negative action is just plain stupid.

So, Ayi won't be continuing on with my husband's successor and his

wife. We wouldn't do it to them. Our predecessor also suffered under Ayi and now we're ready to break the misery chain. I wanted to give Ayi plenty of notice but the plethora of advice from those who've been-there-done-that has been to give her 24 hours' notice, with no onward referrals. This sticks in my craw and it's going to be really tough and yes, I'll take it on my conscience for a long time to come, but alas, Ayi has been the one to create this ending, not me.

Very soon it will be time, and thankfully Xiansheng has informed me he'll be the one to do it while I hide in the bathroom, shaking. Even after all the drama, I can honestly say there will be no regrets, not even over her dismissal, and if you can say that about life, then you have come very far indeed.

Travelling with the Kids

Our last big overseas holiday

We love to travel, and living in Beijing has made jetsetters of our kids. They've not only seen several different countries since we first moved here, they've also totally submerged themselves in China in all its fabulous incarnations — from Chengde to Hainan.

Truth be told, though, it's not always been easy travelling with tots in tow. I'm sick of juggling the weather with the seasons with the flying hours with the distance, with the dodgy stopover options, school vacation times, work commitments, horrendous high-peak seasons and Chinese national holidays. It can be a real feat in logistics gelling these elements into a cohesive, low-stress family adventure.

Then there's the packing, like when we visited winter and summer all in one trip. Never again. For my husband and me, packing is easy: two pairs of walking shoes, an iPod and we're out the door. With kids, you need a master's degree in suitcase origami and a perennial supply

of Tiny Teddy biscuits. From the essentials to the just-in-case items, it can be a little nightmarish, when all you really want is easy as peasy pie.

So, when booking our trip to Vietnam and Cambodia over Christmas, I played it safe. If it had been just us grown-ups, we'd have booked flights and voyaged on a wing and a prayer but because two travel mites are tagging along, things are a little different.

Basically, we've booked every living moment in advance, from the flights to the bowl of pho noodles on Thursday, 1 January at 12.17 p.m. on Hung Vuong Street, Hanoi. We've even booked the sunset over Angkor Wat, for goodness' sake. We've got the cars, the guides, the hotels, the restaurants, the markets — all in sight, all locked in. My brain is so jam-packed with information that you could use my head as a View-Master: just look through my eyeballs and see a travel guide on Vietnam.

You see, we want to relax and *enjoy* our holiday rather than agonise over rumbling tummies and blisters and how much to pay for a cyclo ride. Yes, we *do* want to spend languorous hours in swimming pools to counterbalance the forced-sightseeing the kids have to bear. Travelling is a time to focus on *each other* as well as the wondrous sights and experiences around us. For me, this artful balance is what holidaying with kids is all about. That, and stress-relief.

With only a week to go until our house is folded-up and packed and sent away, with only a week left of school and to shop for our Hoi An Christmas and to attend farewells and get this book you're now reading finished, you could say I'm a ball of tightly wound springs. This brain is so crammed full, I'm surprised it's remembering to make me breathe.

Yes, there's the packing but there's also the kids, the friends, the city, Christmas, family, Christmas cards, teachers, and festive hot chocolate to make. Tomorrow we are having an early Christmas Day, complete with roast dinner and gift-opening with Jie Jie and Smoothie, but there's also book promos in January when we return from Vietnam, more farewells, skating on Hou Hai, and trying to decide which restaurant to choose for our Last Chinese Supper.

Coupled with wondering where to place all our furniture in the new house in Australia and how overwhelming it's going to be to cruise the aisles of Coles — well …

Let's just say I'm gagging to be on that plane to Ho Chi Minh City and let the stress, drama and self-imposed hysteria slip by.

Ayi Trumps Us Yet Again

Spooky

You won't believe this but I just have to tell you it's the absolute truth even though you may think I'm making it up (I'm not). It still sends shivers down my spine. Sure, I understand the concept of coincidence, but in a place where 'coincidental' happenings are an almost daily occurrence, well, it still sends shivers down my spine. (Yes, I've been known to frisk my own clothes and peek underneath café tables for bugs. Bugs that crawl, *of course*.)

Here is what happened.

Last night, on our way home from dinner with friends, Xiansheng and I agreed, in private, in the car and all alone, that Ayi would be retrenched with 24 hours' notice. This afternoon when she came in to work, Ayi handed me a letter that extolled our virtue as a saintly employer and informed us that, when we leave Beijing, she would retire and would not continue on with our successors.

Initial reaction? *Phew!*

Second reaction? *Spooky …*

Third reaction? Suspicion.

In a way, of course, I'm delighted. I can feel the strain of the sacking slide off my back like a duck/water combination. But I also feel suspicious, and frankly, a little short-changed. Ayi has somehow, amid all the drama, still managed to come out on top. She has essentially

resigned before we could even taste the satisfaction of giving her a teensy bit of comeuppance. I'm also pretty much convinced she thinks this voluntary resignation will give her the right to retirement pay.

When she handed me the letter, I knew what it was before I even opened it. I knew because that is just the way of life in Beijing, and that is the way of the 'coincidental occurrence' in this place.

I suppose this strange episode is all good and well, but our family is very much the master of its own ship now. We are writing our own destiny. We are the ones to make the decisions for us, and we stand by that right.

Ayi is on the way out and our family is on the way up. I couldn't be happier.

Changes

The older you get, the harder it is

Sometimes, when I leave the house and walk around Beijing, I notice changes like they've just risen up and slapped me on the back of the head. Those changes, of course, have been there a while, but sometimes it just takes a while to notice.

Today I went to a local department store and a few unusual things occurred. Firstly, a Chinese man held a door open for me. I was so surprised, I said 'thank you' instead of '*xie xie*'. The last time a man opened a door for me in Beijing was around three years ago and he was Middle Eastern. Surprisingly, I've had doors held open by Chinese *women* on a few occasions, but the men still haven't cottoned on. Until today.

The next change I noticed was when I entered a café to see it filled with 75 per cent Chinese as opposed to 75 per cent Western. Then I noticed a new spot selling profiteroles, like those filled with French

pastry cream. I also noticed the rapidly increasing level of English being spoken everywhere; so much so, it's irritating when they lead the conversation away from Mandarin (and hence, my chance to practise the language).

I also notice the coffee is getting better. Not so milky and frothy but really tongue-tanging and bitter, strong and smooth. Another thing I notice is stylish dressing. The Chinese are dressing better, toning it down, loosening things up, losing the bling-before-midday sparkles and be-studded hooker boots, and throwing on a chic scarf and flats instead.

Yes, things are a-changing, not just the skyline and the economy but the everyday moments. It's wonderful but it's also a little sad. China is who she is, and it would be remiss for this deeply historical country to fall headlong into the pit of the West. Let's hope she carefully struts that fine tightrope balance between the past and the future without compromising her soul. With the horrendously rapid way things are changing, it will be an acrobatic marvel if she can hold her balance.

Having lived here for almost four years, I can safely say that if anyone can do it, China can.

A Merry Beijing Christmas

Miss you most at Christmas time

Christmas in Beijing has become more and more festive since we arrived in the capital. There are fairy lights, Christmas trees, plastic snowmen and skinny Santa Claus sightings galore. You'll also find burgeoning ornament wonderlands in Lai Tai and Liangma flower markets — bigger and better than ever before, and the foreign Christmas fairs and bazaars around town are a marvel to behold.

Every Beijing Christmas, there's been a festive fantasy in our house: feathery green garlands, seven (yes, seven) be-baubled Christmas trees,

the aroma of mulled wine and mass gingerbread production lines. We get together with friends, drink bubbles, nibble my mum's Christmas cake, find a Santa's knee to sit on, and watch the skies for any trace of snowfall. Yes, yes, there's even that indefinable Christmas spirit, undeterred by multicultural barriers and firm-standing atheist states.

But this year will be very different for us, alas, because our house will be all but packed and gone. There'll be nary a Christmas bauble in sight; just a bare floor and perhaps a single pine tree needle. And seeing as though I am Mrs Clause reincarnate, this prospect is a little soul-destroying for me and my two wee Christmas elves. So we're up and outta here, and celebrating the festive season in Vietnam.

Don't panic, I've emailed Santa. He's delivering stockings to Hoi An, and I'm sure we'll be able to track down a glass of bubbles or two. But there'll be no roast turkey dinner, no crackers, no hot pudding with custard. For us this year, Christmas will be Vietnamese spring rolls and a dip in the swimming pool.

In a way, I'm glad to abscond our last Christmas in Beijing. It's because I'm tired of the emptiness. We've celebrated Christmas with some wonderful people in the capital but there's still that emptiness, that tender pit in the belly that only family and old friends can fill. It's hard enough dealing with the absence of those long gone without also pining for those across the oceans. Let me just say this: if you play 'Miss You Most at Christmas Time' even once, I'm a melted puddle on the floor.

You may have noticed how much our family loves Christmas, and it seems apt that our Beijing life is ending shortly after the Festive Season and quite literally days before China celebrates a new lunar year. It all seems purposely designed. It wouldn't feel right entering a new Chinese year when our hearts and minds have already packed and gone.

Change is good. We're moving on, and this Christmas is a watershed time for our family. It heralds significant change: our shiny new life, about to unfold.

And with that I say: 'Merry Christmas to all. May all your days be bright — no matter where you are.'

We're Going Home

Why fight it?

So. I've made a decision and it's a very important one. I've decided that I'm *not* going to give up this Beijing life. I'm not going to slip into the mundanity of suburbia from whence I came.

I may not be able to buy *jian bing* (breakfast crêpes) on the streets in the morning. I may not be able to nip into Ya Show for the latest ad-free television series on DVD. I may not be able to watch little old ladies perform *tai chi* by the roadside in the early morning light, nor delight in the partners ballroom dancing in the parks at twilight. I may not crack open ridiculously fresh pomelos for breakfast each morning nor bask in the mass of tofu possibilities available at the wet market, but I'm going to try my hardest to keep this life going, even if it's smack bang in the middle of Aussie suburbia.

Don't get me wrong, Australia is a glorious place to live and I'm a great Aussie patriot. I'm quite desperate for the warm embrace of familiarity we'll experience upon going home, and seeing my children hug and squeeze their homeland is going to be an *enormous* thing. How I ache for the easy, pristine, relaxed, familiar life of Australia. The fresh air, the surreal blue skies, the laid-back amiability, the solid four seasons, the availability, the variety, the honesty, the openness, the warmth, the gum trees, the sporting hysteria, the liquorice bullets and lolly bananas.

How I crave the waft of a barbecue meandering through the neighbourhood, the swoop of a magpie and the cackle of a kookaburra. How I miss the Banksia trees and the wildflowers and digging my hands into the earth to make a hole and pop in a daffodil bulb. How I miss the stunning range of fresh food, the supermarket aisles bursting with cereal boxes and breads, the picnics in the park where you can play cricket on the grass. I even miss the Aussie accent, for goodness' sake.

However, while familiarity is a wonderful thing, I am also nervous about it. I'm nervous about going home and slipping into a familiarity and an ease that takes us off our toes, that steals away the shortness of breath, the drive and the intensity and the energy that comes from challenging situations.

So what I'm going to do is tap into that invisible undercurrent of energy to be found anywhere in the world if we look hard enough, and I'm going to keep thriving on that Beijing energy, even inside a house ringed by gum trees and hovering blue sky.

Sure, I'll have to drive the kids to school, scrub toilets and, God forbid, cook dinner. But I'll do it with gusto while simultaneously keeping a finger on the pulse of all that *is* happening in my new town. Of the cultural, spiritual, dynamic elements that so easily get lost in the humdrum of everyday life, especially when that everyday life is within your own culture and heritage. It's so easy to get lost in your own culture and heritage without the smack-in-the-face polarities and disparities of living Elsewhere.

How blessed we've been to have had this once-in-a-lifetime opportunity to spread our wings in China. Trust me, I won't be leaving here without a full understanding of the gifts this has given our family.

Nonetheless.

It's time to go home.

Dear China

Zai jian

In these last weeks before we leave, I've begun thinking about the things I'd like to say to you. And I really don't know where to start, so forgive me if I ramble.

Before we came to live with you, to be perfectly honest I hadn't heard great things. I heard you were a little cold and a teensy bit pre-

occupied with your own history. I also heard you carried a lot of baggage and that you found it hard to make new friends or to let down the barriers long enough to get to know someone really well. This worried me somewhat, but I do have faith in human nature, and I decided to give you a go.

When we first arrived, I was surprised at how wrong the rumours were. Sure, you were a little standoffish, even surprised to see me, but you soon warmed up and made me feel welcome.

Since then, we've had a mostly easy relationship; sometimes you won't listen and sometimes you insist on things being your way. Sometimes you thrive on complicating things for the hell of it but there's also been a lot of give and take, a lot of acceptance.

To be honest, I won't miss your often puerile nature. I won't miss the way you covet money nor your starry-eyed, calculated greed and complete miscomprehension of the term 'repeat business'. I won't miss the imbecilic red tape that straps up even the simplest transactions of everyday living. I won't miss the scarcity of sunsets and rainbows and birds and butterflies and frogs. I won't miss the filth, the crowds, the pushing and shoving and the inability to form a queue. Lord knows, I won't miss the roads.

What I *will* miss are the years of secret history, pain and joy etched into the faces of the little old men, fanning themselves in their singlets in the *hutong* alleyways. I will miss the fat, shaven-headed babies in their bamboo prams, flashing their family jewels through split pants. I will miss the soft, gentle call of sellers in laneways, drifting to the high-rise buildings above. I will miss the addictive food sellers on the street, the superlative Beijing dumpling, the markets bursting with fresh produce, the provincial farmers cycling their carts into town with nuts and seeds and fruit and chinaware.

I will miss the silk and the baubles and the talented artisans. I'll miss the tender, funny, miscommunicated relationships with locals. I'll miss both the crabby cab drivers and the ones you want to take home for dinner. I will miss the parks and the tea and the vistas and the ancient buildings straddled by high-tech skyscrapers. I will miss the

spectacle — the acrobats, the ceremonies, the temple fairs, the crackers, the celebrations that only the Chinese know how to do so well.

It hasn't always been easy. Living with you has been frustrating and infuriating and challenging, too. But it has also stretched my soul wide open and crammed in culture and spirit and tolerance and understanding and maybe even a little patience.

So China, I want to thank you.

Thank you for making me feel comfortable when I felt most alone. Thank you for having patience with me when I was at my most Western — when I was rude, harried or impatient with your ways. Thank you for not staring at me in horror when I was at my worst, but rather with an innate curiosity and acceptance. Thank you for making me gasp and clutch my hands to my chest at your beauty, at your rawness, at your talent and scope.

Thank you for accepting me into your world — I am so aware that living here in your home was a privilege not a right, and I am so grateful to you for the opportunity.

And, most importantly, above all else — thank you for making me love you. How I will miss you.

Tania, and her loving family

Glossary

Aodaliya jia you! (ow dali ya, jee-ah yo) Go Australia!, literally: 'Australia add oil' or 'press down on the accelerator' or 'go'!

April Gourmet expat supermarket

ayi (aye-ee) maid, literally: auntie

bai jiu (bye-jeoh) a clear, toxic rocket fuel used to expose the inner contents of your stomach, literally: 'white alcohol'

baozi (bao-zr) bread dumplings

Beijing (bay-jing) literally 'northern capital' – the 'j' is not soft

Beijingfan (bay-jing-fun) food endemic to Beijing

Beijingren (bay-jing-ren) local Beijing people

bing (bing) egg pancakes

bu xie (boo shee-eh) no problem, you're welcome, literally: 'don't thank'

Chang'an Jie (chung-un-jeeay) the east–west road that divides Tian'anmen from the Forbidden City, literally: 'long peace street'

da sha (dah sha) big building

dongxi (doong-shee) 'thing'

Dongzhimen (doong-jrr-mn) a north-eastern, inner area of Beijing

er hu (er hoo) a traditional lute-like instrument

feng (fung) wind

fu huo jie kuai le! (foo hwar jee-yeh kwai la) Happy Easter!

furen (foo-ren) madam

gong fu (goong foo) kung fu

gong xi fa cai (goong shee fah tsai) said to others during Chinese New Year, literally: 'wishing you enlarge your wealth'

guanxi (gwan-shee) social and business connection

hao le! (how la) great! (among a million other meanings)

haw chips sweet, dried discs of haw fruit

hutong a type of narrow street or alleyway formed by lines of traditional courtyard houses

Jenny Lou expat supermarket

jian bing (jee-an bing) breakfast crêpes

jian de (jee-an de) real

jiao (jee-ow) cent, also called *mao*

jiaozi (jee-ow-zr) dumpling

jie jie (jee-eh jee-eh) big sister; little sister is *mei mei*

kuai (kwy) slang for money, literally: 'piece' or 'unit'

lao (lao) old

laoshi (lao-shr) teacher

laowai (lao-why) foreigner, literally: 'white devil', we are also called 'big noses'

mafan (mah-fun) trouble

mama huhu (mama hoo-hoo) so-so, not bad, okay

mei you (ma-yo) don't have

ni hao (nee-how) hello

ni hao ma? (nee-how-mah) how are you?

nin hao polite form of *ni hao*

pengyou (pung-yo) friend

pu tao jiu (poo tao jee-oh) wine

pu-erh (poo-err) a type of black tea that comes in a solid block and is renowned for its healthful properties, including aiding weight loss

qi pao (chee-pow) traditional Chinese dress

ren (ren) people

shengdan kuai le! (shung dun kwy le) Happy Christmas!

tai tai (ty-ty) wife

The Jing expat slang for Beijing

Tian'anmen (tee-un-ah-mn) the world's largest city central square, right in the heart of Beijing, just south of the Forbidden City, literally: Heaven Peace Gate

ting bu dong (ting-boo-dong) I hear you but I don't understand what you're saying

Tsingtao (tsing-tao) brand of local beer

wei (way) hello, when answering the telephone

wo (war) I, me

xiansheng (see-an-shung) husband or 'sir'

xie xie (shee-eh shee-eh) thank you

xin nian kuai le! (shin nee-an kwy la) Happy New Year!

yuan (yoo-an) Chinese currency, approximately six *yuan* to the Australian dollar

zai jian (zy jee-an) goodbye

Special thanks to the wonderful team at Exisle Publishing for knowing this book would touch women of all cultures and life experience, and especially publisher Anouska Jones for making the experience such a creative pleasure.

Thanks to my beautiful China dolls and endless inspiration — Ella and Riley — and lastly, thanks also to Beijing.

'This book rewrites the myth of the full-time expat mother.'

— Lee Mack, Managing Editor, *City Weekend Beijing*

'Both funny and insightful, McCartney's utterly honest account is a must read for anyone with an interest in China, in refreshingly frank memoir or in the subject of motherhood — whichever country you choose to learn it in.'

— Jenny Niven, Associate Director of the Wheeler Centre

'At once touching and humorous, accessible but full of food for thought.'

— Barbie Robinson, ArtyFacts broadcaster, ArtSound FM 90.3/92.7

'Hilarious! Kathy Lette eat your heart out!'

— Dani Moger, mother, Melbourne

'In *Beijing Tai Tai*, McCartney skilfully blends amusing anecdotes, personal family moments and the joys and frustrations of parenthood with glimpses of Beijing and China as seen through the eyes of an intelligent and insightful, well-travelled observer.'

— Susan Whelan, World Literatures Feature Writer, Suite 101

EIJING TAI TAI